A STUDENT'S GUIDE TO PLACEMENTS IN HEALTH AND SOCIAL CARE SETTINGS

From Theory to Practice

Other books you may be interested in:

Dilemmas and Decision Making in Social Work
Abbi Jackson   ISBN 9781914171208

Social Work and Covid-19: Lessons for Education and Practice
Edited by Denise Turner   ISBN 9781913453619

Out of the Shadows: The Role of Social Workers in Disasters
Edited by Angie Bartoli, Maris Stratulis and Rebekah Pierre   ISBN 9781915080073

The Anti-racist Social Worker: stories of activism in social care and allied health professionals
Edited by Tanya Moore and Glory Simango   ISBN 9781914171413

www.criticalpublishing.com or contact our distributor Ingram Publisher Services, telephone 01752 202301 or email NBNi.Cservs@ingramcontent.com

CRITICAL PUBLISHING

A STUDENT'S GUIDE TO PLACEMENTS IN HEALTH AND SOCIAL CARE SETTINGS

From Theory to Practice

**EDITED BY
SIMON WILLIAMS
AND DIANA CONROY**

First published in 2022 by Critical Publishing Ltd

All rights reserved. No part of this publication may be reproduced, stored in a retrieval system, or transmitted in any form or by any means, electronic, mechanical, photocopying, recording or otherwise, without prior permission in writing from the publisher.

Copyright © 2022 Simon Williams, Diana Conroy

British Library Cataloguing in Publication Data
A CIP record for this book is available from the British Library

ISBN: 9781914171598
This book is also available in the following e-book formats:
EPUB ISBN: 9781914171604
Adobe e-book ISBN: 9781914171611

The rights of Simon Williams and Diana Conroy to be identified as the Authors of this work have been asserted by them in accordance with the Copyright, Design and Patents Act 1988.

Cover design by Out of House
Text design by Greensplash
Project Management by Deanta Global Publishing Services, Dublin, Ireland
Printed and bound in Great Britain by 4edge, Essex

Critical Publishing
3 Connaught Road
St Albans aL3 5RX

www.criticalpublishing.com

Contents

Meet the editors vii

Meet the authors viii

Introduction 1

PART 1
Pre-placement 5

1 Being prepared 7
Simon Williams and Diana Conroy

2 Reflection 21
Liz Eate, Zuzia Goddard and Sarah Barley-McMullen

3 Emotional resilience 34
Toni-Marie Benaton, Pauline Green and Fran Fuller

4 Anti-oppressive practice 47
Jodie Low, Ben Wyke and Sarah Barley-McMullen

PART 2
During placement 65

5 Working within the context of an agency 67
Claire Connor and Nigel Down

6 Placements in challenging settings 82
Jackie King-Owen and Claire Ambrose

7 Managing your placement and supervision 95
Diana Conroy, Nigel Down and Helen Morgan

8	Technology and digital literacy *Valerie Fletcher, Tom Matthews and John Hills*	108
9	Resource of self *Diana Conroy*	122

PART 3
Advanced skills — **137**

10	Interprofessional learning and working *Jodie Low, Liz Eate and Fran Fuller*	139
11	Involving others *Vita Snowden and Gavin Jinks*	154
12	Managing projects *Simon Williams*	168
13	Measuring impact *Tim Rosier*	182

Index — *199*

Meet the editors

Simon Williams is Assistant Discipline Lead for Social and Community Studies at the University of Derby. With over 25 years experience in the field of youth and community work, and an experienced senior lecturer, Simon has a vast experience of hosting and souring student placements, to create the best possible student experience.

Diana Conroy has wide experience of working in well-being, health and social care. She has worked as a Advanced Social Work Practitioner and Approved Mental Health Professional in a Community Mental Health Team and is a qualified psychotherapist. Diana currently works as a Senior Lecturer, teaching mental health and psychological therapies and researches the impact of trauma and traumatic stress.

Meet the authors

Claire Ambrose

Claire Ambrose has worked in the fields of education and health for over thirty-five years. She has held a wide range of senior leadership and management positions in both education and health, being responsible for managing staff, resources, curriculum, and quality. She is a qualified secondary school teacher and has worked in Schools, Colleges of FE, Universities and for Ofsted. Her previous education quality assurance roles include preparing organisations for inspection and leading inspections, carrying out 100s of teaching and learning observations. She has been employed as a Senior Lecturer at the University of Derby for 15 years and won awards as Lecturer of the Year and Inspirational Teacher of the Year.

Sarah Barley-McMullen

Sarah Barley-McMullen has over 35 years of community and youth work experience. Within this time, she has spent 14 years as an academic in this field, and 3 years as the Diversity and Inclusion Lead, both at the University of Derby.

In 2019, Sarah was made Stonewall Role Model of the Year for her culture change work within the University. More recently, as Chair of her hometown LGBT+ Pride community organisation, Sarah has been shortlisted as LGBT+ Community Organisation of the year by the National Diversity Awards.

Throughout her career, reflection on and in practice has been pivotal in enabling challenge, action and change to take place within her work.

Tonimarie Benaton

Tonimarie Benaton is a Registered Social Worker and a Senior Lecturer in Social Work in the School of Applied Health, Psychology, and Social Care at Derby University. Tonimarie has over 16 years of experience in the field of Children and Families Social Work including work with Children in Care, Adoption, Training, Education, Independent Visiting, and Independent Reviewing Children in Care. She is currently undertaking her DPrac in Health and Social Care in Social Work and The Assimilation of the Child's Voice. She is actively involved in research relating to Vicarious Trauma of Social Work Students, Post 16 Children in Care, and Children in Care and Creative Interventions.

Claire Connor

Claire Connor has been a social worker for over 15 years. She began her career in the voluntary sector as a practitioner and manager within the field of child sexual exploitation (CSE). She developed innovative programmes to support young people affected by CSE including the experiences of young men and boys. Claire took her social work experience into education. She worked on several programmes as a lecturer and also authored safeguarding and professional practice modules at the University of Derby. Claire now works for the NHS as a CAMHS Mental Health Practitioner. She continues to lecture alongside providing supervision for social work students as a Practice Educator. She also teaches Pilates within a Derby based wellbeing centre which she manages.

Nigel Down

Nigel Down had experience of working in the field of Youth and Community Development Work for over 30 years before moving to teach at the University of Derby. Nigel's professional practice experience has been mainly with both local authority services for children and young people, and with voluntary sector community organisations. Throughout his Youth Work practice, he was mainly involved in working with 'hard to reach' groups and with young people displaying challenging behaviour. He worked as a senior service manager for 13 years, having responsibility for workforce training and development within his management portfolio. Nigel graduated from the University of Derby in 1995.

Liz Eate

As a registered adult general nurse, Specialist Community Public Health Nurse and specialist in teenage pregnancy, Liz is currently Interim Discipline Lead for Social and Community Studies at the University of Derby. Her research interests include the language of joint serious case and domestic homicide reviews; interprofessional working in child protection and safeguarding and the experiences of students and practitioners who work with children and/or families; the use of technology to enhance the learning of students in the health and social care arena; diversifying the curriculum; and interprofessional learning for undergraduates not only in health and social care but drawing in other colleges and programmes too.

Valerie Fletcher

Valerie works is a Senior Lecturer in the School of Health at Leeds Beckett University, where she is Post Graduate Diploma Course Leader, supervises dissertations and teaches on the MA Integrative Psychotherapy courses and is a Fellow of the Higher Education Academy (FHEA), enjoying helping students to learn and flourish into successful professional practitioners. Valerie also runs a private practice as an Accredited (BACP) Counsellor / Psychotherapist, specialising in working with Trauma, Abuse, Bereavement, Mental Health Diagnoses, Depression and Anxiety. Alongside her successful Private Practice, she is working as a Psychological Therapist/ Counsellor within the NHS, has previously worked as a Nurse and within Prison and School settings. Valerie is undertaking research into resilience amongst mental health and counselling students, the evidence base behind therapies for depression, inclusivity and decolonisation of services and supporting students working with clients with a personality disorder diagnosis.

Fran Fuller

Fran Fuller is Interim Head of School for Allied Health & Social Care, a registered social worker and is currently researching Child Protection and Interprofessional Learning (Ed D). Fran has been an academic for nearly 20 years and prior to this was a training officer and child protection officer. Fran was a member of the British Association of Social Workers and was Chair of BASW UK for 5 years (2010). Currently, Fran is Chair of the Professional Development Committee.

Zuzia Goddard

Zuzia Goddard is a qualified and registered social worker as well as being a qualified Practice Educator. She has over 25 years' experience within the health and social care field. She is a Fellow of the Higher Education Academy and holds a Master of Education from the University of Derby. Her interests are in Safeguarding Adults with a focus on substance use and misuse.

Pauline Green

Pauline Green is a former course director and academic lead in Social Work and Social Care, University of Derby where she worked between 1999 and 2021. She is a registered social worker, qualifying in 1984 and worked in a wide range of statutory settings in both children and adult services.

John Hills

John Hills is a senior lecturer at Leeds Beckett University and leads on the MA Integrative Counselling course, which is a route to professional qualification. He is a BACP accredited pluralistic therapist in private practice with particular theoretical interest in Existentialism and Acceptance and Commitment Therapy. His PhD centres upon the meanings and patterns of therapeutic change, and this is an ongoing interest. John is currently researching into the social determinants of mental health and their implications for the work of counselling and psychotherapy.

Gavin Jinks

Gavin has been a qualified social worker since 1990. He had wide ranging experience across the adult service spectrum before moving into Learning and Development with Derby City Council. He played a key role in creating and delivering a training course for Practice Educators while working for Derby City. He qualified as a counsellor in 2001 and has worked as a Senior Lecturer at the University of Derby since 2012. Gavin has written and presented at a significant number of national and international conferences on issues relating to student engagement. He is a Senior Fellow of the Higher Education Academy and has won awards at the University of Derby for his work on creative teaching, student mentoring and student engagement.

Jackie King-Owen

Jackie King-Owen has been a qualified social worker since 1979 and an independent practice educator since 1983. She has worked mainly in the charitable and voluntary sector running a housing with care organisation for 25 years and employing 650 staff including 12 social workers. She set up an in-house social work training unit (known as PEPE) which offered placements to over 50 students. Following early retirement in 2015, Jackie joined the University of Derby as an associate lecturer, then a lecturer in Child, Family, Health and Wellbeing, completing her PGCE in 2019. She is currently a part time staff tutor at the Open University, leading on the social work degree courses in the Midlands region and service user involvement strategy for the OU in England. She is a doctoral researcher in health and social care and a helpline volunteer, supervisor and paid trainer for Cruse Bereavement Care. Her three adult children are all qualified social workers too!

Jodie Low

Jodie is a Director of Free 2 Talk CIC delivering Youth Work; Parenting and Counselling with disadvantaged communities in Northamptonshire. Her role in the organisation is in operational leadership and funding and resourcing. She is a Senior Lecturer for University of Northampton, teaching on MA in Youth & Community Leadership with JNC; BA in Social Care and Community Practice and the Fdn in Health & Social Care. Prior to this she worked as a Senior Lecturer at Derby University's Department of Health and Social Care; module leading on Youth Work, Protecting and Safeguarding Children and Professional Practice. Before joining the University of Derby in 2012, Jodie led training for Northamptonshire County Council and delivered lectures and placement supervision for the University of Northampton. Jodie's research experience has utilised a range of methods, and her research focus currently is on youth violence, exploitation and contextual safeguarding. She is JNC Qualified Youth & Community Worker, has an MA in Community Education and a BSc in Psychology. She is a HEA Fellow with Postgraduate Diploma in teaching at Higher Education.

Tom Matthews

Tom Matthews is a lecturer within the Psychological Therapies and Mental Health subject group at Leeds Beckett University. Tom combines lecturing with working as a Clinical Psychologist in the NHS, third and private sectors. Tom's work as a Clinical Psychologist has predominantly been with young people and families, working in ways which support them around their psychological wellbeing within both generic and specialist NHS child and adolescent mental health teams. His interest and experience in systemic thinking is rooted in this work, and underpinned his involvement in the chapter within this book. Tom has supervised students and trainees from disciplines whilst on placement, increasingly utilising digital technology to do so during the recent Covid outbreak. He therefore writes from the position of educator, supervisor and clinician.

Helen Morgan

Helen Morgan is Programme Lead and admissions tutor for the BA (Hons) Health and Social Care. She has been at the university since 2015; prior to that she worked in FE and prior to that as a Registered General Nurse in critical care. She is also a qualified Operating Department Practitioner. As part of her nursing career, she spent time working with residential care homes and nursing homes to both train staff and develop staff to deliver the highest possible care to service users and patients. She is passionate about teaching and feels that her broad experience has led her to develop skills in many areas and she can bring these to the classroom. As well as the University of Derby she worked at the University of Bradford and developed a Foundation Degree in Dementia Studies.

Tim Rosier

Tim is a Senior Lecturer in Social & Community Studies at the University of Derby. As well as teaching and module leadership, he has responsibility for Youth Work & Community Development placements within the discipline. Prior to academia, he had a varied career in the Criminal Justice System working as a Probation Officer, a specialist in the counter-radicalisation arena and as a senior project manager for a faith-based VCSE working with juvenile and young offenders in custody. His research interests include youth work and youth justice, evidence-based youthwork practice, professional identity formation, chaplaincy work with young people, faith-based community work, and desistance from crime. Tim is on the Council of the Institute for Youth Work and an Associate Member of the Alliance for Youth Justice.

Vita Snowden

Vita was a family carer for over 11 years and, alongside that role, set up a successful, innovative, social enterprise for family carers in a local community; the model that was developed recognised how important peer support and community activities are to the wellbeing and rights of family carers. She is currently undertaking a PhD that explores community activities for family carers under the Care Act 2014. Vita has extensive experience working as a practitioner, a manager, and an entrepreneur within third sector organisations. She is a qualified social worker and Practice Educator, having provided numerous placements for students within her Social Enterprise. She currently works for the University of Derby lecturing within the undergraduate and postgraduate social work programmes.

Ben Wyke

Ben's background in social care and education covers over 35 years. Voluntary work in a day centre led to a development post with Derby Mind and then a post with Derbyshire County Council as a Community Living Instructor for people with a learning disability. Ben went on to spend 20 years in community based mental health services in Derby as a Support Worker, Social Worker, Approved Social Worker and Community Mental Health Team Manager subsequently becoming Senior lecturer and latterly Programme Leader for the Social Work Degree at the University of Derby, until 2020. As a practitioner Ben supported students as a practice educator and then taught on the practice learning module at university whilst also tutoring students on placement. Ben currently works part time for the Care Quality Commission as a Mental Health Act Reviewer a role he has held since 2007.

Introduction

Placements are a period in a student's studies that are often full of excitement and anxiety in equal measure; they can be the place where students are able to excel and evidence how effective they are in their practice, but at the same time students are fully aware of being evaluated as part of this, and the complications this can bring. We remember our own time as students – thinking about placement and the opportunities it could provide, and wanting to prove to ourselves to those we were working with, so we could demonstrate competence and that we knew what we were doing. We were also both mature students and came to studies from practice, so of course we knew what we were doing! Once we started our first placements, we soon realised that we knew so little and had so much to learn; it was a humbling experience!

Placements are much more than just the student and there are three main parties involved: first is the student, second is the organisation and third is the university itself. These three aspects form a partnership that seeks to provide a space for students to excel, explore and create new knowledge. Simon had the experience of existing in all three areas – student, organisation and university – and as such been able to see how things are mirrored across parties. For example, when he hosted students on placement, he remembers 'spring cleaning' – tidying the office, making sure our policies were refreshed, even if they were good for another year, making sure he was super organised – why? Because he was both excited and anxious at the same time. We would think the same questions as students – what if they don't like me? What if they complain about me to the university? What if I look like I don't know what I'm doing? So often we were mirroring the thoughts, emotions and experiences of the student as a supervisor! But as practitioners, we both loved hosting placements; it was a huge benefit to us as professionals, but also for our organisation. Not only did students bring themselves and were an 'extra pair of hands', but more so they brought the latest research and theory and their critical minds; we were able to engage in debate about what we did and why, helping make sense of practice and enabling critical reflection.

Simon remembers working with one student in their final year of study; they were a confident student, and they had worked well together for several weeks. Simon had organised a trip for some local young people to visit the local police station, meet and greet officers, see the holding cells and try on the uniforms, to help build some bridges between the young people and the local police force. The student took him to task and challenged him about this project; they engaged in discussion, and Simon learned about the student's own personal experience with the police. Through this, they were able to make the event better, making sure the police were involved in learning – just as much as the young people. The event was improved, thanks to that student.

When working at the university organising placements, we were always thrilled to hear feedback and what was happening across the field. Students were and are having a huge impact across the health and social care sector, not just in terms of delivery, but also in organisational development. Every year there is a list of the positive changes students have made to the organisations locally and nationally. Therefore, it is not surprising why we are both passionate about placements and seek to provide support for students undertaking them.

Placement is a huge learning opportunity for all parties involved, but, as already said, can equally be filled with anxiety and uncertainty. As academics, we argue that the theory we teach is to support our profession; theory helps us make sense of and react to situations; theory helps us develop and respond to need; theory helps us question the why and the how, giving understanding and context. As lecturers we encourage students to drive into the theory and wrestle with the concepts to develop a critical thinking which they can apply to practice. And this ideology is what has led to this book. So often students can feel theory is detached from their practice. They learn about theory in the classroom, look at models and quotes and maybe even apply it to a case study, but when you encounter real lives on placement, it can seem like theory flies out the window. We have therefore designed this book so that students can reflect on and experience the real connection between theory and practice.

We have asked for a range of authors with lots of different experiences, many of whom hosted students on placements, and most are involved in teaching placement modules or organising placement arrangements. We hope that this collective pool of knowledge will provide a wide and varied aspect to the theory presented and the approach of the book. We recognise that different professions use different languages for certain aspects, and throughout the book authors have used the terminologies that best suit their professions. We hope this enables readers of this book to see and explore the wider aspects of placement and study in the health and social care sector.

The book has been designed in three parts. The first section looks at the preparation needed before placement, how students can apply the theory to ready themselves for the practice they will face and make sure they are equipped to deal with some of the common issues with placement. The second part of the book deals with being on placement and the issues that can present themselves while undertaking the placement. The third section looks at aspects that might be for students in their final year, or students who are trying to stretch themselves as part of their experience. Throughout the book we have shared the chapters with real-life students and asked them to provide 'hacks' – key bits of advice – to our readers. Throughout the chapters you will find these 'student hacks' in boxes and we hope that this will help our readers be more confident on their placement.

The book has 13 chapters and starts with Chapter 1 on preparation for placement. This chapter helps students to develop a 'placement mindset'; it explores how students can prepare themselves, emotionally, physically and theoretically, so they are ready to engage in the placement experience. Chapter 2 has a detailed look at reflection, arguing that reflection is key to students learning about themselves and their work, exploring the different approaches to reflection that students can adopt on placement. Chapter 3 follows with a discussion on emotional resilience and looks at the theory that will help students develop resilience to work with people in the wider contexts of their lives. Chapter 4 concludes the first section looking at anti-oppressive practice, including key theories that help students be prepared to recognise and challenge oppressive behaviour, building on previous chapters so that students can reflect on and explore their own bias.

The second section of the book starts with Chapter 5 which looks at the wider context of working with an agency; it explores the theories that student will need to be able to work within the mechanisms of an organisation and recognises some of the challenges of being a student on placement. Chapter 6 expands on this to look at working in challenging settings. Placements will often encounter difficult and ethical situations and this chapter explores the theory to support students to engage in difficult situations such as whistleblowing. Chapter 7 continues to support students through theory to respond to managing the relationship between student and their supervisor; this chapter helps students explore the theory of effective supervision and power dynamics that are involved. Chapter 8 explores the role and impact of technology on placement; it wrestles with the theory of digital literacy in a people-orientated business and how digital tools could support a student's practice. The section finishes with Chapter 9 which explores the theory of and use of self; how students can recognise their strengths and areas for development and use their personality attributes in practice.

The final section of the book starts with Chapter 10 which explores the theory behind interprofessional working and how this is a common concept, but often misunderstood. The chapter helps students apply theory to be able to work well with other agencies and individuals. Chapter 11 explores theoretically how students can involve others, looking at how we gain meaningful feedback to explore and develop our practice. Chapter 12 examines managing projects; how theory can support student skills of negotiation and planning as well as dissemination of information. Finally, this section, and the book, finishes with Chapter 13 which explores measuring our impact. This chapter encourages students to explore the frameworks that affect how we measure impact and what are effective ways of developing this.

We hope that this book is a resource which supports you as students on your journey through studies and placement. We also hope this book is useful to those who host students on placement to support the theoretical development of both parties. Students in health and social settings make a huge difference in the lives of individuals and groups, in training and as qualified and graduated professionals. We wish you all the best in your studies, placements and future career.

Simon Williams and Diana Conroy

Part 1
Pre-placement

1 Being prepared

Simon Williams and Diana Conroy

Introduction

Placement can be an exciting time for students; there is the anticipation about engaging in real-world learning, gaining work-based skills and seeing what future working could be like (Juznic and Pymm, 2011; Jones, Green and Higson, 2015). However, while preparing for placement many students can experience a range of emotions. A report on student's mental health found that those engaging in theoretical and practice work can develop stress in addressing a *'theory practice gap'* on placement (Student Minds, 2017, p 21), which is the challenge of integrating academic and theoretical knowledge into real-world, clinical practice. Students can question their own abilities and skills, be concerned about building professional relationships and struggle with anxiety around assessments, success and practical logistics in regard to placement (Parker, 2008; Melincavage, 2011; Lam, Wong and Leung, 2006). However, a student well supported by an understanding of theory can be better prepared to not just cope but succeed, developing critical skills for practice in a real-world context. Placement presents an opportunity to test out and explore whether models and concepts actually work in the real world, in a supportive environment where there is less pressure to be the expert. One of the crucial elements this chapter will discuss is the ability to develop a 'placement mindset', a firm grasp of what is required intrinsically to give the best chance of the placement being a meaningful and enhancing experience.

The focus on a 'placement mindset' will be the key theme, and this chapter seeks to debate what skills are needed to develop this, such as emotional intelligence, attitude, critical thinking and application of theory. This should help students be fully prepared to cope with change and for challenges on placement, as well as reflect on professional and personal development.

This chapter will cover:

- What is a placement mindset?
- Practical preparation
- Emotional intelligence
- Applying theory to practice

What is a placement mindset?

Meier and Kropp (2010) define mindset as '*A mental attitude. It shapes our actions and our thoughts*' (p 179). Dwerk (2010) expands on this idea, discussing that individuals can hold two types of mindset: 'fixed' or 'growth'. As an example, a student who goes into placement with a fixed mindset might think that their intelligence is not something they can change and if they did not understand a theory initially, that's that. However, a student with a growth mindset would realise that they need to apply themselves and be resilient in their approach, recognising that they are able to learn something that does not initially make sense. A further example is Einstein who had to put in the hard work and dedication to become the genius that he was. While we are not all Einstein, it does illustrate how much a student 'puts in' matters and goes back to that old saying 'what you put in, you get out'. The research also suggests that engagement and open-mindedness are critical, with students who adopt these attributes growing their abilities and intellectual capacity (Dwerk, 2010).

As well as consciously choosing to have a growth mindset for placement, thinking and reflecting on what a student's best hopes are from placement will create a frame of mind that could set them up for a positive experience. The term 'best hopes' (Ratner, George and Iveson, 2012, p 63) comes from an approach called Solution Focused Brief Therapy (SFBT), which found that focusing on positive outcomes and goals encourages the mind towards these. To develop this approach, students might undertake writing through a reflective journal as a helpful exercise to really think about what they want to realistically achieve and get out of placement. It could start with a sentence like 'if I was to get all that I wanted out of placement, I'd know this had happened because …'. Then students might list that they had understood how attachment theory works in babies, had the opportunity to run a group or design an intervention. As well as being clear and specific about hopes, the exercise will help grow a more optimistic and positive attitude. Research has also demonstrated that cultivating optimism can have a considerable impact on real-world (and thus placement) experience, as thinking optimistically means that when problems occur, they are viewed as temporary, and generally having a 'can do' attitude means that students are likely to be more resilient to stress and setbacks (Seligman, 2018). Additionally, a student honestly reflecting on their general life attitudes and thinking style can be an important part of psychological preparedness.

Another useful exercise is for students to consider if they are a glass 'half full' or 'half empty' person. This can identify potentially pessimistic thinking and increasing awareness of this means that a choice can be made to think positively rather than focusing on negatives. Being optimistic has been found to protect oneself from stress and growing a positive disposition or 'dispositional optimism' (Conversano et al., 2010, p 26). Developing a positive mindset could mean that a student going into placement is more likely to feel hopeful and therefore cope with challenges better. For example, let's consider two students going into the same placement. On the one hand, Michael focuses on how stressful placement will be, what additional money and time is needed to arrange childcare and how tired he will be at the end of the day, and his goal is to get through and simply pass. On the other hand, Ama, also a parent, is thinking about what she wants to learn and how many skills she can build and is looking forward to seeing what she learns from fellow practitioners in the real world. Ama is envisaging getting to the end of placement and feeling good, and with lots of new knowledge and skills. In placement she has that 'can do' spirit and as a result could have better relationships with supervisor and colleagues, and is energised rather than drained by the experience, leading to being offered many more interesting learning opportunities than Michael.

As well as students thinking about 'best hopes' to create a positive experience, there is evidence to suggest that imagining what Peters et al. (2010) named as your 'best possible self' is associated with growing and maintaining optimism. In a study, participants who spent five minutes a day visualising their best possible self significantly increased their optimism (Meevissen, Peters and Alberts, 2011). For students preparing to go on placement, writing down a list of their skills, qualities and competencies, then visualising using these in action regularly before placement could help assist in psychological preparation. However, we cannot blame Michael for feeling anxious about starting placement; the evolutionary adaption of the brain's threat system is often activated at the prospect of doing something new and uncertain – that it is the mind at work, one that has a flawed design and negative bias means that a self-compassionate approach needs to be taken (Gilbert, 2010). Rather than blaming the self for experiencing negative thoughts, students going into placement can understand via this model that this is simply the brain at work, in the way it has been programmed – like the software that runs in computers.

Using tools such as mindfulness with self-compassion can calm the situation. Mindfulness enables the emotion to be acknowledged with awareness and non-judgement that makes it the cornerstone of calming the systems in the body that react to threat, and coupled with self-compassion offers a range of ways to relax the threat system – including bodywork approaches such as soothing rhythm breathing and exercises to build a compassionate self, such as letter writing. There are a range of these on the website run by The Compassionate Mind Foundation (2015).

Kabat-Zin (2013) pioneered the use of mindfulness meditation to treat chronic illnesses and recurrent depression four decades ago to enable participants to observe their thoughts and feelings and the way to manage these. Furthermore, a review of empirical studies into mindfulness on psychological health found that it increased well-being and helped regulate emotion and behaviour (Keng, Smoski and Robins, 2011).

> *Placement may not be what you expected; however, by staying positive and making the most of opportunities it can help you find an area of the profession you would not have originally considered.*
>
> Mackenzie, Youth Work and Community Development

The purpose of this is to enable a more objective and non-judgemental self-exploration that builds skills of objectivity and insight. When strong emotions or reactions are involved, the ability to step back in a considered way is lost. Thus, being aware and being able to soothe the self when stressed mean that students are not run by their emotions and are more available to learn as the brain is not preoccupied with these other matters.

Being able to build tolerance for difficult feelings is a critical skill that can help in managing stress and to foster resilience (Gilbert, 2014). Chapter 3 looks at resilience in detail, but Thompson's (2015) idea about realism is an important one to discuss here. Having a positive, open mind but also being realistic about what placement may bring can help regulate and manage anxiety and stress.

It also takes courage to acknowledge that a student might feel fearful about starting placement. These fears may be around juggling academic work or other demands such as caring or parenting, but also about the reasons that students come into the helping professions in the first place. There is some evidence to suggest that placement demands for students in the helping professions compared to others can have additional stresses, with requirements for students to work with client groups who may be experiencing crises, multiple and serious stressors and who often have a history of being abused or traumatised in some way (Cunningham, 2014; Harr et al., 2019). Furthermore, some students will have their own difficult histories or circumstances that call for them to challenge automatic responses or behaviours. Take Krystna, for example, a mother of three, who has been assigned a placement in a child protection social work team. Krystna is used to offering care and comfort to her children when in distress, and needs to consider how she will cope and hold professional boundaries when seeing children in difficult situations, where her first instinct may be to offer a hug or reassurance.

Personal effectiveness and emotional intelligence

Thompson (2015) defines personal effectiveness (the ability to make good use of internal and external resources and self-management) as a range of attributes that includes self-awareness, time management, stress management and being realistic and resilient. Self-awareness is key to building greater emotional intelligence (EQ), a concept first brought to light by the work of Daniel Goleman, who suggested that having emotional, rather than intellectual intelligence was an important attribute, particularly in the helping professions, as it equips us with the ability to recognise our own and others' emotions (Moss, 2017). However, Murphy (2006) suggests that EQ is a vague, undefinable concept that is difficult to grasp or measure, with claims of its importance overstated. Furthermore, there are cultural and social constructions as to how EQ is understood, as well as Gardiner's (1983)

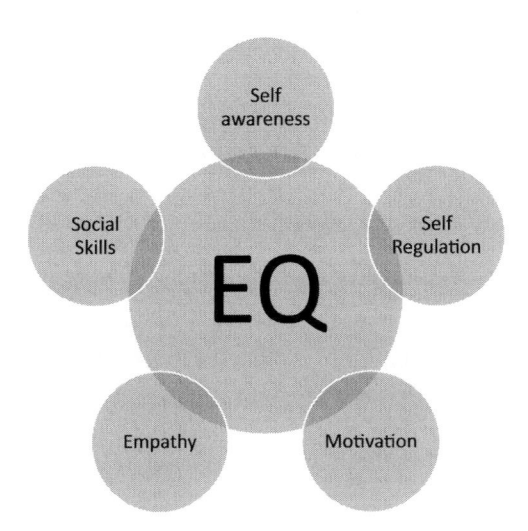

Figure 1.1 Concepts of emotional intelligence

seminal theory that suggests there are various types of intelligence including intra-personal. Goleman's theory could be compared to this aspect of Gardiner's work. However, Goleman (1998) expands on the concept of intra-personal and defines five key areas (see Figure 1.1).

1. Self-awareness – knowing what you are feeling and being able to accurately name emotions in the moment (being in touch with your emotions).

2. Self-regulation – managing emotions and responses in an appropriate and proportionate way (not being ruled by emotions, blowing up or breaking down, recovering from setbacks).

3. Motivation – initiative, persevering and reaching goals (being committed to improving and striving to achieve what you set out to do).

4. Empathy – tuning into and trying to understand the emotions and perspectives of others (trying to walk in someone else's shoes).

5. Social skills – interacting with others, cooperating, negotiating (working well in a team, getting on with others).

Moreover, Mayer and Salovey (1997) conceptualise this in their definition of EQ.

The ability to perceive accurately, appraise, and express emotion.

The ability to access and/or generate feelings when they facilitate thought.

The ability to understand emotion and emotional knowledge.

The ability to regulate emotions to promote emotional and intellectual growth.

EQ is a capacity and skill that relies of high levels of consciousness. However, it also means that this is the responsibility of the individual (Lindebaum, 2009), and while personal responsibility is key, students and placements are not stand-alone entities but part of wider systems. An approach that overemphasises the individual and ignores other factors such as class, race or cultural and systemic problems that occur in systems and organisations is arguably one that is simplistic and reductionist. Thompson (2016) observes that individuals are heavily influenced by their culture and society and ignoring these can lead to piecemeal and oppressive practice. Students, therefore, need to understand that EQ is more than just about understanding the self and others. Nevertheless, there is no denying that EQ is a useful attribute to foster; it is strongly linked to being able to build good relationships with others (social skills) and empathy and is the '*new yardstick*' (Goleman, 1998, p 7) by which employees are being measured. Of course, this begs the question on how to recognise emotions in the first place, which can sometimes be no easy feat. However, as discussed above, mindfulness is a good approach to becoming aware of these. If EQ suggests that motivation is one of its core components, then engaging in tools and practical methods such as mindfulness is critical practice for purposefully paying attention to the present moment, observing and accepting thoughts and feelings non-judgementally. Other practical and useful tools to think about in placement and building consciousness are to use the Johari window (see Chapter 9) and/or complete a self-audit via a SWOT analysis.

Reflective practice is one of the most beneficial tools that helps students develop self-awareness, it helps guard us from tunnel vision in our personal or professional life by allowing us to consider the wider perspectives of a narrative and enables a productive and efficient response.

Wayne, Youth Work and Community Development

Self-audit SWOT analysis

A SWOT analysis grid is a structured, analytical way to examine themes around strengths, weaknesses, opportunities and threats (Helms and Nixon, 2010). Students going into placement can find this a helpful tool to identify different elements that influence the experience. Strengths and opportunities are what are helpful, while weaknesses and threats are what are generally harmful. These could be internal or external. Moreover, when a student going into placement considers these, a systemic analysis can be incorporated that will give depth to the exercise. Some examples of these are shown in Figure 1.2.

The model is an approach to critically evaluate and prepare for placement. As well as thinking about what could go wrong (weaknesses and threats), it also considers what could go right (strengths, opportunities).

A few things that I really found useful as a mature student with prior experience was just to be humble and have a Positive Mental Attitude. I had to remember that work is diverse and can take many forms and practices, therefore I must be flexible. Reminding myself of this helped me go into placement with an open mind and get the most out of the experience.

Barney, Youth Work and Community Development

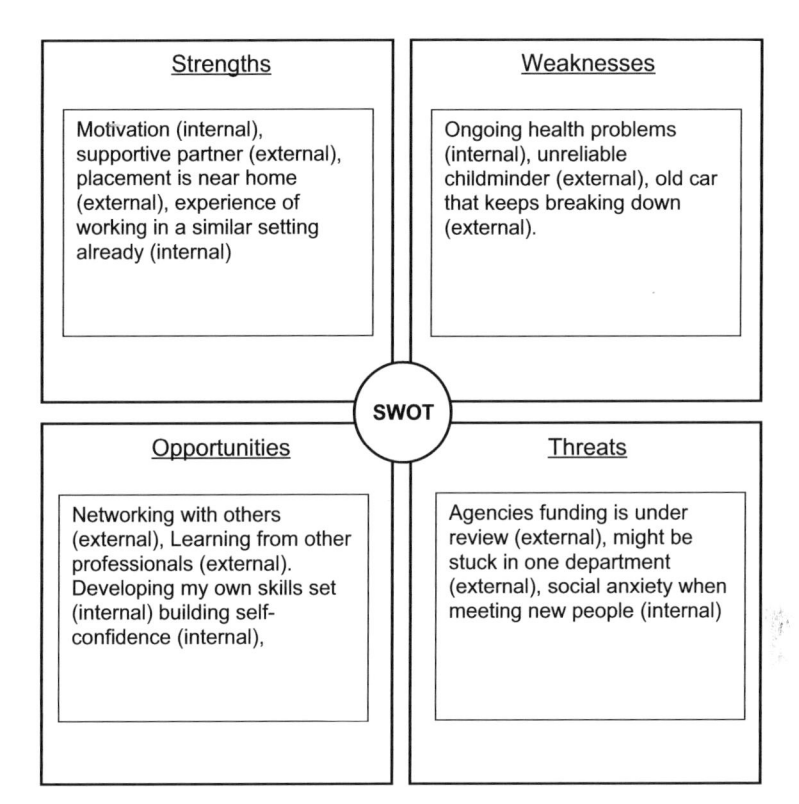

Strengths	Weaknesses
Motivation (internal), supportive partner (external), placement is near home (external), experience of working in a similar setting already (internal)	Ongoing health problems (internal), unreliable childminder (external), old car that keeps breaking down (external).

SWOT

Opportunities	Threats
Networking with others (external), Learning from other professionals (external). Developing my own skills set (internal) building self-confidence (internal),	Agencies funding is under review (external), might be stuck in one department (external), social anxiety when meeting new people (internal)

Figure 1.2 SWOT analysis example

Students going into placement have a good number of assets and skills already, and focusing on these is a good way to build confidence. As noted, the brain has an inbuilt negativity bias, which is why a criticism stays and a compliment can be hard to receive (Carlson, Martin and Buskist, 2013). Self-confidence is a student believing that they can do things and make the best of placement. It is not to be confused with ego or being unrealistic; it is about what a student thinks they can do. As already discussed, having a positive attitude and being open to experience comprise a helpful way to approach placement, and this will help build confidence (Hasson, 2017).

Practical preparation

In developing the 'placement mindset' a student also needs to consider practical aspects of preparation, and many of these can be unique to their chosen course – for example, preparation might involve completing tutorial records, professional progress reflections, attendance records etc. These often require careful time management prior to placement. However, students may also have external factors affecting placement experiences, for example, caring responsibilities, transportation methods or having an additional need such as a disability. These internal and external factors can lead to an increase in stress around the placement experience, and therefore should be discussed at the earliest opportunity with your placement organisation team, who help provide, or signpost to, support. Students are the experts of what is affecting their lives and their personal needs – however, if this is not communicated to other key people (module leaders, support staff, supervisors) it is impossible to provide a structure of support. Therefore, students need to be honest about their worries and concerns about placement. Universities and placement agencies want students to succeed and excel, yet often students express that by discussing their personal needs they are creating difficulty or lowering expectations of agencies and supervisors (Kendall, 2016). However, the reality is that all workplaces have to make reasonable adjustments for workers based on protected characteristics such as gender, race and religion under The Equality Act 2010, and this is a common practice that many supervisors will be experienced in and happy to accommodate.

Additional to the mental and practical is the theoretical preparation needed for a constructive 'placement mindset'. Some students think that they can just arrive at placement and 'get on with the work'; however, university placement often comes with a greater expectation – students should be translating the theory gained from their learning experiences into their placement experience. There is, therefore, a need to develop critical thinking about applying theory to practice as part of a healthy 'placement mindset'.

What is theory?

Theory is in constant flux; new research and approaches are being constantly developed and updated. While this is appropriate and useful, it could lead to confusion for students on placement about what would be considered best practice, especially where organisations are not working with the most recent research. Therefore, it is important to understand what theory is, how to wrestle with it and how to apply it. Being confident about what theory is and how to be critical of it is at the core of the placement experience. Students attend university for a variety of reasons, including engaging in learning, gaining academic reputation and being better equipped for future careers (Neves and Hillman, 2018). Lecturers engage in teaching in a range of different styles, and students might engage in large lectures, group work, workshops, practical sessions and so on. Students show their learning through a range of assessments (Zhang, 2010, Sander et al., 2010, Smith, 2018). This learning is usually assessed by the student response to and engagement with theory. Theory, therefore, becomes the core centre of all university learning (Avis, Fisher and Thompson, 2015). Placement modules are a key part of students' learning as placement takes the taught and debated theory from the classroom and assessments and compares it to real-life working practices. This can lead to the development and reforming of theory and, therefore, working practices, while also encouraging reflection on an individual's own professional values and understanding (Russell, 1997; Smith et al., 2007; Clarke et al., 2014).

However, the placement experience can also provide significant challenges; in the current field of health and social care, constantly evolving issues such as a lack of finance, marketisation of services, neoliberalism, modern technology and competence of staff (British Medical Association (BMA), 2017; Jones, 2015; De St Croix, 2016) can impact on students. These challenges and the effect on placement will be explored more in Chapters 5–7. This can sometimes lead to students engaging in placement with disgruntled workers, poor practice and absent supervisors. Therefore, university teaching should enable students to be fully prepared through good theory development.

Theory is something that students are expected to debate, yet some might not have the skill of identifying theory. For example, some students have described theory as follows.

- 'Anything written in a book.'
- 'An idea that has a model attached to it.'
- 'Ideas that have been informed by research.'
- 'What the lecturer says I need to include in my assessment.'

There is often a conflicting understanding of theory, especially when it could be argued that all the above is accurate. Wacker (1998) suggests that some theory is *abstract and does not have to be applied or tested to be a "good" theory* (p 362). This allows the concept of theory to enter an imaginary space of ideas. Any idea could be counted as theory, and in modern society with open access to a range of social media, students can be exposed to a wide variety of ideas, many of them that have not been applied or tested to become a 'good theory'. However, this concept is not just difficult for students to understand as Ryn and Heaney (1992, p 316) note:

> *When academics, researchers, and theoreticians talk about theory to their practitioner colleagues, are they heard to be discussing something that is commendable and useful (systematically organized knowledge), unapproachable and out of reach (abstract knowledge), or pitiful and unusable (an assumption or guess based on limited knowledge or information)? This is a crucial question.*

The quote suggests that even those who are engrossed in theory on a day-to-day basis can often misunderstand its meaning. If academics cannot agree on an understanding of theory, how can they expect students to? However, at its very core a theory is an idea; that idea is then researched to be evident and changes to practice are made. This can be seen in the situation below:

Intelligence and ethnicity

An idea was formed that genetically people of different ethnic groups had varied levels of intelligence, with some groups being more or less intelligent than others. Nobel Prize winner and renowned geneticist James Watson has made several statements on the IQ difference between black and white individuals. The results of IQ tests 'evidenced' that white people have a higher IQ. This idea was 'proven' through research and reinforced by further research and academics. However, thankfully, several individuals were critical of this theory and used their own ideas and research to show that the differences in IQ scores can be attributed to several factors such as environment, the impact of poverty, the cultural aspect of testing, IQ testing being devised by white men and many other factors. Critical research highlighted the racially homogenous culture of the field of science (Harmon, 2019). The idea of ethnic groups having lower IQ is now generally not accepted, thanks to intensive and critical research. While this is an extreme example, it highlights the effect of ideas (especially by those in positions of privilege, power and influence) providing credibility and affecting culture, thinking and practice. Most importantly, it highlights the need to be critical of theory, so that practice is up to date, but also to prevent great harm to groups and individuals.

The importance of applying theory to practice

Many academics strongly believe that practice should be informed and developed through theory, yet some students can come to the end of their studies with no real concept or understanding of how that theory has been applied to their practice. This is demonstrated in the case study below:

Billy is a final-year student, giving a presentation on the third and final placement of his studies. Billy demonstrated some excellent work, including critical discussion of theories and Billy's supervisor heaped praise on his practice, even offering him a job. However, when asked by the academic why he worked in a particular way, Billy responded, 'I don't know, I just do it'. This frustrated the academic, as the excellent work Billy had completed was not a result of luck, divine gifting or DNA – it was a result of three years' hard study and research. Billy had clearly demonstrated a critical understanding of theories but could not articulate how those theories had informed his own practice.

Students might talk about 'natural ways of working', or 'I just did it' approaches, but these 'normal ways' of working are often developed by theory and experience. Billy had reached a point where he had become competent with theory to the point that it became a natural part of his work. An example of this can be found in other areas of learning, for example, learning to drive. While learning you have to think carefully about what to do and when; however, as you become more competent, you no longer spend as much time thinking on these things – it becomes 'natural'. This is often referred to as the competence ladder (Bradley, 1997) (see Chapter 2 for more detail). This can be the same in our professional practice. While at university students are surrounded by theory; however, students must not move away from critical reflection and practice, recognising the role of theory in their practice.

So how do students move from an understanding of theory to the application of it? And how do you think critically about theory? To make sense of this, the journey with the learning can be described with the model shown in Figure 1.3.

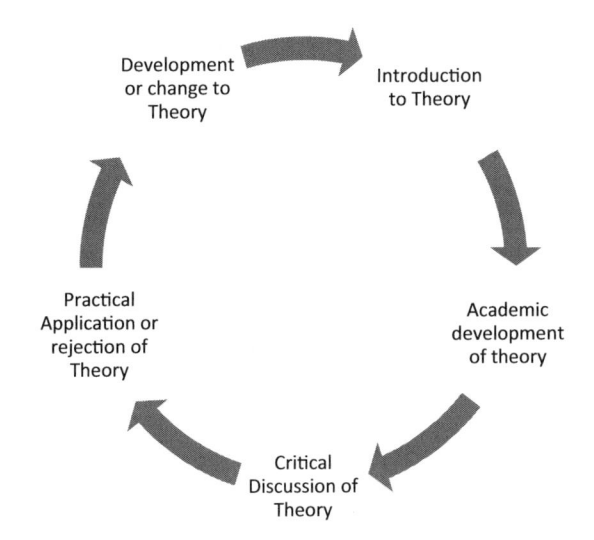

Figure 1.3 Cycle of theory development

This model starts with the introduction of theory; this is the presentation of the idea, which might be based in research or might simply be an idea. Students can then engage in academic development of the theory; the theory is read about and compared to other ideas and theories, which leads to a critical discussion of the theory. This might include questions like 'What needs to change?', 'Is the process linear or circular?', 'Is the concept based on current society?'. With a critical understanding of the theory, a student applies this to practice and explores the real-life working, which may lead to a full rejection of the theory or a useful application of the theory. This moves to the development or change of theory, for example, steps might be added or the direction of travel might change. This leads to the development of a new theory that then continues the process.

The issue here is that in the academic environment, students may not get past the critical discussion of theory until they are involved in practice/placement. This could lead to the students' practice becoming stunted and undeveloped. For the placement mindset to be successfully developed, shifting the stance from seeing theory as 'only in books' to actively searching for and/or applying examples of it is an important component.

Conclusion

This chapter has explored various ways a student can prepare for placement including practically, mentally, emotionally and theoretically through developing a placement mindset. Figure 1.4 provides a representation of its key elements.

Being able to approach placement from these different aspects will enable students to consider the various opportunities and challenges that placement may present them with

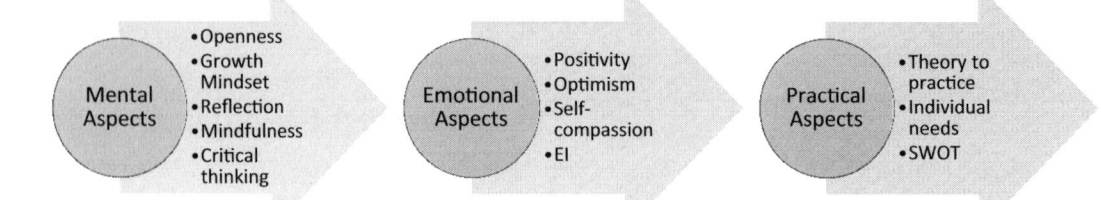

Mental Aspects
- Openness
- Growth Mindset
- Reflection
- Mindfulness
- Critical thinking

Emotional Aspects
- Positivity
- Optimism
- Self-compassion
- EI

Practical Aspects
- Theory to practice
- Individual needs
- SWOT

Figure 1.4 Placement mindset

and grow preparedness to recognise and manage them. Personal effectiveness is crucial to make good use of all the resources students have available to them, including the model shown in Figure 1.4. By using some of the approaches and tools covered here, such as mindfulness, visualisation, emotional intelligence and SWOT analysis, a student can build self-awareness. As well as mental and emotional preparation, practical aspects are an important element of becoming ready to start placement; considering how theory is linked to practice, and while the definition of theory is mixed and varied and can lead to lack of clear understanding of its role and implication, at the heart of the issue is that theory is an idea of the how and the why, enabling students to take classroom learning into practice. However, theory should be treated as an ever-evolving process alongside the ever-evolving working practices of the field. The same is with emotional preparation, which needs to be seen as a dynamic process of development affording the opportunity for both personal and professional growth.

References

Avis, J, Fisher, R and Thompson, R (2015) *Teaching in Lifelong Learning: A Guide to Theory and Practice*. Milton Keynes: Open University Press.

Bradley, F (1997) From Unconscious Incompetence to Unconscious Competence. *Journal of Adult Learning*, 9(Issue 2):20–21.

British Medical Association (2017) *The Ethical Implications of the Use of Market-Type Mechanisms in the Delivery of NHS Care*. London: British Medical Association.

Carlson, N R, Martin, G N and Buskist, W (2013) *Psychology*. 5th ed. Harlow: Pearson Education.

Clarke, C, Martin, M, Sadlo, G and de-Visser, R (2014) The Development of an Authentic Professional Identity on Role-Emerging Placements. *British Journal of Occupational Therapy*, 77(5):222–29.

The Compassionate Mind Foundation (2015) *Resources*. Available awww.compassionatemind.co.uk/resources (accessed 02 June 2010).

Conversano, C, Rotondo, A, Lensi, E, Della Vista, O, Arpone, F, and Reda, M A (2010) Optimism and Its Impact on Mental and Physical Well-Being, *Clinical Practice & Epidemiology in Mental Health*, 6: 25–29.

Cunningham, M (2014) Teaching Social Workers about Trauma: Reducing the Risk of Vicarious Traumatization in the Classroom. *Journal of Social Work Education*, 40(Issue 2):305–17.

De St Croix, T (2016) *Grassroots Youth Work*. Bristol: Policy Press.

Dwerk, C (2010) Mindsets & Equitable Education. *Principal Leadership*, 10(5):25–29. DOI: 10.2174/1745017901006010025.

The Equality Act (2010) Available at www.legislation.gov.uk/ukpga/2010/15/contents (accessed 24 June 2021).

Gardner, H (1983) *Frames of Mind: The Theory of Multiple Intelligences*. New York: Basic Books.

Gilbert, P (2010) *Compassion Focused Therapy: Distinctive Features*. London: Routledge.

Gilbert, P (2014) The Origins and Nature of Compassion Focused Therapy. *British Journal of Clinical Psychology*, 53: 6–41. DOI: 10.1111/bjc.12043.

Goleman, D (1998) *Working with Emotional Intelligence*. London: Bloomsbury Publishing.

Harmon, A (2019) James Watson Had a Chance to Salvage His Reputation on Race. He Made Things Worse. *New York Times*, 1 January [online]. Available at: www.nytimes.com/2019/01/01/science/watson-dna-genetics-race.html (accessed 21 June 2021).

Harr, C R, Brice, T S, Riley, K and Moore, B (2019) The Impact of Compassion Fatigue and Compassion Satisfaction on Social Work Students. *Journal of the Society for Social Work & Research*, 5(2):233–49.

Hasson, G (2017) *Confidence Pocketbook*. Chichester: Capstone Publishing.

Helms, M M and Nixon, J (2010) Exploring SWOT Analysis – Where Are We Now? A Review of Academic Research from the Last Decade. *Journal of Strategy and Management*, 3(3):215–51. DOI: 10.1108/17554251011064837.

Jones, C, Green, J and Higson, H (2015) Do Work Placements Improve Final Year Academic Performance or do High-Calibre Students Choose to do Work Placements? *Studies in Higher Education*, 42(6):976–92.

Jones, R (2015) The End Game: The Marketisation and Privatisation of Children's Social Work and Child Protection. *Critical Social Policy*, 35(4):447–269.

Juznic, P and Pymm, B (2011) Students on Placement: A Comparative Study. *New Library World*, 112(5/6):248–60.

Kabat-Zinn, J (2013) *Full Catastrophe Living*. London: Piatkus.

Kendall, L (2016) Higher Education and Disability: Exploring Student Experiences. *Cogent Education*, 3(1)

Keng, S L, Smoski, M J and Robins, C J (2011) Effects of Mindfulness on Psychological Health: A Review of Empirical Studies. *Clinical Psychology Review*, 31(6):1041–56.

Lam, C, Wong, H and Leung, T (2006) An Unfinished Reflexive Journey: Social Work Students' Reflection on their Placement Experiences. *The British Journal of Social Work*, 37(1):91–105.

Lindebaum, D. (2009) Rhetoric or Remedy? A Critique on Developing Emotional Intelligence. *Academy of Management Learning & Education*, 8(2):225–37.

Mayer, J D and Salovey, P (1997) What is Emotional Intelligence?. In Salovey, P. and D. (Eds.), *Emotional development and emotional intelligence: Educational implications* (pp. 3–34). Basic Books.

Meevissen, Y M C, Peters, M L and Alberts, H (2011) Become More Optimistic by Imagining a Best Possible Self: Effects of a Two Week Intervention. *Journal of Behavior Therapy and Experimental Psychiatry*, 42(Issue 3):371–78. doi.org/10.1016/j.jbtep.2011.02.012.

Meier, J D and Kropp, M (2010) *Getting Results the Agile Way: A Personal Results System for Work and Life*. Bellevue: Innovation Playhouse.

Melincavage, S (2011) Student Nurses' Experiences of Anxiety in the Clinical Setting. *Nurse Education Today*, 31(8):785–89.

Moss, B (2017) *Communication Skills in Health & Social Care*. Los Angeles: Sage.

Murphy, K (2006) *A Critique of Emotional Intelligence: What Are the Problems and How Can They Be Fixed?* London: Psychology Press.

Neves, J and Hillman, N (2018) *2018 Student Academic Experience Survey*. Available at www.hepi.ac.uk/2018/06/07/2018-student-academic-experience-survey/ (accessed 26 March 2019).

Parker, J (2008) When Things Go Wrong! Placement Disruption and Termination: Power and Student Perspectives. *The British Journal of Social Work*, 40(3):983–99.

Peters, L M, Flink, I K, Boersma, K and Linton, S J (2010). Manipulating Optimism: Can Imagining a Best Possible Self be Used to Increase Positive Future Expectancies? *The Journal of Positive Psychology*, 5(3):204–11.

Ratner, H, George, E and Iveson, C (2012) *Solution Focused Brief Therapy: 100 Key Points & Techniques*. Hove: Routledge.

Russell, T (1997) *Teaching about Teaching*. London: Routledge.

Ryn, M and Heaney, C (1992) What's the Use of Theory? *Health Education Quarterly* 19(3):315–30.

Salovey, P and Sluyter, D J (eds) (1997) *Emotional Development and Emotional Intelligence: Educational Implications*. New York: Basic Books.

Sander, P, Stevenson, K, King, M, and Coates, D (2010) University Student's Expectations of Teaching. *Studies in Higher Education*, 25(3):309–23.

Seligman, M. (2018) *Learned Optimism: How to Change Your Mind and Your Life*. London: Nicholas Brealey Publishing.

Smith, K, Clegg, S, Lawrence, E and Todd, M (2007) The Challenges of Reflection: Students Learning form Work Placements. *Innovations in Education and Teaching International Journal*, 44(2):131–41.

Smith, L (2018) *Taking an Active Approach to Lectures Using Flipped Learning, Play and Digital Technologies*. Available at: www.heacademy.ac.uk/knowledge-hub/taking-active-approach-lectures-using-flipped-learning-play-and-digital-technologies (accessed 26 March 2019).

Student Minds (2017) *Grand Challenges in Student Mental Health*. Available at www.studentminds.org.uk/uploads/3/7/8/4/3784584/grand_challenges_report_for_public.pdf (accessed 26 March 2019).

Thompson, N (2015) *People Skills*. 4th ed. London: Palgrave MacMillan.

Thompson, N (2016) *Anti-discriminatory Practice*. 6th ed. Basingstoke: Palgrave MacMillan.

Wacker, J (1998) A Definition of Theory: Research Guidelines for Different Theory-Building Research Methods in Operations Management. *Journal of Operations Management*, 16:361–85.

Zhang, L (2010) Thinking Styles: University Students' Preferred Teaching Styles and Their Conceptions of Effective Teachers. *The Journal of Psychology*, 138(3):233–52.

2 Reflection

Liz Eate, Zuzia Goddard and Sarah Barley-McMullen

Introduction

Reflective practice is a useful tool for practitioners and students to develop self-awareness and a greater understanding of current situations, and to enable appropriate responses. Therefore, to ensure that trainee health and social care practitioners are effective, there is a necessity to be reflective and reflexive in practice (Drake and Heath, 2011). Students must seek to ensure that they are reflective to *'recognise, take authority over and responsibility for [our] own personal and professional actions, identity, values and feelings'* (Boulton, 2014, p 10). Additionally, students need to combine reflection with reflexivity to *'find strategies to question our own attitudes, theories in use, values, assumptions, prejudices and habitual actions; to understand our complex roles in relation to others'* (Boulton, 2014, p 7). This chapter will explore a questioning approach that practitioners need to develop towards their own practice through engagement in reflective and reflexive practice.

This chapter will also identify how reflection and reflexivity can enable practitioners to learn from analysing experience as well as methods of analysis, the place and value of theoretical concepts as well as professional knowledge in the reflective process. It will then go on to explore the premise that reflective practice is not about finding the truth, but rather making sense of a situation to help inform and develop practice. Theories and models will be used and applied to demonstrate how different reflective approaches can create different outcomes. The chapter will conclude with a suggestion of building a reflective practitioner toolkit that uses the resources and resilience of self in a complex and ever-changing environment.

This chapter discusses:

- Definitions and types of reflection
- Understanding a model of competence and its impact on reflection

- Reflexive versus reflective practice
- Models of reflection, including comparisons
- Applying reflection in practice
- The SAROL toolkit

What is reflection?

It can be argued that throughout our lives we learn from our experiences, whether it be physical or emotional ones. Knott and Scragg (2010) link this premise to the works of John Dewey (1933) who saw reflection as '*the continual re-evaluation of personal beliefs, assumptions and ideas in the light of experience and data and the generation of alternative interpretations of those experiences and data*' (p 5), suggesting that experiences will shape the way in which we approach situations in the future. For example, as children we may have fallen over after running too fast and grazed our knees. The next time we run, we may be slower, remembering the pain of the last time. Over time, we learn when we can and cannot run fast as we begin to consider the environment, the weather, our footwear, etc. So, by reflecting on and considering what had happened before, we adjust our behaviour to change the outcome of falling over again. That is, we use our knowledge and experience to predict and consider what may happen again in the future. This then suggests that by reflecting, we look at what has gone before to change or inform the way things will happen going forward. In practice, reflection can be defined as '*the capacity to reflect on action to engage in a process of continuous learning*' (Social Care Institute for Excellence, 2020). Meaning that our day-to-day experiences will shape and inform the way in which we learn, process and develop our approaches. For example, asking the questions, 'What did I do?' 'What went well?' 'What did not go as well?' 'What do I need to do differently in the future?' Without this skill, we may be left making the same mistakes repeatedly, leaving us as incompetent and potentially dangerous practitioners.

Howell (1982, pp 29–33) recognised the importance of reflection in understanding how learning could affect competence. This is demonstrated in the conscious competence model (Figure 2.1).

Howell proposed four stages to the cycle.

Unconscious incompetence – this is the stage where you are not even aware that you do not have a particular competence. For example, you become so confident that you no longer ask for guidance and believe that you know and understand the processes fully. At this stage you are in danger of believing that you already 'know it all' and approach each task with that belief. You no longer consider doing things differently as you believe that the way in which you are doing things is the 'right way'.

Conscious incompetence – this is when you know that you want to learn how to do something, but you are incompetent at doing it. For example, this links to you starting your placement. Here you will be unfamiliar with the building, the service

```
        UNCONSCOUS        →        CONSCIOUS
        INCOMPETENCE              INCOMPETENCE


                                       ↓
          ↑

        UNCONSCIOUS       ←        CONSCIOUS
         COMPETENCE                COMPETENCE
```

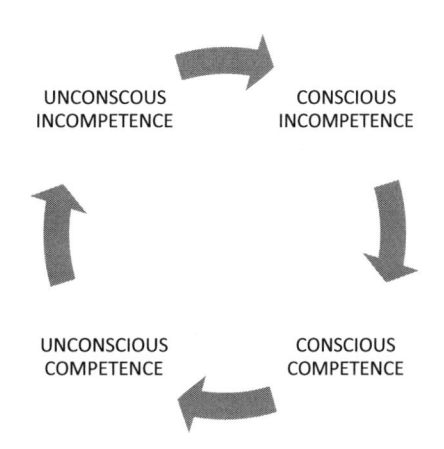

Figure 2.1 *Competence cycle*

> or the group of individuals you are going to be working with. You may at this stage be feeling deskilled and anxious about making mistakes – doing or saying the wrong thing. You are very aware of your practice and how you approach individuals.

Conscious competence – this is when you can achieve this particular task, but you are very conscious about everything you do. For example, as you become more familiar with your placement, you may be feeling a little more confident. You ask questions and make sure you follow the correct processes and check out with your supervisor if you are not sure about anything. You have begun to complete tasks without feeling as anxious about them. You also approach individuals with more confidence and knowledge.

Unconscious competence – this is when you finally master it and you do not even think about what you have such as when you have learnt to ride a bike very successfully. For example, as you progress through your placement, you are given more independence and welcome this as your confidence has grown and you feel able to manage tasks without as much help or supervision. You feel confident about the processes and ask fewer questions. You will undertake tasks without as much planning as you will have knowledge and experience of doing them already several times.

Without the ability to reflect on our practice and interactions, there is a risk of becoming unconsciously incompetent. This could leave practitioners in danger of making mistakes and not acknowledging new and innovative ways of working with others in order to achieve more positive outcomes (Howell, 1982).

Reflection can also be used to try to understand why others are behaving or responding in the way that they do. A reaction to the interaction, their personal circumstances or some other factor (whether environmental or political) could be influencing and impacting on their interactions too. While practitioners need to be self-aware, they should also be aware of the wider social impacts and be able to *'tune in to the bigger social picture that plays such an important part in shaping people's lives'* (Thompson and Thompson, 2018, p 23).

What is reflexive practice?

While reflection deals with the learning gained from the experience, reflexivity is about how the learning is then applied to change the way in which we practice. For example, having reflected that the way in which you are communicating is not working, you are able to respond by changing your communication style to suit the situation/individual. Here, the change is how your use of self is influencing the practice directly.

D'Cruz, Gillingham and Melendez (2007) considered three ways of understanding what it means to practise reflexively.

- *To understand and be aware of the social situation and social problems that influence decision-making.*
  Thompson (2010) takes this idea further, saying that *'everyone is a unique individual, but each of us is an individual in a social context'* (p 59). This means that social workers not only need to be aware of specific factors that impact on an individual, they should also have interest in the wider context in relation to personal, cultural and structural factors that are also present.

- *To understand and be aware that knowledge of theories and research gives practitioners power over those they are interacting with.*
  Power is inherent in social care practice, with French and Raven (1965, cited in Forsyth, 2013) identifying five types of power within social care relationships, legitimate power, expert power, reward power, referent power and coercive power. Appearing to know everything about a person's life or circumstances can inadvertently create a feeling of disempowerment for individuals who may feel that they have lost power over their own narrative.

- *To understand and be aware of the relationship between thoughts and feelings.*
  Fook (2002) defined reflexivity as understanding the influence of 'self' in practice. Some health and social care education often focuses in on the understanding of 'self' and being able to recognise how personal values can (and do) impact on attitudes and values and subsequently practice. Chapter 9 covers resource of self in detail, and includes suggestions as to how you can understand yourself better. For example, embedded within professions are the professional values which underpin further the importance of understanding how personal values can impact on thoughts and feelings.

Consequently, while models of reflection can give us the theoretical knowledge to analyse our practice, reflexivity demonstrates the application of our understanding to practice, considering the individual, their social context as well as the influence of 'self' on our thoughts and feelings. As Thompson points out, theory without practice or indeed practice without theory can be as dangerous as each other (Thompson and Thompson, 2018).

Models of reflection

Considering the importance of reflective and reflexive practice, it is useful to understand some of the models of reflection which are available to support you in this process. Common models used by practitioners are those by Gibbs, Kolb, Schon and Beard.

Gibbs (1988, Figure 2.2) suggests that one way to analyse an event and learn through reflection is to consider the description of the event, how you felt about it, an evaluation and analysis of feelings and why things happened as they did. If you are able to draw from research and your own tacit as well as experiential knowledge on the subject, Gibbs then believes that reasonable conclusions can be reached and an action plan can be created for if the event is ever faced again. This way of reflecting is often encouraged after the event has happened as more time can be given to the reflection and the rationalisation of feelings.

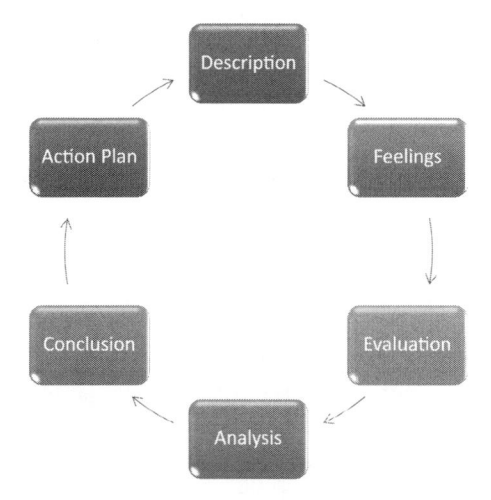

Figure 2.2 Gibbs's reflective cycle (1988)

Schon's model of reflection (1983, Figure 2.3) suggests that reflection is a process that can happen consciously over time. Schon believes there is benefit in reflecting retrospectively on practice as well as at the same time as practice is occurring. This model enables the practitioner to:

- reflect prior to the event, **FOR action** to plan ahead and weigh up some of the pros and cons of different approaches;

- reflect at the time of the event, **IN action** by constantly considering the situation which you are in, and change how you are acting immediately to improve or change the situation (reflexivity);
- and finally, to reconsider the event, reflecting **ON action** enabling the changes and building of good practice which are needed for your future effective practice.

Reflection FOR practice (Planning prior to the event)
- Considering outcomes which need to be achieved
- Planning for possible resources needed (inclusing staff)
- ensuring that risk assessments are dynamic and in place

Reflection IN action (at the time of the event)
- The experience of self
- Thinking about practice, acton and impact at the time
- Acting immediately

Reflection ON action (after the event)
- Reflecting retrospectively
- Considering what might be done differently next time
- Using new knowledge or theoretical perspectives learned from study, to inform the how the reflector processes feelings and actions surrounding the event.

Figure 2.3 Schon's model of reflection (1983)

Kolb's experiential learning cycle (1984, Figure 2.4) again suggests that there is great value to be had by reflecting after practice has taken place and provides practitioners with a useful way of applying theory to practice. Initially Kolb (1984) suggests that there is a concrete experience which happens; this is followed by a reflective observation where you can reflect on the experience. Abstract conceptualisation follows where you analyse the event, making connections to new ideas and learning from your experience before actively experimenting, planning and trying out your ideas, conclusions and learning.

Beginning with the 'concrete experience' stage – what is the practice-based situation which requires further thought or consideration? Where is the situation taking place? Who is involved? What is going on?

Next Kolb moves on to the 'reflect on experience' stage. Be honest with yourself here about what is going on. What is really happening and what really needs to happen? Why are the practitioners doing what they are doing? What are the responses of the individual that you are working with? This is the stage where the practitioner needs to make their own meaning.

The third section is where Kolb encourages you to take what you already know and the meaning you have made from it and apply new ideas or theory, which enables you to

Reflection · 27

Plan Active Experimentaion 'REVIEW'

Concrete Experience 'DO'

Abstract Conceptulisation 'ADD THEORY AND LEARN'

Reflecton on Experience 'REFLECT'

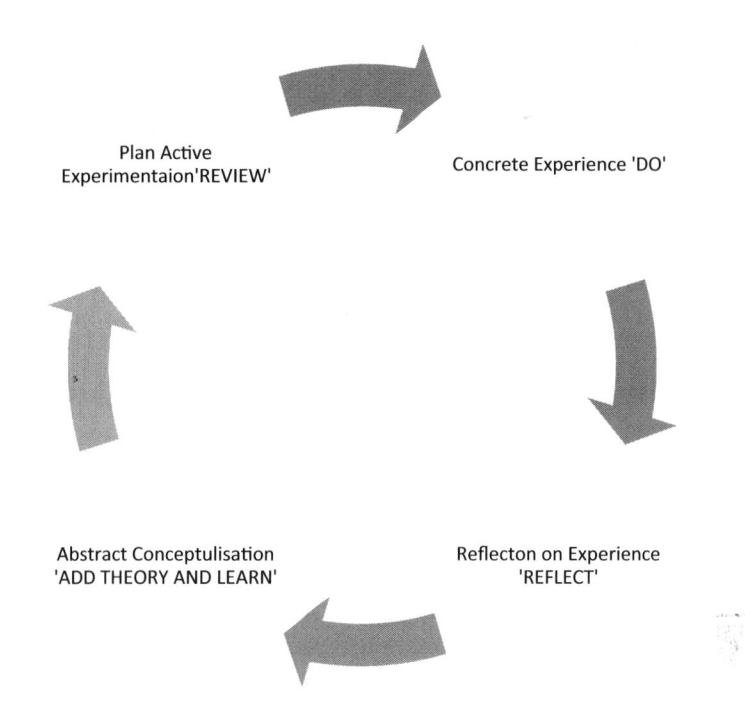

Figure 2.4 *Kolb's experiential learning cycle (1984)*

see the situation and responses from a different perspective. It may be that you are working with a group of young people who all got on really well when they first met; however, after the second week of engaging with them as a group and introducing a new activity, individuals begin to argue with each other, and the structure of the group begins to crumble. As a practitioner there is the potential here to begin to doubt your skills as a worker and keep trying to find a way to patch up the fallout that has occurred. However, applying Tuckman's (1965) theory of the stages of group process, you can understand that often groups go through a storming stage in their development. Being able to apply a new idea or a theory to a situation brings a new level of understanding to the reflective practice situation and enables you to learn more about your practice. The individual you are working with will also benefit considerably from your reflective practice and professional knowledge, as they also have the ability to learn and grow, or, as Einstein suggested, if the educator focuses on providing the right conditions for learning, the learning will happen naturally.

Kolb's final stage of his learning cycle is around planning active experimentation, to review where your practice is considering the previous three stages. This stage can be the most enlightening as it enables you to take stock of the journey you have travelled through and the process of the application of reflection to practice. It can also enable you to consider, in a more informed way, where your next steps could lead you.

Beard (2010) has more recently expanded on Kolb's experiential learning cycle (1984) to consider how your emotions influence reflection. Beard (2010) suggests that every person has a sense of being or an inner self, this being the culmination of our experiences, genetics and self-awareness. It is suggested that this sense of being is internal and encompasses our ethics, values and the sense we have already made of the world which then impacts on our future experiences. Beard posits that we have a sense of belonging which is both social, in that it encompasses the people who we are with, and environmental. It could be seen that 'inclusion' is also a factor in our sense of belonging encompassing how long we have been with an organisation, whether we are seen as a professional in our own right and whether there are structures in place which would support us to have difficult conversations and deal with challenging situations.

When an event occurs that is reflected on, we begin by experiencing it externally with our senses. Beard (2010) suggests that the more senses that are used the more we can learn from, understand and recall an experience or event. The five known basic senses are sight, touch, hearing, smell and taste. During the event, information comes to us from the external force and enters our brains to be processed. At this point, as the information enters our brains, the focus of the reflection moves internally and causes us to 'feel' with a range of emotions (Schoeller and Dunaetz, 2018).

Gross (2020) suggests that in order that we can act in a more considered manner rather than in a manner where we act on our 'fight or flight responses', we need to build the capacity to manage our emotions or 'self-regulate'. Gross (2020) describes this as evaluating a situation objectively, whereas Griffin and Tyrell (2001) discuss that when we feel intense emotions, we lose the capacity for rational thought by focusing in on the perceived threat to us, which causes us to react before we have considered the situation and evaluated how our differing reactions may be received. Griffin and Tyrell suggest that we should essentially zoom out to develop our capacity for rational thought, stopping us from acting in a way which does not meet our personal or professional values (Gross, 2020) and allowing us to move forward to what Beard (2010) describes as the knowing stage. In placement, emotional challenges face students at regular intervals, from a nerve-wracking first day to a visit to a client that upsets or distresses us. Being aware of our feelings but being able to step back from them so we are not lost in them means we are not lost in reacting and can better weigh up what is actually going on.

Knowing is described by Beard as organising and processing the information in order to understand it better and suggests that initially we understand and evaluate or 'process' an event by analysing the parts, synthesising or combining the elements by relating theory to the practice and using our current knowledge to further understand the issues. By comparing and contrasting ideas together, then using this to converge the ideas, we are able to solve the situation or issues which have arisen. Beard observes that this is a transformative process which changes us and helps us to learn from an event, which then impacts on our sense of being, thus completing the reflective and learning cycle.

Figure 2.5 is a comparison of the different models of reflection discussed here – by knowing these, students can chose the most appropriate one to apply.

Gibbs (1988)	Schon (1983)	Kolb (1984)	Beard (2010)
• Process driven. • Professional and personal development • Retrospective reflection. • Learning through repition. • Learning from reflection and analysis for next time. • Useful for developing Personal as well as Leadership skills through the repetition of process. • Applicable to many professions.	• Process driven. • Professional and personal development • Planning based on prior information and knowledge. • Learning in the moment as well as from reflection and analysis for next time. • Useful for developing individual, team an organisational approaches to events and practice	• Process driven. • Professional and personal approach to own professional development. • Learning preferences can be accomadated. • Transformation of experience and theory in to knowledge applied to practice. • Continuously created and recreated. • Learning from reflection and analysis for next time. • Applicable to many professions. • Useful for personal and professional development.	• Process driven. • Professional and personal approach to own professional development. • Learning preferences can be accomadated. • Transformation of experience and theory in to knowledge applied to practice. • Continuously created and recreated. • Learning from reflection and analysis for next time. • Applicable to many professions. • Useful for personal and professional development • Also considers how our previous experiences impact on our continuing knowledge learning and development • Looks at the impact of our emotions and senses on how we may react to new situations

Figure 2.5 Comparing reflective models

Applying reflection in practice

The idea of reflective practice suggests that we need to adopt a questioning approach to what we do in our practice. In professional practice, we therefore need to be questioning:

- our understanding;
- what we believe to be true;
- our assumptions;
- our attitudes;
- our actions;
- our values;
- our academic, professional and personal knowledge;
- the way we work;
- the outcomes of our work.

From this, we can see that reflective practice is about the process of learning from analysing our experiences of self, others and situations. Skilled practitioners use different forms of knowledge to develop practice – knowledge of skills, of resources and of competencies needed. Practice informs knowledge and knowledge informs practice. Gould and Taylor (1996) suggest that when we practice in a reflective way, we can develop a new approach to professional learning through developing our own professional knowledge. Professional knowledge is made up of our understanding of theory and practice alongside a systemic analysis of experience. This is confirmed by Eraut (1994) when he suggests that professional knowledge is based on intuition, understanding and learning from practice. This idea of creating our own professional knowledge through reflective practice is not, according to Robb (2007), about discovering the 'truth'. Instead, it is to enable us as practitioners to make sense of experiences of practice and ultimately to inform practice.

To apply this, we need to question how we understand reflection in relation to our experience, knowledge and practice. We need to be able to do this prior to an event, while an event is happening and after an event has occurred. For the practice of reflection to embody professional or personal learning, these areas need to be addressed dynamically and be underpinned by theory.

Petty (2009) discusses good learning taking place only when the right conditions are created for the learners to make their own meaning or find their own understanding of a situation. The limitation of this is that conditions need to be right, and someone will only be able to construct new knowledge around the limitations of their own experience. The advantage of this, however, is that if the right conditions can be created, then limitations will grow and the learning will become embedded. Consequently, from starting with what we already know and then moving on to applying our own constructs of meaning to the situation through applying theory, we can essentially discover something new which will align with the purpose of the event – or it will encourage further reflection and consideration.

Understanding learning theories can be crucial in professional practice with all groups. Reflection on learning can enable all manner of different aspects of practice to be developed and positive change to be achieved. Jappe's (2010) Three Ps model (Professional: Personal: Private: approaches to practice) explores how trust can be developed between the professional practitioner and the child/young person, through making greater connections on a professional (boundary setting) and personal (trust building), but not private level. The 'private' level is the practitioner's rest and recovery place. An understanding of behaviourist styles of learning, based on the works of Pavlov (1927) and Skinner (1976), is where we learn from reward and motivation may be at the heart of one individual's learning preference, while a humanist approach, which was set out by Rogers (1961), translates emotions, personal growth and development into structures of confidence building, resilience and self-esteem, which Rogers believes will be at the heart of how another child/young person is able to find a way of engaging with you as a practitioner.

In summary, reflection in professional practice enables a practitioner to consciously stop, think and plan what they are going to do, what they are doing, why they are doing it and how it could be done differently next time (Kolb, 1984). You can only be a reflective practitioner if you apply reflexivity and relate theory and other professional knowledge to practice with every event you engage in, and you learn from each situation (Boulton, 2014). Practice and learning have knowledge at their heart, and reflective-based practice is always most effective when working with others (Eraut, 1994).

The reflective practitioner toolkit – SAROL

How we reflect is as important as why we reflect, to be consistent in our approach to reflective practice. There are skills and knowledge that you will need to draw on, both at a moment's notice as well as when planning for future work streams. Having a 'toolkit' in your collection of professional resources is essential in professional practice. It will arm you with not only the resources of self and others, but also an awareness of what the outcomes of a situation could look like. Arguably these resources will be different for everyone; however, for reflective and reflexive practice, they will need to be around the following five areas forming the acronym **SAROL**.

1. **Situation evaluation**
   Evaluate the situation. What is it? Who is involved? Where is it taking place? Why has the situation occurred? What else do you need to know about the situation?

2. **Action**
   What is going on? Who is doing what? What happened? What did not happen? What needs to happen next?

3. **Response**
   How does everyone involved respond to what is going on? What influenced these responses? How were your responses received? Which theories support your thinking? What practical resources might you need to respond? What worked, what did not and why?

4. **Outcome**
   How does the situation end? What are the consequences? What are the outcomes and next steps for everyone involved?

5. **Learning**
   What have you learnt from the responses and outcomes within the process? Think about what you would do again and what you would not. Think about the resources that were used – which helped, which did not? How have you recorded what took place? Is this kept safely?

Using a questioning approach throughout the SAROL reflective/reflexive process will enable you to view the situation thoroughly, enabling different layers to be discovered as your experiences and knowledge as a trainee professional practitioner increase. This is a crucial part of being a reflective practitioner.

In conclusion, this chapter has discussed the importance of reflective and reflexive practice on placement, and how students can use different models to utilise this. By comparing models of reflection, students are better placed to select an appropriate model and learn effectively from it. Reflection is influenced by a wide range of issues, including personal values, knowledge and experiences; so it is vital that students use the valuable tool of reflection to understand themselves and their practice better. Relating theory to practice and reflective outcomes to feed into critical evaluation (reflexivity), analysis of events and professional learning is critical to enable you to develop into safe and effective practitioners. Having a sound way in which reflection can be applied to practice to enable trainee practitioners to access appropriate resources and achieve the best outcomes can be supported by using toolkits such as the SAROL to analyse and improve practice.

References

Beard, C (2010) *The Experiential Learning Toolkit: Blending Practice with Concepts*. London: Kogan Page.

Bolton, G (2014) *Reflective Practice – Writing and Professional Development*. 4th ed. London: Sage.

D'Cruz, H, Gillingham, P and Melendez, S (2007) Reflexivity, Its Meanings and Relevance for Social Work: A Critical Review of the Literature. British Cultivating Reflexivity in Social Work Students: A Course-Based Experience. *Journal of Practice Teaching & Learning*, 11(1):54–74. DOI:10.1921/ 175951511X651959.

Dewey, J (1933) *How We Think: A Restatement of the Relation of Reflective Thinking to the Educative Process*. Boston: D.C. Heath & Co Publishers.

Drake, P and Heath, L (2011) *Practitioner Research at Doctorate Level – Developing Coherent Research Methodologies*. London: Routledge.

Eraut, M (1994) *Developing Professional Knowledge and Competence*. London: Falmer Press.

Fook, J. (2002) *Social Work: Critical Theory and Practice*. London: Sage.

Forsyth, D R (2013) *Group Dynamics*. 6th ed. Belmont: Wadsworth.

Gibbs, G (1988) *Learning by Doing: A Guide to Teaching and Learning Methods*. London: Further Education Unit.

Gould, N and Taylor, I (1996) *Reflective Learning for Social Work: Research, Theory and Practice*. University of Michigan: Arean Publishing.

Griffin, J and Tyrell, I (2001) The APET Model: Emotions Come First. *Human Givens Journal*, 8(1).

Gross, R (2020) *Psychology: The Science of Mind and Behaviour*. 8th ed. London: Hodder Education.

Howell, W S (1982) *The Empathic Communicator*. University of Minnesota: Wadsworth Publishing Company.

Jappe, E (2010) *Handbook for Pedagogy Students*. Frederiksberg: Frydenlund.

Kolb, D A (1984) *Experimental Learning: Experience as the Source of Learning and Development*. Englewood Cliffs: Prentice Hall.

Knott, C and Scragg, T (2010) *Reflective Practice in Social Work*. Exeter: Learning Matters.

Pavlov, I P (1927) *Conditioned Reflexes: An Investigation of the Physiological Activity of the Cerebral cortex*. Oxford: Oxford University Press.

Petty, G (2009) *Teaching Today A Practical Guide Fourth Edition*. London: Nelson Thrones.

Robb, M (2007) *Youth in Context: Frameworks, Settings and Encounters*. London: Sage.

Rogers, C R (1961) *On Becoming a Person: A Therapist's View of Psychotherapy*. Boston: Houghton Mifflin.

Schon, D (1983) *The Reflective Practitioner: How Professionals Think in Action*. London: Temple Smith.

Schoeller, D and Dunaetz, N (2018) Thinking Emergence as Interaffecting: Approaching and Contextualizing Eugene Gendlin's Process Model. *Continental Philosophy Review*, 51(Issue 1):123–40.

Skinner, B F (1976). *About Behaviorism*. New York: Random House.

Social Care Institute for Excellence (SCIE) (2020) *Reflective Practice*. Available at: www.scie.org.uk/workforce/induction/standards/cis02_personaldevelopment.asp#:~:text=Reflective%20practice%20is%20defined%20as,see%20what%20you%20can%20learn (accessed 25 May 2021).

Thompson, N (2010) *Theorizing Social Work Practice*. Basingstoke: Palgrave Macmillan.

Thompson, S and Thompson, N (2018) *The Critically Reflective Practitioner* Basingstoke: Palgrave Macmillan.

Tuckman, B W (1965) Developmental Sequence in Small Groups. *Psychological Bulletin*, 63:384–99.

3 Emotional resilience

Toni-Marie Benaton, Pauline Green and Fran Fuller

Introduction

This chapter introduces the concept of emotional resilience and how it can help to prepare students to succeed on placements. Being resilient can help students to feel confident, have a rewarding placement experience and develop strategies to continue to develop their resilience. To encourage an understanding of emotional resilience, the chapter begins by exploring the origins of the term 'emotional resilience' and considers research relating to emotional resilience in children and adults. Definitions of emotional resilience are also examined which include a wide range of aspects relating to the individual such as personal traits, attributes, skills and experience, as well as social, cultural and environmental factors.

The chapter continues by explaining how students need to be able to show their capacity to manage the day-to-day responsibilities that a placement brings, thus highlighting why an understanding of emotional resilience is so important. Being aware of what emotional resilience is enables students to develop strategies for keeping emotionally and physically safe. The chapter concludes by presenting different ways that students can use their emotional resilience to enhance their skills in practice in order to cope with the varied demands of the profession.

This chapter discusses:

- What is emotional resilience?
- Why is emotional resilience important for placement?
- How can students develop emotional resilience?
- How can emotional resilience be used in practice?

What is 'emotional resilience'?

The term 'emotional resilience' was first used by Werner (1971), best known for her 40-year longitudinal study involving 698 children living in Hawaii, which investigated the effects of trauma and deprivation on children (Werner and Smith, 2001). The children were assessed at different stages throughout their lives: at birth, during adolescence and at 32 years of age. The research was interested in trying to find out why a proportion of the children growing up with adverse life conditions had avoided becoming involved in some of the expected adolescent behaviours, such as teenage pregnancy, substance misuse and unemployment. The results from the study indicated that resilience was linked to the children having a good attachment, if not with a parent, with significant others in their lives such as peers, a teacher or step-parent. It also established that resilience should be viewed as a process, rather than a trait, and that it developed over time (Zolkoski and Bullock, 2012). The findings of the study were endorsed by other theorists interested in resilience at the time. Garmezy (1973) studied recovery rates for schizophrenic patients, and Rutter (1975) explored the idea of 'protective mechanisms' being utilised by children to deal with risk factors in their lives.

Definitions of emotional resilience

According to Hurley, Martin and Hallberg (2013), any definition of emotional resilience includes a wide range of aspects relating to the individual, in terms of personal traits or characteristics, as well as social, cultural and environmental factors, as outlined in Figure 3.1.

From a psychological perspective, theorists such as Bowlby (1951) and Rutter (1975, 1985, 2007) considered emotional resilience to be a characteristic that developed in childhood. Bowlby's (1953) maternal deprivation theory proposed that children who grew up having formed secure attachments in their childhood were more likely to have positive mental health, self-confidence and high self-esteem later in life. This heralded a change in thinking about the definition of resilience, from one of individual traits being the main determining factor to that of taking into consideration certain processes involving risk and protective factors that might enhance resilience (Aronwitz, 2005).

This shift in thinking was demonstrated by Collishaw et al. (2007) who, to gain an understanding of what made some people more resilient than others, undertook a research study in 1964 of 571 children, aged 9–10 years to 44–45 years. The children were selected because they were known to the local authorities as having been physically or sexually abused. When interviewed and tested in adulthood, half of the participants showed no adverse psychological or emotional effects. The findings indicated that the most important factor in remaining resilient was having good-quality relationships in childhood, which included positive parenting (not normally associated with abuse), good peer support and having parents who were in stable marital relationships.

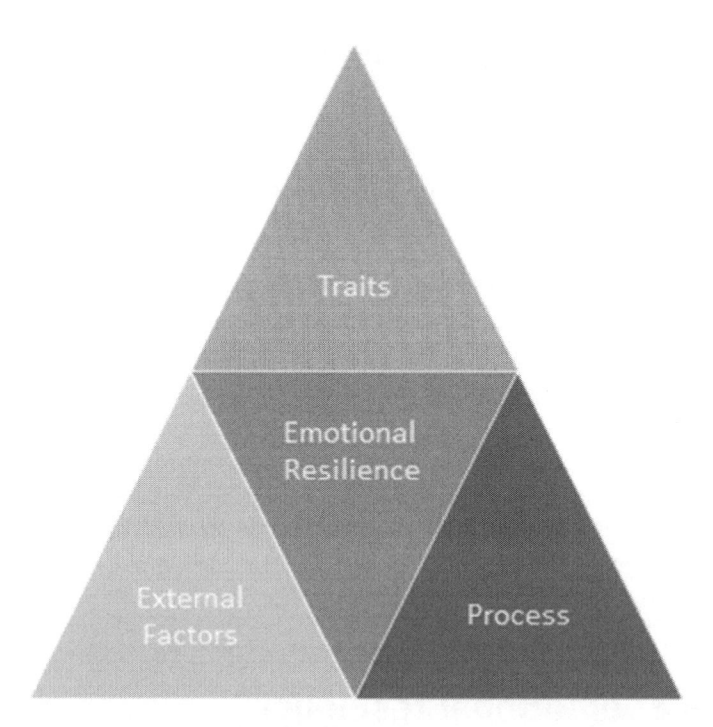

Figure 3.1 Components of emotional resilience

Ungar (2006, 2008, 2012) was critical of the fact that most of the research on children and young people's resilience concentrated solely on personality traits or protective factors such as secure and supportive attachments, as well as being based on a westernised point of view. Findings from the study in 2006, an international resilience project involving over 1500 at-risk young people from 11 countries in 5 continents, evidenced that there were aspects to resilience which were associated with culture and environment, which could promote healthy emotional and psychological growth and resilience. According to the study, there was a lack of recognition in literature and research that resilience was a process which could vary and be dependent upon culture and context. Ungar's (2006) definition of emotional resilience highlighted that:

> *Resilience is both an individual's capacity to navigate to health resources and a condition of the individual's family, community and culture to provide these resources in culturally meaningful ways.*
>
> (p 55)

Ruch, Turney and Ward (2010) maintained that there were a wide range of factors associated with resilience which included optimism and self-motivation, coupled with a particular set of skills and abilities such as problem-solving and coping mechanisms, which seemed to make it possible for people to 'bounce back' from adverse situations. According to this research, a combination of intrapersonal traits and interpersonal skills enabled individuals to remain resilient while working in environments which were often unpredictable and risk laden, similar to those that might be encountered by students on placement.

Adamson, Beddoe and Davys (2014) defined resilience as being a process which is constantly changing and developing. They considered that working in caring professions demanded the ability to be able to cope with high levels of emotional labour in terms of high caseloads, increased paperwork, limited resources, constantly changing policies and procedures and poor supervision. These factors could have a significant impact on emotional resilience, and they proposed that, with experience and over time, individuals were able to employ strategies to cope in order to not become overwhelmed. However, this did not mean that those individuals would never feel stressed or unable to cope. Knowing that experience can be linked with resilience is encouraging for students, as placements will provide a wide range of opportunities to develop their experience.

In summary, the definitions outlined in this section highlight the fact that emotional resilience is a multifaceted concept, and that no one definition is likely to suit all. Different professions will consider it to have a meaning that is pertinent to them and will connect it to the type of work being undertaken and the people involved.

> *Until reading about emotional resilience as being a thing, I thought more along the lines of you either had it or you don't, and I am quite a strong character, so I've never paid close attention to it. I feel I understand it more, that saying 'no man is an island' came to mind.*
> Rachel, Social Work

While on placement students will have the opportunity to reflect on what it is that makes them feel more resilient. It is possible that students will view resilience as a personality trait, but as the research indicates, it is also likely that if the placement is experiential and supportive, students will start to make links with other factors that may increase their emotional resilience.

Why is emotional resilience important for placement?

Placements can be an exciting time for students as they move away from the confines of academic settings and formal curriculum learning into a new environment, such as hospitals, prisons, educational facilities, local authority departments and voluntary agencies, offering students the opportunity to learn by '*doing*' (Chui, 2009). This is achieved by working directly and indirectly with a range of professionals and service users. The placement is where students develop their ability and capacity to identify themselves as a professional (Nixon and Murr, 2006), by taking on and adapting to the role and responsibilities set out by the organisation and in working to relevant policies, procedures, legislative law and in managing the complex dynamics of interprofessional and interdisciplinary working. This, though, is complex in nature, with students often having to balance continued academic study alongside placement reports and other commitments such as family and work-related or financial pressures. This can lead to placements being presented as a daunting experience, undoubtedly creating feelings of anxiety or stress which can impact on individual well-being (Collins et al., 2010; Kinman and Grant, 2017).

Emotional resilience can be seen as akin to wearing a *'multifunctioning coat'*, acting as an agent in maintaining a safe and warm environment and protecting oneself from the effects of working in an emotionally charged sector. The provision of comfort creates sustenance in building self-confidence and esteem to navigate the world. Having a coat that adapts to the environment enables a foothold to be made, in what constitutes realistic expectations of self through prioritising and exploring the use of assertiveness. It can provide a better chance of developing self-efficacy, which is to be proactive even in the face of great adversity, creating motivation to develop self-determination and a steadiness in one's sense of self. Finally, emotional resilience is interrelated to a deeper level of understanding in making sense of adverse experiences, creating opportunities for personal and professional growth (Grant and Kinman, 2012; Bunce et al., 2019).

How can students develop emotional resilience?

Having established that emotional resilience is not necessarily a trait someone is born with, it is worth considering how it is developed. Individuals all develop strategies to manage stressful situations, consciously or subconsciously, and this is dependent on individual traits and internal/external resources with a common theme being the prior learning experience of the individual.

Learning need and resilience

The arrival onto placement can be both an exciting opportunity and an anxiety-provoking experience filled with a variety of expectations. It is important for students to remember that as a learner, prior knowledge and experience will influence any assumptions of the learning experience. Students may have adopted a particular learning style or way of working; so understanding any learning need is a good starting point. As adult learners, it is important to recognise the importance of different characteristics of individual learning, such as how a person may take on new information and the impact of the environment in relation to physical, cultural and social elements. Knowles (1990) relates this to adult learning, a concept which highlights the difference between children and adults.

Marton and Säljö (1976) highlight two distinct approaches to learning: *'surface'* (memorising information and a lack of reflection of its meaning) and *'deep'* (understanding the application of theory into practice with greater analysis of reflection and meaning). This suggests that the element of reflection can be seen as building professional competency, increasing opportunities for self-development and enhancing individual emotional resilience. However, within placements this can create anxiety about what to reflect on, why and how, reducing opportunities for personal and professional growth. Students can struggle to understand the concept of reflection and the reality can be daunting, particularly when being observed or assessments are being undertaken. A useful mechanism is to think of reflection as moving away from a culture of compliance (what needs to be done to pass!) into a culture of what the learning means, personally and professionally. This generates opportunities to stimulate thoughts and feelings both internally and externally on any aspect of the learning experience.

Furthermore, Säljö's (1979a, 1979b) discussion recognises distinctive differences in how people learn and that the individual's approach to learning is an important factor to consider because it incorporates self-efficiency; the 'student' becomes more aware of themselves and the demands placed upon them in relation to the learning environment.

> *Resilience will provide an opportunity for me to enhance self-awareness and enable the generation of new strategies to cope with the demands of a statutory children placement and family life.*
>
> Blessing, Social Work

As such, students are better able to manage, adapt and take on new responsibilities which become a core feature, particularly in relation to placements and the development of self (Beesley, 2020). A key component to consider here is that mistakes are part of the learning experience and that effective strategies in exploring these are essential (Sicora, 2019). Therefore, it is vital to have a robust system in place to support continuous reflective development.

How can emotional resilience be used in practice?

As well as understanding what emotional resilience is and why it is needed, understanding how emotional resilience can be used in practice is important, and one which needs time and preparation to develop and master. Emotional resilience is not something that can just be attained overnight. It is the combination of the individual's ability to acknowledge, manage and overcome negative stresses that impact on their personal and professional role and responsibilities and to find personal meaning within them (Klohen, 1996; Youssef and Lathans, 2007).

In facilitating the development of resilience in practice, understanding the connection between emotional resilience and emotional intelligence is useful because it allows for the further development of the conscious and the unconscious state of knowing. Goleman (1996) coined the term 'emotional intelligence' as exploring the individual's disposition in managing and sustaining one's own and others' emotional responses. As a student acknowledging the influx of stimulus, its impact upon self, actions and professional insight is essential, as it offers an opportunity to create effective and successful learning experiences. Morrison (2007) further highlights Goleman's (1998) definition of emotional intelligence as a useful set of concepts for students to consider, arguing that understanding emotions is critical in practice (Table 3.1).

Table 3.1 Emotional intelligence definition adapted by Morrison (2007)

Goleman's (1998) definition of emotional intelligence adapted by Morrison (2007)	
Self-awareness	Relates to the individual's capacity to understand their abilities, levels of confidence, feelings and emotions, their impact on self and practice, how this affects others and how, in turn, this impacts upon their sense of self and ability and capacity to adapt
Emotional resilience	Is the individual's ability to thrive in stressful environments, by developing strategies which build on managing stress through the development of accessing appropriate support and resources
Motivation/drivers	Connects with ambitions and achievements and the ability to keep moving forward even in times of great adversity
Empathy/sensitivity:	Is the capacity to be able to acknowledge or anticipate the behaviour or emotional state of others, to be able to '*walk in their shoes*' (Hogan, 1969) and adapt responses, emotions and interventions accordingly
Influence/rapport	Can be identified as a strengths-based approach, in that it is an essential component in developing, engaging and sustaining relationships by using positive interactions which build upon trust, motivating the individual and the potential for success and change
Intuition	Acknowledgement of instinctive feelings or emotions of a situation without conscious reasoning of the why and being aware of its importance
Conscientiousness	Refers to the ability to be honest, trustworthy and mindful of work being undertaken in order to persevere in completing work to a high standard

A student that can develop these abilities in placement will be able to combat some of the negative stresses that can arise, such as complex team dynamics. This connection between emotional intelligence and emotional resilience enables the student to 'make sense of a situation' both internally and externally and act appropriately (Howe, 2008). The student learns to recognise the impact of the environment on their actions and consider the most appropriate way forward and protect their own well-being. Having developed the concept of what emotional resilience is and how to develop certain attributes, it is important for students to think about other areas that might create anxiety and where particular strategies or techniques may be useful. The remainder of this chapter explores these concepts.

University and placement

Self-development is an important factor to consider in placement. Students may be undertaking practice alongside academic study, which can feel isolating as well as overwhelming, particularly if expectations and processes are different. Many students on placement move from writing in the third person to the first person with the completion of portfolios that explore application to practice. These new ways of thinking and writing, as well as managing individual priorities, can create feelings that are uncomfortable. As such, it is important for students to be aware that such feelings or emotions are normal, and seen as a positive feature, particularly in relation to the development and continuation of emotional resilience. Such acceptance can enable a student to move out of a comfort zone to access relevant services, most notably the library and study skills (Wilson and Flanagan, 2019). The student's ability to expand and develop these connections also resonates with self-efficiency, which, according to Wilks and Spivey (2010), enables students to manage stress from both the perspective of practice placements and the accompanying academic work. The self as a resource is explored in Chapter 9.

Students may also be on placement away from their peers or an environment completely alien to them. Students will of course have access to a formal induction process where the day-to-day practicalities of what a placement will offer in relation to cases or individual pieces of work are likely to be provided. However, the impact on emotional well-being or the dynamics of the placement may be minimised, as highlighted by Grant and Kinman (2012), by students acknowledging and disclosing feelings of anxiety. Therefore, navigating support services available is a particularly useful exercise as it can demonstrate the student's capacity to find solutions, prioritise workloads and take on new information in what Greer (2016) identifies as a proactive approach. This can then create a buffer zone where emotional resilience can be further promoted, and more successfully achieved, because the relationship between the self and support mechanisms are in sync.

Making connections and talking

While on placement students will come across a variety of different people and organisations and will have to draw on knowledge of 'how to communicate'. This can be extremely challenging, as no two service users will have the same set of needs, and organisations will have different priorities and eligibility criteria. Students are likely to take on the roles and responsibilities of the agency which may incorporate certain behaviours or actions such as a more authoritative stance when working with legislation, policies and procedures. If left unsupported, students can feel physically and emotionally exhausted leading to stress, burnout and feelings of incompetence (Lloyd et al., 2002; McFadden et al., 2015). It is therefore important to consider that students require the opportunity to develop their knowledge base of understanding the basic facets of verbal communication. Tsang (2007) explored the concept of orality and literacy in social care, highlighting the need for students to consider the importance between oral language and written communication; that is, the connection between practice in an oral mode (the appearance, tone of voice, gestures and arousing emotions in a way that can engage the whole person) and the role of written communication (evidence-based practice through academic papers, work-related reports, proposals and letters). Such considerations can inevitably enable the student to create a repertoire of different strategies in relation to communicating with a range of individuals, communities and organisations. For example, a student may feel nervous about developing rapport and move straight into an assessment process. Here the tone of voice may become more assertive or professional jargon may be used due to a lack of skill in navigating appropriate language to identify the core features of what is being discussed. As such, a student will need to develop skills to strike balance, providing an appropriate level of technical terminology in layman terms. For example, explaining that 'eligibility criteria' means 'what you can access based on your circumstances'. It is also worth noting that students need to be mindful of the impact on their own language. Rai's (2004) study makes clear the complex nature of students whose first language is not English and the complexities that this can raise in relation to oral communication and written reports. Some words are lost in translation and there can be a conflict between students wanting to speak the same language as a service user while remaining mindful of how this can be interpreted.

Report writing

Report writing can invoke an array of feelings which students need to address both in the day-to-day activities on placement and in relation to their academic study. Taylor and Handy (2013) make clear that social care can become focused solely on facts, meaning that information exchanged can be seen in isolation. Taking the time to invest in the emotive meaning of discussions and the context of language referred to can reinforce a better analysis of the situation, thus creating opportunities for greater discourse and understanding of the service user's perceptions (Tsang, 2007). Emotional resilience and intelligence acknowledge these elements, and incorporating them into practice and having access to free resources are a useful way for students to develop their skill sets for report writing.

Supervision and how to engage effectively (see Chapter 7 also)

For students on placement, supervision and the time to talk to another professional is essential. Supervision does not work in a vacuum. It is an opportunity for students to be able to explore and focus on the learning opportunities provided, unpick difficult dilemmas and explore feelings and emotions experienced in day-to-day interactions with service users, organisations and other professionals (Rajan-Rankin, 2014). The **SHARE** model (Finch et al., 2018) is a useful way to think about not only the direct experience with service users and organisations, but also in sharing this experience within supervision.

SHARE stands for:

S – seeing

H – hearing

A – action

R – reading

E – elevation

The SHARE model encompasses a humanistic and multi-sensory way of working and presents the scope to create a pathway to move away from a one-dimensional model of 'describing' a particular issue into multifunctional and co-operative practice. It enables the student to reflect on all aspects of the experience including their own thoughts and feelings and how these have impacted on actions or behaviours. The model also draws on the wider factors impacting upon professional practice such as structure and power and how these shape and influence analysis and responses in meeting the needs of the individual at the centre of the process.

To summarise, coping styles and problem-solving techniques are important factors in dealing with the demands of the profession and create self-identity and professional competence in placements (Rajan-Rankin, 2014; McFadden et al., 2015). As Goleman (1996) highlights, individuals who can adapt by changing their perspectives will reduce the impact of burnout; so, being emotionally resilient in practice is essential. As this section has identified, there are a range of ways that emotional resilience can be utilised and built upon via academic study, placements, effective communication and supervision.

Conclusion

This chapter has highlighted that emotional resilience is a key factor in being able to work effectively in the caring professions. The student's awareness of emotional resilience is paramount to ensuring that emotional resilience is viewed as being an essential part of the process in becoming a professional; it is what enhances professional competence and accountability. Students may feel bombarded with information on placement but placing this into the context of what is achievable will not only develop emotional resilience, but also enable the management of the placement and create opportunities for success.

Students may enter placements with thoughts of trepidation, excitement and worry which can increase individual levels of anxiety. However, placements offer students the potential to become part of a practice-based workplace to develop and enhance their skill base, and emotional resilience can change and develop as students become more experienced. Therefore, as this chapter suggests, placements should be embraced by students, because they play an essential role in providing opportunities to develop resilience, through working with a wide range of service users and problematic issues.

Finally, this chapter has demonstrated that moving from academic study to practising in 'real-life' situations can be a daunting experience for students. To assist with this transition, the chapter has outlined strategies to cope with the emotional demands of the job and presented several techniques that can be utilised by students while studying, on placement and in practice.

References

Adamson, C, Beddoe, L and Davys, A (2014) Building Resilient Practitioners: Definitions and Practitioner Understandings. *British Journal of Social Work*, 44(3):522–41.

Aronwitz, T (2005) The Role of 'Envisioning the Future' in the Development of Resilience among At-Risk Youth. *Public Health Nursing*, 22(3):200–08.

Beesley, P (2020) *Making the Most of Your Social Work Placement*. London: Sage.

Bowlby, J (1951) *Maternal Care and Mental Health*. Northvale: Jason Aronson Inc.

Bowlby, J (1953) Some Pathological Processes Set in Train by Early Mother Child Separation. *Journal Mental Science*, 99:265–72.

Bunce, L, Lonsdale, A J, King, N, Childs, J and Bennie, R (2019) Emotional Intelligence and Self-Determined Behaviour Reduce Psychological Distress: Interactions with Resilience in Social Work Students in the UK. *British Journal of Social Work*, 49(3):2092–111.

Chui, W H (2009) First Practice Placement. *The Journal of Practice Teaching and Learning*, 9(2):10–32.

Collins, S, Coffey, M and Morris, L (2010) Social Work Students: Stress, Support and Wellbeing. *British Journal of Social Work*, 40:963–82.

Collishaw, S, Pickles, A, Messer, J, Rutter, M, Shearer, C and Maughan, B (2007) Resilience to Adult Psychopathology Following Childhood Maltreatment: Evidence from a Community Sample. *Child Abuse and Neglect*, 31(3):211–29.

Finch, J, Tedam, P and Maclean, S (2018) *SHARE - A New Model for Social Work*. Lichfield: Kirwin Maclean Associates Ltd.

Garmezy, N (1973) in Masten, A S and Tellegen, A (2012) Resilience in Developmental Psychopathology: Contributions of the Project Competence Longitudinal Study. *Development and Psychopathology*, 24:345–61.

Goleman, D (1996) *Emotional Intelligence: Why It Can Matter More Than IQ*. London: Bloomsbury.

Goleman, D (1998) *Working with Emotional Intelligence*. London: Bloomsbury.

Grant, L and Kinman, G (2012) Enhancing Well-Being in Social Work Students: Building Resilience in the Next Generation. *The International Journal Social Work Education*, 31(5):605–21.

Greer, J (2016) *Resilience and Personal Effectiveness for Social Workers*. London: Sage.

Hogan, R (1969). Development of an Empathy Scale. *Journal of Consulting and Clinical Psychology*, 3(3):307–13.

Howe, D (2008) *The Emotionally Intelligent Social Worker*. Basingstoke: Palgrave Macmillan.

Hurley, D J, Martin, L and Hallberg, R (2013) Resilience in Child Welfare: A Social Work Perspective. *International Journal of Child, Youth and Family Studies*, 4(2):259–73.

Kinman, G and Grant, L (2017) Building Resilience in Early Career Social Workers: Evaluating a Multimodal Intervention. *The British Journal of Social Work*, 47:1979–98.

Klohen, E (1996) Conceptual Analysis and Measurement of The Construct of Ego Resiliency. *Journal of Personality and Social Psychology*, 70(5):10670–1079.

Knowles, M (1990) *The Adult Learner-A Neglected Species*, 4th ed. London: Gulf Publishers.

Lloyd, C, King, R and Chenoworth, L (2002) Social Work Stress and Burn Out: A Review. *Journal of Mental Health*, 11(3):255–65.

Marton, F and Säljö, R (1976) On Qualitative Differences in Learning: Outcome and Process. *British Journal of Educational Psychology*, 46(1):4–11.

McFadden, P, Campbell, A and Taylor, B (2015) Resilience and Burnout in Child Protection Social Work: Individual and Organisational Themes from a Systematic Literature Review. *British Journal of Social Work*, 45(5):1546–63.

Morrison, T (2007) Emotional Intelligence, Emotion and Social Work: Context, Characteristics, Complications and Contribution. *British Journal of Social Work*, 37(2): 245–63.

Nixon, S and Murr, A (2006) Practice Learning and the Development of professional practice. *Social Work Education*, 25(8):798–811.

Rai, L (2004) Exploring Literacy in Social Work Education: A Social Practice Approach to Student Writing. *Social Work Education*, 23(2): 149–62.

Rajan-Rankin, S (2014) Self-Identity, Embodiment and the Development of Emotional Resilience. *The British Journal of Social Work*, 44(8):2426–42.

Ruch, G, Turney, D and Ward, A (2010) *Relationship Based Practice: Getting to the Heart of Practice*. London: Jessica Kingsley Publications.

Rutter, M (1975) *Helping Troubled Children*. Harmondsworth: Penguin.

Rutter, M (1985) Resilience in the Face of Adversity: Protective Factors and Resistance to Psychiatric Disorder. *British Journal of Psychiatry*, 147(6): 598–611.

Rutter, M (2007) Implications of Resilience Concepts for Scientific Understanding. *Annals of the New York Academy of Sciences*, 1094:1–12.

Säljö, R (1979a) *Learning in the Learner's Perspective: Some Common Sense Conceptions. Report from the Institute of Education University of Gothenberg, No 76*. Washington: ERIC Clearinghouse.

Säljö, R (1979b) Learning About Learning. *Higher Education*, 8:443–51.

Sicora, A (2019) Reflective Practice and Learning from Mistakes in Social Work Student Placement. *Social Work Education*, 38(1):63–74.

Taylor, D and Handy, H (2013) Adult Learning Theories: Implications for Learning and Teaching in Medical Education: AMEE Guide No. 83. *Medical Teacher* 35(11):1561–72.

Tsang, N M (2007) Orality and Literacy: Their Relevance to Social Work. *Journal of Social Work*, 7(1):51–70.

Tulley, G (2009) *Teaching Life Lessons through Tinkering*. Available at www.youtube.com/watch?v=hvHViFcOekw (accessed 24 November 2021).

Ungar, M (2006) Nurturing Hidden Resilience in At-Risk Youth in Different Cultures. *Journal of the Canadian Academy of Child and Adolescent Psychiatry*, 15(2):53–58.

Ungar, M (2008) Resilience across Cultures. *British Journal of Social Work*, 38(2):218–35.

Ungar, M (2012) Social Ecologies and Their Contribution to Resilience, in Ungar, M (ed) *The Social Ecology of Resilience – A Handbook of Theory and Practice*. New York: Springer-Verlag.

Werner, E E, Bierman, J M and French, F E (1971) *The Children of Kauai: A Longitudinal Study from the Prenatal Period to Age Ten*. Honolulu: University of Hawaii.

Werner, E E and Smith, R (2001) *Journeys from Childhood to Midlife: Risk, Resilience, and Recovery*. Ithaca: Cornell University.

Wilks, S C and Spivey, C A (2010) Resilience in Undergraduate Social Work Students: Social Support and Adjustment to Academic Stress. *Social Work Education*, 29(3):276–88.

Wilson, E and Flanagan, N (2019) What Tools Facilitate Learning on Placement? Findings of a Social Work Student-to-Student Research Study. *Social Work Education*, 40(4):535–51.

Youssef, Y and Luthans, F (2007) Positive Organisational Behaviour in the Workplace the Impact of Hope Optimism and Resilience. *Journal of Management*, 33:774–800.

Zolkoski, S M and Bullock, L M (2012) Resilience in Children and Youth: A Review. *Children and Youth Services Review*, 34(12):2295–303.

4 Anti-oppressive practice

Jodie Low, Ben Wyke and Sarah Barley-McMullen

Introduction

For students on placement, a vital area of discussion will revolve around practice that is anti-oppressive and the need to consider a commitment to principles of tackling oppression and discrimination throughout their work. Inequality is growing in the developed world with corresponding increases in ill health, falling levels of well-being and deepening levels of hate crime. Collectively, this continues to set the scene for the seeming acceptance and growing support of oppression and discrimination through political leadership, impacting on the services, service providers and users of those services where students are on placement.

Society continually shapes and moves our behaviour, thoughts and feelings. Students, as with all people, are vulnerable to the power in the structural systems and processes of society. Their developing of knowledge, skills, experience and understanding does not make them immune to the pressure and power of society. Consequently, anti-oppressive practice should be an ongoing dialogue throughout placement, not something that is achieved as a tick box exercise but an ongoing process of reflection. It is vital that students recognise that effective anti-oppressive practice needs to permeate through both their professional and personal lives and through the values which drive, motivate and commit them to challenge and tackle social injustice. It is therefore a key aspect of practice that a student needs to understand on placement.

This chapter will begin to enable students to identify what oppression and discrimination looks like, how they create barriers to change and what the barriers look like in different people's lives. This will enable students to begin to understand how to implement strategies, working anti-oppressively to challenge and change the behaviour and actions which perpetuate discrimination and oppression in the lives of the people you are working with. This chapter lays the foundations for anti-oppressive practice by exploring the key language, concepts and behaviours of oppression, power, self, culture, identity and diversity. It provides an overview of essential models and theory which can be used to underpin and empower anti-oppressive practice. By then moving this theory into practice, the chapter offers practical reflections to act. It provides a guided pathway to key milestones and checkpoints for planning how practice will challenge oppression effectively. It examines approaches to maintain the implementation of a practitioner's commitment to principled anti-oppressive practice by ensuring the bedrock of continual critical reflection.

This chapter discusses:

- The value base for anti-oppressive practice
- Diversity and equality
- Internalisation
- Tackling oppression
- Empowerment
- Conscious anti-oppressive practice
- Reflective practice

The value base for anti-oppressive practice

Practice in supporting people is underpinned by common principles and values which align to human rights of dignity, fairness, equality, respect and independence. These are written into legislation within member states through the Universal Declaration of Human Rights (1948). As supporting services for people are frequently found where human rights become contested, compromised or contravened (Wilkinson and Pickett, 2011), students on placement will find themselves working with individuals facing challenges resulting from the growing global inequality witnessed today. Consequently, students will be faced with the fundamental challenge of practising anti-oppressively to support and uphold an individual's human rights.

Anti-oppressive practice recognises common features within definitions of oppression, including a process of dehumanisation, objectification and denial of existence. Oppression is the immobilising effect on a group of people restricting their human rights (Caldwell and Bennett Leighton, 2018; Chouhan, 2009). Anti-oppressive practices, therefore, will be reflected in the actions taken by students to challenge, lobby, advocate and influence for social change. By doing so, this challenges the norms, culture and structures that allow, enable and deepen the roots of oppression throughout structures, systems, cultures and behaviours within society (Dalrymple and Burke, 1995; Burke and Harrison, 1998). Anti-oppressive practice also recognises discrimination. Discrimination is a behaviour or action which negatively impacts on people due to their social and diverse characteristics such as race, gender or class (Thompson, 2016). Oppression is the outworking of discrimination which controls the power, mobility and agency of groups of people through the experience of repeated, widespread, systemic injustice (Deutsch, 2006).

For the student it is therefore important to recognise that anti-oppressive practice is not an add-on activity or process when supporting people.

> *Good quality relationships are fundamental when working with young people. Hence building rapport with the young person and establishing good interpersonal relationships helps in getting to know them better by understanding their experiences and identity. In understanding their experiences and identity we embrace their differences and similarities; this therefore helps in reducing prejudice and oppression by supporting them effectively.*
>
> Shirley, Youth and Community Leadership

It reflects a distinct value base. It needs to be woven throughout daily practice, embedded in every interaction and experienced and perceived by users of services as genuine respect. Such anti-oppressive, non-judgemental approaches can foster the trust in relationships and begin to normalise difference.

Diversity and equality

Understanding diversity recognises that we are all unique. This uniqueness reflects several factors such as our background, life experiences and beliefs, and will be discussed in more depth to consider what impacts on these factors. Students need to develop their awareness of their own diversity and that of others, to then practise addressing equality issues. Chapter 9, 'Resource of self', has some exercises which can help students build self-awareness. Individual, cultural and structural factors create inequality in society (Thompson, 2006). Equality seeks to address the resulting inequalities in status, rights or opportunities.

Students on placement will work with a diverse range of people reflecting different backgrounds, experiences and beliefs. Although not an exhaustive list, their diversity may encompass age, race, ethnicity, gender, culture, religion, disability, class and sexuality. Considering these descriptions of social characteristics enables students to start to make sense of how these impact on people and in turn the equality of their experience. For example, an older adult who is unfamiliar or lacks confidence with using the internet may have a very different experience of shopping or managing finances than a younger person brought up in the internet age. This may mean their need for support to enable equality of opportunity and access to services may be very different. So, by attaching a social characteristic or label, students can start to understand and analyse the behaviour and interaction that people experience. A further example of this may be the female in a heterosexual relationship who is completing most caring responsibilities as a parent. If this reflects a cultural norm based on her gender, students can then consider the similarities and differences between people's experiences, and opportunities as parents based on gender. They may then need to consider how they can raise awareness and address inequality in their practice.

Labelling theory can be helpful here to understand society's impact on diversity. Becker's labelling theory (1963) argues that society labels people, for example, old or young, male or female, as in the example above. Becker argues that this creates stereotypes attached to the label. A stereotype is characterised by fixed and generalised beliefs associated with a group or person. For example, a person labelled as old might stereotypically be considered wise, or alternatively forgetful; a label can therefore generate both negative and positive beliefs. Becker's theory focuses on how 'deviancy' becomes defined according to labels. For example, media representation linking being young, black and male to criminal violence (Cushion, Moore and Jewell, 2011). This not only develops a generalised belief in society but also can lead to internalisation (explored later) of that belief by the individual or group. Any violent act being committed by a black male, whatever the context, has the cyclical effect of reinforcing the label. Becker (1963) argues that the shared meaning and expectations of a label are set by those with power and authority in society.

If we accept that labelling theory is correct, then students need to be consistently reflective of this in their approaches, observations and behaviours when working with people. Students need to recognise that as practitioners and members of society, although labels can be helpful in understanding the narrative of someone's experiences, labels also have the potential to generate stereotypical expectations. For example, it can be argued that there is a current focus on early intervention and preventative services which require vulnerability matrices and screening tools to predict the likelihood for a person to require supporting services. Such tools are powerful, particularly for safeguarding, providing a means to understand risk and vulnerability. They may, however, reinforce an objective approach to systematically working with people, allowing and encouraging stereotypical judgement and expectations by services resulting in discriminatory and oppressive approaches. Students therefore need to be critically reflective of the potential for services they are involved with to be disempowering towards the individual.

When working with groups, students must be conscious that a diversity of people creates diversity of experience and knowledge within a group. Where people are brought together with different backgrounds, identities and life experiences, there will be a diversity of opinions, perspectives, values and principles. Consequently, students may find that the potential of diverse groups is greater than is found within non-diverse groups, who may possess more limited experience and knowledge; this may also reflect that where there is conflict between differing perspectives, this challenges the accepted norm. Recognising diversity naturally alerts us to what makes individuals different and sometimes unique. The key for students on placement is found in harnessing the potential power of diverse groups (Lindsay and Orton, 2014). For example, a group of young people, in different school years, from different identity groups with a range of knowledge, experience and skills can be influential, be successful in challenging circumstances that the school system creates, drawing on the range of their members' experience to overcome adversity, such as the oppressive culture of excluding students who may have disabilities or having lower expectations of students from less affluent backgrounds or with English as a second language. It is the collective power of the diverse student group which will force change in the school systems.

For a student working with groups, facilitating the exchange of knowledge and experience demonstrates working anti-oppressively to promote the power of a group. However, a student may find a less diverse group as naturally having a more harmonious group functioning and therefore an ease in developing shared meaning and energy for similar goals. These groups may be less problematic for a student and consequently working anti-oppressively by developing their group functioning, team strength and resilience could be overlooked (Brandler and Roman, 2015). Their potential is restricted by the narrower experience and knowledge (Jackson, 2007). A student needs to recognise that the power of a non-diverse group is more likely to be set and limited by their location in their social system and can collude with the inequality between groups (Cameron Kelly and Varghese, 2018).

A student on placement working with groups may consider the value of bringing together diverse groups as collectives, seeking to reduce inequality between groups. Such collectives have greater potential to identify common shared experience of inequality through critical thinking and subsequently challenge oppression through a critical mass, thus creating a movement (Love, 2013). Where different people recognise their shared meaning, develop their shared goals and enable their group functioning to act as one, collectives embrace the power of their diverse experience and knowledge. This collective power can challenge the surrounding social systems to reduce the injustice and increase the equality between people; these are the central tenets of the humanistic values of group work proposed by Glassman (2009). Equality can often be confused with being treated the same as everyone else; however, it is more than responding to difference and celebrating diversity. It includes addressing the wider understanding of individual need and levels of oppression.

Internalisation

Internalisation is the process by which the social norms, values and discriminatory behaviours are adopted by the individual (Berger, 1966, cited in Thompson, 2016). A person conforms fully with the dominant societal view. For those students familiar with the film *Django Unchained* (2012), the internalisation of oppression is clearly demonstrated in the character played by Samuel L Jackson, who despite himself being a black African slave fully adopts the beliefs, attitudes and behaviours of his white owners towards his fellow black African slaves, in turn oppressing them as he has been oppressed. In doing so he demonstrates internalised oppression, described by Lipsky (1987, p 6) as *'turning upon ourselves, upon our families ... upon our own people ... the oppression of the (dominant) society'*.

A student on placement might observe whether service users have adopted a view of their social, cultural and structural surroundings that reflects the accepted norms and oppressive attitudes of the mainstream social order. This may be demonstrated through their personality, behaviours and lived codes of ethics. For example, has a young offender internalised the view that they are destined for a life of criminality, have little value in society and will never hold down a job? It is important to understand that internalisation is not a conscious process. The individual's subconscious steers them towards behaviours that reflect the mainstream collective conscience of society, accepting and acknowledging these as social facts and truths (Smith, 2014). A student may then recognise that the individual can be both discriminator and discriminated, believing in and accepting the consequences of not following the mainstream social order.

Goffman's work on the self-concept (1959, 1963) further supports an understanding of internalisation. This considered that human behaviour operates as a script which is written by society and assumed through the roles that we play. This 'self-concept' is created through adopting shared meaning and identification of our sameness with others (Erikson, 1950); uniqueness within identity is developed through conflict and comparison with others. Once sameness is assumed, shared definition and categorisation of the sameness highlight expectation and create the shape of roles, discourse and interactions, thereby creating a script for roles we play (Goffman, 1963). An example of internalisation becoming increasingly apparent is in the dominant paradigm around welfare benefits where we see the oppressive issue of media framing (Niblock and Bindel, 2017) reporting claimants as 'scroungers' and 'lazy' resulting in young people becoming a population of 'hidden jobless' fearing the sanctions of the welfare system and being negatively labelled. In many instances, young people are opting to take on criminal lifestyles to earn their money rather than making legitimate claims (Higgins et al., 2018; Windle, Moyle and Coomber, 2018; Smeaton, 2009; Stephen, 2009). This becomes increasingly challenging in the face of social media. Without professional edit and conduct for publication, the editor is the audience, meaning that whatever variant of popularism is prevalent that becomes the dominant response. Young people are subsequently moved to the margins of society through collective pressure to adhere to glamorised norms and values such as cosmetic surgery or gang lifestyles, which thrive on capitalistic consumption and materialism. This results in a cycle of discontent and dissatisfaction with the self-concept they hold of themselves (Dahl, Argo and Morales, 2012). For students on placement, this understanding of internalisation can help with recognising why users of services across the spectrum may appear trapped within negative cyclical behaviours.

Tackling oppression

How to tackle oppression in practice is a challenge which will be faced by students, as it is for practitioners. Primarily it must begin with students themselves and how each individual promotes equality, inclusion and belonging. There is no one-size-fits-all approach, but an awareness of our own power, how we use our power and how we enable and empower others is an excellent starting point (Doel and Sawdon, 1999).

Freedom from discrimination through Freire's (1968) concept of mutual humanisation is pivotal in bringing anti-oppressive theory and practice together in health and social care. This is where both the student and service user see each other as subjects who think, feel and do, not just as objects to be filled with knowledge. They work in collaboration for a common goal. Greater understanding and recognition of the inherent and social intersections of self are also important in tackling oppression, as this enables an individual to become their whole self, particularly when seeking to work in partnership or collaboratively with others. In this way the student (subject) may be able to move consciously from being seen as an 'object', controlled by budgets, procedures and time, to a subject who 'knows and acts' in a person-centred way for the greater good of individuals and communities. This may be considered a process of personal empowerment whereby the power is reclaimed by both the student and the community, and the resources of self and others needed in partnership and collaborative work begin to become accessible and available to all.

Thompson (2018, p 237) in his PCS model (2006, Figure 4.1) considers that discrimination occurs on three levels – personal, cultural and structural. Thompson suggests that personal empowerment weakens the power of controlling cultural discrimination and in turn erodes structural principles, increasing the chance of achieving change in the longer term. From a practice perspective, this idea can be developed to suggest that when students feel and are empowered, they will be able to build stronger partnership and collaboration. This is achieved through having the confidence to find their own voice and space within the relationships they build with service users and other professionals. For example, a student should expect to be working with increasing independence as their placement progresses. Failure to enable this may reflect that structural discrimination, possibly based on a culture towards students, is present in the organisation. If this is the case, then support from tutors and supervisors should be sought to challenge this. Additionally, when students are more conscious and political in their approaches to tackling apparent oppression, everyone can benefit from this shared awareness; if you know where oppression comes from, you know where to focus your action. Consequently, through understanding the

PCS Model

Thompson, N. (2006) Anti-Discriminatory Practice, Palgrave

- Personal
- Cultural
- Structural

Discrimination occurs at three distinct levels

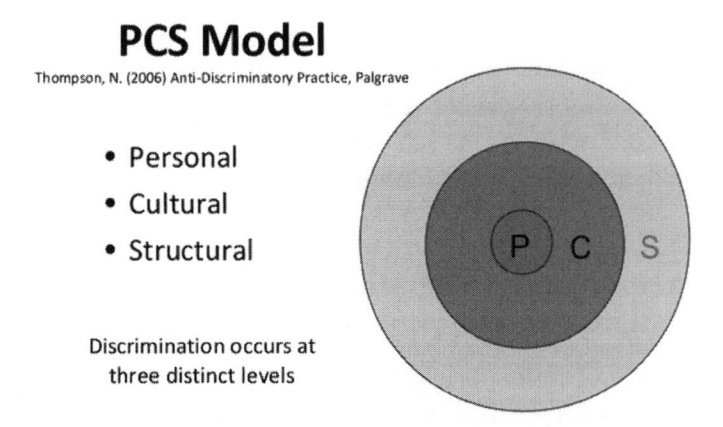

Figure 4.1 PCS model

reality of the impact of oppression, this can be challenged by students on placement through working with individuals and communities on a personal level.

Similarly, students on placement may be able to work more collaboratively if they are more confident about the contribution they bring, and the contributions needed from others.

> *When working with young people it's absolutely right to ask them to show you the way, just because we are older does not mean we know best. I often have no idea what their words mean in a contemporary context so it's good to learn – this helps me understand other young people better, especially those who may be less confident or less able in articulating themselves and helps me understand their worlds in a much deeper way.*
>
> Laura, Youth and Community Leadership

If they are also more engaged and critically reflective of the whole process of change, transition and transformation, they can ensure that the process of reclaiming power in a situation, while not without difficulties, is received by individuals and communities with less fear and uncertainty.

Empowerment

By its very nature, empowerment is a process of change, a mechanism leading to individuals, communities and organisations gaining control over their lives (Rappaport, Swift and Hess, 1984). It is also a central feature of principled approaches to anti-oppressive professional practice and therefore one that needs to be clearly understood by students in both theory and practice.

With its roots in Freire's (1968) thinking around critical and dominated consciousness, empowerment is the process of awakening the confidence needed to tackle the personal, cultural and structural (Thompson, 2006) dominance of oppressive approaches used by 'those in power'. These approaches are used to control and repress people to keep the power with the few and not the many. We see this increasingly in the factors which underpin the progressive levels of poverty and inequality in the UK. For example, as a result of the coronavirus pandemic which swept the world in 2020, many of the areas in UK society which already had increasing levels of poverty and inequality were exacerbated by the spot light of government decisions about where funding should go. It was therefore people on zero hours contracts in the gig economy, many of whom were already on the edge of poverty, who were not supported financially by the UK government's furlough scheme. It was women who worked part time in the retail and hospitality industry who lost their jobs first, because it is mostly women who take on part time work to fit around child care (Ferguson, 2020), and it was domestic violence mainly towards women that was aggravated and spiked significantly during the government's lockdowns throughout the country (Horley, 2020).

For people to be able to see themselves as valued and respected individuals, equipped to reject the oppressive structures which limit their education, occupation, and health, individuals need to understand the power that they can own for themselves. In addition to this, they need to be able to channel this power in ways which enable them to act and stand up for themselves when faced with losing control of factors which disrupt their lives, as well as the wider community and society. Friere (1968) suggests that the greatest solution to oppression is liberation through education. Students on placement therefore face the considerable challenge of both learning from individuals and families who may feel so left behind and oppressed in social and community settings, while seeking ways to empower them as a professional in training. Friere (1968) argues that through education an individual can learn to think critically in life, not merely to accept what is written but instead to question and critically discuss knowledge and behaviour and thus respond in an empowered way. In practice this can enable individuals to make better choices and decisions which can in turn transform their lives and the lives of the people around them. Friere (1968) calls this critical consciousness for social transformation. As a student on placement, enabling individuals to feel confident to use their voice and call out conscious discrimination and oppression, is an empowering state for the individuals and communities.

Conscious anti-oppressive practice

The principle of anti-oppressive practice is central to ethical and value-based practice when working in social and community settings. It is therefore also one of the few areas that are relatable in every practice-based module for students on placement. Consequently, students need to either navigate their own experiences of discrimination and oppression to demonstrate empathy for others, or become open enough to listen to and learn from the narratives of the service users they are working with, to understand and empathise.

On placement, students will often work with service users whose history and ongoing daily experience is one of oppression, and whose experience of the very service purporting to support them, is also one of structural oppression. Anti-oppressive practice may be perceived as a glib patronising statement from a caring professional, unaware of their role in oppression. As has been identified, oppression has at its core inequality; inequality arising from lack of opportunity due to circumstance of birth, gender, culture, race, age, disability, relationships and, ultimately, a lack of power.

Thompson's (2006) PCS model provides a possible template for a student to reflect on their potential as an oppressor on personal, cultural and structural levels, which may be argued provides the crux of being anti-oppressive. The model encourages reflective analysis of the part culture plays in understanding oppression and discrimination through emphasis on the individual experience on a personal level being steeped in their cultural context. The model proposes that the complexity of oppression cannot be understood by individual experience; therefore, cultural context must also be understood. This is ever more important with the growing levels of violence and crime that are being exposed through a developing understanding of exploitation in society. Firmin (2020) highlights the need to rewrite systems responding to contexts, to incorporate an educated understanding of 'social fields' that operate a code of conduct, that are validated by culture and written off by processes of dehumanisation. Consequently, when reflecting on culture, it is best for students to approach this in partnership with people to avoid imposing personal bias and discrimination which can cloud the development of the cultural picture.

Students should consider their culture through the analogy of an iceberg (Hall, 1976; Figure 4.2) as an opportunity to create a visual representation of culture. It is worth noting that when completing the cultural iceberg, it is not a statement of what the individual believes in or acts on; it is an appreciation of the wider cultural context to the personal experience. In a similar vein, the structural forces of society contextualise culture; these

Consider culture as an iceberg. The section of the iceberg which is out of the water is the elements of culture we can see. Below the water line is all the elements which we need to explore through discussion, active listening and professional relationships.

Choose a person, family or community you work with. Against each element add specific examples of their culture. For example:
Dress: casual sportswear
Attitude to materialism: no waste

Dress:
Food:
Vocations:
Language:
Routines:
Religious practice:

Parenting:
Values:
Family roles:
Relation to authority:
Biases:
Beliefs:
Rules of conduct:
Work ethic:
Attitude to education:
Attitude to materialism:
Concept of justice:
Humour:
Gender roles:
Personal space:
Expectations:

Review your cultural iceberg, what elements of the structural level maintain or attempt to change the culture?

Figure 4.2 Cultural iceberg

can be recognised as comprising the 'infrastructure' of society such as the systems, processes and drivers of our economy, education, media, legislation, healthcare, welfare etc. The structural level for many is the most abstract level of the model. Thompson (2006) argues, this is the layer which is *embedded in the fabric of society*'; it is the legislation, the policies, the institutions that reinforce and maintain oppression in culture. The further from the personal level, the less power an individual has and consequently less ability to understand, influence and create change.

A student may feel they understand an individual's oppression, but the action needed to counter, rather than exacerbate this, is challenging and raises ethical practice dilemmas. Take for example the homeless person begging on the street. This person is likely to be experiencing a complex mix of social and health-related issues in addition to their basic housing need. What is the anti-oppressive response to such a person, should you be on placement working in a street outreach project? In proposing to answer this, it may be helpful to return to consider the view of Freire (1996) who considered education the means to the liberation of the oppressed, education requiring the active involvement of both oppressed and oppressor. Any action that is anti-oppressive is surely focused on liberating the individual to understand and experience opportunity beyond the boundaries exerted by societal norms. This approach proposed that liberation occurred through critical thinking, mutual humanisation and partnership. In the case of being anti-oppressive towards the homeless individual how could this apply? Critical thinking in this case might require the student on placement to seek to analyse the potential impact of any action in liberation of the individual. The danger here is to assume knowledge of what is best for the individual based on unconfirmed judgements, influenced by stereotypical societal views. To progress would obviously require some form of interaction, so there is the need for mutual humanisation, to engage with the person not the image. This, it is suggested, is at the heart of the challenge posed to achieving anti-oppressive practice. Freire spoke of *'the affirmation of human beings as persons'* (Freire, 1996, cited in Irwin, 2012, p 31). It is not suggested here that the homeless individual is less human, but it can be argued that society's perception is such, and there is a psychological barrier, created by internalisation, to be overcome. Recognition here of the individual as a daughter, a son, maybe a father or a mother, having a past and a future, is essential to challenging the stigma surrounding the image. Once the barrier presented by humanisation of an individual is recognised and addressed, the principle of partnership may have a chance to develop. This may be through empathy, a mutual experience of humanity and a real chance to critically and mutually explore ways to empower (Adams, 2008; Rappaport, Swift and Hess, 1984). This is of course idealistic, but it is suggested the principles are sound. To really engage with any individual, anti-oppressively, it will take time, consistency of approach, clear expectations, motivational coaching, mutual benefit (Adams, 2008) before a shared experience of humanity can occur, thereby enabling progress in empowering through responding to both immediate and longer-term needs. This constitutes an example of an anti-oppressive practice approach, transferable to most practice in social care, community development and education. It needs to be recognised here that continuity is vital, which therefore presents a challenge for any student on a time-limited placement. In this instance, engaging with an individual anti-oppressively to develop an ongoing working relationship will have limited value if that ceases once placement ends. Reassurance to an individual that support will continue if appropriate needs to be communicated and agreed at the commencement of any work by a student and before exit.

Similarly, as a student on placement one key support is supervision (see Chapter 7). Supervision needs to be experienced anti-oppressively; there is a need to build a partnership based on trust, accountability and respect. Having these qualities within your supervisory relationship will result in discussion of personal and professional issues that enables learning and development as an effective practitioner. It may be assumed that many students who seek careers working to support disadvantaged groups and individuals set off with 'good intentions' driven by a core commitment to, and a degree of understanding of, social justice and a desire to support not oppress. For the individual, or group, the good intentions of a student, however, are not enough. There is a need to reflect on understanding the experience of oppression and consider the approaches and skills that are needed to engage anti-oppressively if liberation is to occur.

My top ten tips for developing anti-oppressive practice as a student on placement:

1. *Don't ever assume you know things about people – experience can help you understand them, but no two people are the same!*
2. *Don't be afraid to ask questions about people and circumstances – but always be respectful.*
3. *When working with young people it's important to know that just because you are older does not mean you know best!*
4. *People are the experts in their own lives, never forget that!*
5. *If you are asking people to do something, make sure you are happy to do it too.*
6. *Difficult conversations are usually the most beneficial in the long term.*
7. *If something isn't working, then there's a great opportunity to learn from it.*
8. *Correct use of supervision and reflection will offer constructive criticism that helps you to grow.*
9. *Listen. Always listen.*
10. *Just because you haven't experienced something, or you don't do it, doesn't mean it isn't happening.*

Laura, Youth and Community Leadership

Reflective practice – unlocking anti-oppressive practice

As a student being reflective in practice is essential in unlocking anti-oppressive practice (see Chapter 2). To consider reflective practice, the most straightforward and accessible model is that proposed by Schon (1983). Schon proposed reflection can occur either 'in action' or 'on action'. *Reflecting on action* Schon considered as occurring after an event. *Reflecting in action* occurs at the time of the event. In this context, for a student to practice anti-oppressively it is ideally also necessary to have engaged in prior reflective thinking, effectively thinking 'on' an action about to take place. For example, consider being required to engage with a young woman with Downs Syndrome who it is feared is being physically, possibly sexually, abused at home. Reflecting prior to engagement would be essential drawing on understanding of oppression, labelling, stereotypes and internalisation, as discussed above. Students might consider what impact the individual's learning disability has on her experience of oppression. Has the label assigned to her limited her 'voice', affected her opportunities, increased her experience of vulnerability? Has the physical and psychological impact of her learning disability affected her methods of communication, her means of expression and her level of understanding? Or should this not be assumed given what we know about the impact of stereotyping? Has internalisation normalised the abuse for her? Furthermore, should she have experienced, or be experiencing, abuse, her vulnerability may be ongoing. How might any intervention impact on this? What is certain is that she is in a position of relative powerlessness in society. This may be strongly impacted by social learning (Bandura, 1977; Miller, 2011), her behaviour being modelled on and impacted by the attitudes and emotions of others around her, and possibly learned helplessness (Seligman, 1975) whereby she becomes a passive recipient, as a result of inescapable prejudice (Cox et al., 2012). Wider critical reflection here may recognise her likely experience of structural oppression, including the impact of a succession of health and social care professionals in her life. These are just some areas a student may reflect on before engaging. While not strictly reflecting on action, the practitioner here will be reflecting on previous learning and experiences, drawing on their own palette of ideas, theories and approaches and reframing these to possibly inform the proposed interaction. This remains very much in line with Schon's (1983) theory of reflection on action, which is clearly a circular, and not a linear, process.

While reflection may engender an understanding of powerlessness in respect to the service users' experience, it must also be acknowledged this may also characterise the experience of the student. Reflection before action may rightly give the student pause to consider if they have the skills and understanding to act appropriately. However, to be anti-oppressive this must not lead to inaction. Time and again serious case reviews have identified a failure on services to act despite concerns being recorded and shared (Brandon et al., 2008). Blom-Cooper's landmark enquiry into the death of Jasmine Beckford (1985) stated '*thou shalt not, not intervene*'. Therefore, for any reflective student aware of social injustice and inequality and power, they have a duty to act, and acting reflectively will aid acting anti-oppressively. However, as a student they must remember they are not acting alone and should use the supervisory support they receive on placement to share concerns, fears and uncertainty and to confirm how best to intervene. Reflection in action occurs during the engagement and is vital to ensure anti-oppressive practice continues throughout. Reflection here needs to come from focused engagement and connection with the individual and having an openness to new understanding as the interaction progresses. Schon described it as permitting oneself to experience *'surprise, puzzlement, or confusion'* (1983, p 68). This links nicely to taking a person-centred approach in any interaction (Means and Thorne, 2007). Being person centred is a widely used concept adopted by practitioners in health, social and community care settings and originates from Rogers's (1961) counselling approach. Congruence is a key tenet of this approach, essentially meaning to stay connected with person, place or time. This links well to the need for humanisation in anti-oppressive practice (Friere, 1996, in Irwin, 2012), as discussed earlier. By sharing reflections with colleagues and proactively exploring this in supervision, students can unlock the complexity of the contexts that people live in and sharpen the accuracy of practice. A conscious, self-aware, reflective student will be developing the ability to understand differing social contexts and utilise collaborative support for the people they serve.

Conclusion

This chapter considered anti-oppressive and anti-discriminative approaches to collaborate and empower individuals. While working as a student on placement, it is important to consider the opening elements of this chapter which recognises the power of diverse groups. Anti-oppressive practice cannot be realised by working with individuals alone. If we were to do this, empowerment is reduced to power within a maintained status quo of inequality. Thompson's (2016) proposal that the further one is from the personal level, the less power one has reaffirms the necessity of encouraging collective action for anti-oppressive practice to be demonstrated on placement. To enable collective action, the journey must continue to include mutual benefit, but there should also be an educative and enabling process, as argued by Freire (1996), thereby developing leadership with people. For students on placement to lead change, they must ensure that the impact of oppression and discrimination is addressed from individual, cultural and structural perspectives to ensure that real change becomes transformational at each of these levels in each service user's life. Consistent and professional reflection enables a student on placement to identify, investigate and tackle inequality and oppression, resisting the oppressive social forces they too are exposed to and are part of. After all, if we are not part of the solution, are we not part of the problem?

References

Adams, R (2008) *Empowerment, Participation and Social Work*. New York: Palgrave Macmillan.

Bandura, A (1977) *Social Learning Theory*. Englewood Cliffs: Prentice Hall.

Becker, H S (1963) *Outsiders: Studies in the Sociology of Deviance*. New York: Palgrave Macmillan.

Blom-Cooper, L (1985) *A Child in Trust: Report of the Panel of Inquiry into the Circumstances Surrounding the Death of Jasmine Beckford*. Wembley: London Borough of Brent.

Brandler, S and Roman, C P (2015) *Group Work: Skills and Strategies for Effective Interventions*. Taylor & Francis.

Brandon, M, Belderson, P, Warren, C and Howe, D (2008) *Child Deaths and Serious Injury through Abuse and Neglect: What Can We Learn? Biennial Analysis of Serious Case Reviews 2003–2005*. London: DCSF.

Burke B and Harrison, P (1998) Anti-Oppressive Practice, in Adams, R, Dominelli, L, Payne, M and Campling, J (eds) *Social Work*. London: Palgrave Macmillan.

Caldwell, C and Bennett Leighton, L (2018) *Oppression & the Body*. Berkley: North Atlantic Books.

Cameron Kelly, D and Varghese, R (2018) Four Contexts of Institutional Oppression: Examining the Experiences of Blacks in Education, Criminal Justice and Child Welfare. *Journal of Human Behavior in the Social Environment*, 28(7):874–88.

Chouhan, J (2009) Anti-Oppressive Practice, in Woods, J and Hine, J (eds) *Working with Young People*. London: Sage.

Cox, W T L, Abramson, L Y, Devine, P G, and Hollon, S D (2012) Stereotypes, Prejudice, and Depression: The Integrated Perspective. *Perspectives on Psychological Science Journal*, 7(Issue 5): 427–49.

Cushion, S, Moore, K, and Jewell, J (2011) Media Representations of Black Young Men and Boys: Report of the REACH Monitoring Project. *School of Journalism, Media and Cultural Studies*. Available at: https://orca.cardiff.ac.uk/28559/1/2113275.pdf (accessed 26 November 2021).

Dahl, D W, Argo, J J and Morales, A C (2012) Social Information in the Retail Environment: The Importance of Consumption Alignment, Referent Identity, and Self-Esteem. *Journal of Consumer Research*, 38(5): 860–71.

Dalrymple, J and Burke, B (1995) *Anti-Oppressive Practice: Social Care and the Law*. Buckingham: Open University Press.

Deutsch, M (2006) A Framework for Thinking about Oppression and Its Change. *Social Justice Research*, 19 (1):7–41.

Django Unchained (2012) Directed by Q. Tarantino, USA: Columbia Pictures.

Doel, M and Sawdon, C (1999) *The Essential Group Worker: Teaching and Learning Creative Group Work*. London: Jessica Kingsley Publications.

Erikson, E H (1950) *Childhood and Society*. New York: Norton.

Ferguson, D (2020) 'I Feel Light a 1950s Housewife': How Lockdown has Exposed the Gender Divide. Available at: www.theguardian.com/world/2020/may/03/i-feel-like-a-1950s-housewife-how-lockdown-has-exposed-the-gender-divide (accessed 05 November 2021).

Firmin, C (2020) *Contextual Safeguarding and Child Protection: Rewriting the Rules*. London: Routledge.

Freire, P (1968) *Pedagogy of the Oppressed*. London: Continuum.

Glassman, U (2009) *Group Work: A Humanistic and Skills Building Approach*. London: Sage.

Goffman, E (1959) *The Presentation of Self in Everyday Life*. New York: Anchor Books.

Goffman, E (1963) *Stigma; Notes on the Management of Spoiled Identity*. Englewood Cliffs: Prentice-Hall.

Greater London Authority (2018) *The London Health Inequalities Strategy*. London: Greater London Authority.

Hall, E T (1976) *Beyond Culture*. Garden City: Anchor Press.

Higgins, A, Benier, K, Shenderovich, Y, Bedford, L, Mazerolle, L and Murray, J (2018) Factors Associated with Youth Gang Membership in Low- and Middle-Income Countries: A systematic Review. *Campbell Systematic Review*, 14(1). Available at: https://doi.org/10.4073/csr.2018.11.

Horley, S (2020) Refuge Reports Further Increase in Demand for Its National Domestic Abuse Helpline Services During Lockdown. Available at: www.refuge.org.uk/refuge-reports-further-increase-in-demand-for-its-national-domestic-abuse-helpline-services-during-lockdown/ (accessed 05 November 2021).

Irwin, J (2012) *Paulo Freire's Philosophy of Education*. London: Continuum.

Jackson, S (2007) Freire Re-Viewed. *Educational Theory*, 75(2):199–213.

Lindsay, T and Orton, S (2014) *Groupwork Practice for Social Work*. London: Learning Matters.

Lipsky, S (1987) *Internalized Racism*. Seattle: Rational Island.

Love, B (2013) Developing a Liberatory Consciousness, in Adams, M, Blumenfield, W, Castañeda, C R, Hackman, H W, Peters, M L and Zúñiga, X (eds), *Readings for Diversity and Social Justice*. 3rd ed. New York: Routledge.

Mearns, D and Thorne, B (2007) *Person-Centred Counselling in Action*. Los Angeles: Sage.

Miller, P H (2011) *Theories of Developmental Psychology*. New York: Worth Publishers.

Niblock, S and Bindel, J (2017) Reframing Reporting of Childhood Sexual Exploitation. *Journalism Practice*, 11(5): 577–91. DOI: 10.1080/17512786.2016.1164613.

Rappaport, J, Swift, C F and Hess, R (1984) *Studies in Empowerment: Steps Toward Understanding and Action*. New York: Haworth.

Refuge (2021) *Service Review 2020/21*. Available at: www.refuge.org.uk/wp-content/uploads/2021/03/Refuge-Covid-Service-Report.pdf (accessed 26 November 2021).

Rogers, C R (1961) *On Becoming a Person: A Therapist's View of Psychotherapy*. Boston: Houghton Mifflin.

Schon, D (1987) *Educating the Reflective Practitioner*. San Fransisco: Jossey Boss.

Seligman, M E P (1975) *Helplessness: On Development, Depression and Death*. San Fransisco: W.H Freeman.

Smeaton, E (2009) Off the Radar and at Risk: Children on the Streets in the UK Housing. *Care and Support*, 12(3):22–27.

Smith, K (2014) *Emile Durkheim and the Collective Consciousness of Society*. New York: Anthem Press.

Stephen, D E (2009) Time to Stop Twisting the Knife: A Critical Commentary on the Rights and Wrongs of Criminal Justice Responses to Problem Youth in the UK. *Journal of Social Welfare and Family Law*, 31(2):193–206.

Thompson, N (2016) *Anti Discriminatory Practice*. 6th ed. London: Palgrave Macmillan.

Thompson, N (2018) *Promoting Equality*. 4th ed. London: Palgrave Macmillan.

United Nations (1948) Universal Declaration of Human Rights. Available at: www.un.org/en/about-us/universal-declaration-of-human-rights (accessed 26 November 2021).

Wilkinson, R G and Pickett, K (2011) *The Spirit Level: Why Greater Equality Makes Societies Stronger*. New York: Bloomsbury.

Windle, J, Moyle, L and Coomber, R (2018) Vulnerable Kids Going Country: Children and Young People's Involvement in County Lines. *Youth Justice*, 20(1–2):64–78.

Part 2
During placement

5 Working within the context of an agency

Claire Connor and Nigel Down

Introduction

The landscape of health and social care has seen unprecedented changes over a significant number of years having been impacted by austerity cuts across the statutory, private and voluntary sectors. This has resulted in the emergence of new and creative ways of working with service users and those who present as in need (Gopee and Galloway, 2017). The statutory sector is now working more closely with a range of organisations, signposting individuals who do not meet stringent service-specific eligibility criteria and referring work to a wide range of health and social care practitioners. Where historically particular intervention was viewed as profession specific, the change in the social care landscape has fostered a more collaborative and fluid relationship where interprofessional working has become pivotal in providing services, particularly for those who present as in need (Dickinson and Carey, 2016).

This chapter will enable students to understand the different types of organisations that currently exist to provide health and social care services. It will include discussion on the role of policy and procedures in contextualising responsibility, the different structures within organisations and understanding the different roles that organisations have in the health and social care sector. There will be discussion on the impact of the political drivers that have and will continue to influence organisational development and functionality, including funding, and the impact of a political agenda on the development of health and social care policy, along with the additional impact of austerity on the way in which health and social care is delivered and to whom. The chapter will also consider the growth of social enterprise in meeting the needs of the changing service delivery landscape.

The chapter will further consider the range of professional job roles such as social worker, youth worker and support worker. Finally, it will consider the wider links between the statutory, private and voluntary sectors, identifying the commonalities and expertise of each professional in delivering the best outcome for those in need. The chapter concludes discussing the need for effective and inclusive interprofessional working.

This chapter discusses:

- Political drivers which shape organisations
- Types of organisations delivering health and social care provision
- The growth of social enterprise in delivering services
- Student expectations and professional growth
- Inclusive interprofessional working

Understanding the landscape

Placements provide opportunities for students to foster knowledge, understanding and skills in the development of funding health and social care provision. Through examining organisational governance, business planning, community engagement, financial planning and partnership development, students will recognise the organisation's sustainable funding strategies. Students need to develop an understanding of the political, social and economic context which underpins the organisation and the service it provides (Walsh, Stevens and Moore, 2000). The ideologies and values of the organisation are often reflected in its organisational vision, mission statement, aims and objectives (Doherty and Horne, 2002). Therefore, students will be able to understand the context of the organisation by identifying social and economic policy which shapes the strategic planning and management of service delivery, together with the ethical and economic implications (Field and Brown, 2020). During a placement, students can examine a variety of mainstream and social enterprise mechanisms by which services are delivered, and develop an understanding of the structure, governance and constitution of organisations. This would include the current and evolving arrangements for contracting and funding across health and social care provision such as service-level agreements, partnership working, procurement and commissioning and the provision of services through community-/user-led organisations and social enterprise.

The political landscape shaping health and social care

The wider delivery of health and social care provision could be considered as a continuum, encompassing a diverse variety of organisations providing an array of services and ranging from charitable status to being managed within the public sector. The political drivers shaping current policy development can see public sector organisations shift position on the continuum, moving away from being funded through public bodies towards an array of alternative funding models (Clarke, Gewitz and McLaughlin, 2001). For example, this became apparent during the 2010s, when local authority-managed youth services saw a significant reduction in funding due to the austerity measures being implemented by the Conservative government. This led to a number of alternative funding and delivery models being explored in order to maintain youth work provision across the country (Local Government Association, 2019), with some authorities opting to commission the delivery of youth provision, some youth services 'spinning out' of the local authority to create social enterprise and community interest companies, and some services remaining within the public sector. This shift in the type of funding which youth services received was able to be recognised due to the fact that the direct delivery of youth services is not a statutory requirement of local authorities. As such, the level of service provision can be determined by the local authority. However, this is not the case for other health and social care services, with the responsibility for specific statutory functions and duties, embedded in legislation such as the Care Act 2014 and safeguarding legislation, remaining with public sector organisations and services.

Public sector organisations are inevitably steered by a political agenda and politically defined goals (Doherty and Horne, 2014) which ultimately determine the desired outcomes and outputs at the end point of service delivery. Whereas charitable, voluntary and private sector services are less pressured by the constraints of a political influence and offer a greater level of autonomy in determining their own desired outcomes. However, this greater autonomy can arguably lead to these organisations redefining their aims in order to 'follow the money' and secure funding from a broader range of income sources by being creative in their approach to attract funding (Beugre, 2017; Clay et al., 2020). Nevertheless, this tactic of shifting focus is debatably endemic of some health and social care services despite the likelihood of 'mission drift' and establishing a broader interpretation of their aims. According to Clarke, Gewirtz and McLaughlin (2001), in an attempt to make organisations behave more 'business like' they have become subject to a number of new pressures. These pressures include the competitiveness of delivering services within a mixed economy of providers, the development of both internal and external 'purchaser and provider' service delivery contract arrangements, and 'quasi' agencies directing the spending of the public purse (Lowndes and Skelcher, 1998). The introduction of this 'new managerialism' approach across public services fuelled the need for service managers to employ an entrepreneurial way of working in order to meet funding targets and outcomes. Debatably, the type of health and social care organisation can be determined by the primary source of resources and its level of accountability (Gopee and Galloway, 2017).

Being exposed to the pressure of funding opened my eyes to the hurdles organisations face. It is not only the voluntary sector that has to fight to remain authentic to its cause. The placement helped me understand the context of the political, social and economic challenges faced by organisations in practice. Understanding these challenges enabled me to further develop my ideas about establishing my own social enterprise, who to approach for funding and what funders expect.

Ruth, Child, Family Health and Well-Being

Professional practice placements can enable students to acknowledge the procurement and contracting relationships which have emerged in community, voluntary and statutory health and social care delivery, while recognising the development of provision within a landscape of a mixed market and in an environment of public and private partnership and multi-agency working.

Partnerships in service delivery

The steady increase in funding pressures for the government purse has paved the way for alternative approaches as a means to finance services. The growing pressures on services, as a result of austerity, budget reduction, longer life expectancy and expensive drug treatments for example, have resulted in an increase in commissioning the private and voluntary sectors to deliver provision across the health and social care sector (Gopee and Galloway, 2017). Osbourne and Gaebler (1991) suggest that although procurement is likely to be a permanent fixture of the future funding and annual budget setting arrangements, it is often considered controversial as it is a shift away from state-delivered services. Creation of partnerships to deliver services is increasing and includes providers from the private, voluntary and community sectors working jointly with the public sector to utilise funds from a variety of sources.

While students are working alongside professionals from across a range of disciplines within the field of health and social care, they will inevitably be involved in partnership arrangements to deliver services, and placement settings can offer students an insight into the complex landscape of delivery partnerships, commissioning and procurement (Field and Brown, 2020).

The growth of social enterprise in delivering services

The UK coalition government in 2011 introduced the Localism Act which gave rise to the then prime minister David Cameron's concept of The Big Society – increasing 'social action' through volunteering and opening-up public services to private and voluntary sector competition. As a result, this generated a significant rise in social enterprise models delivering health and social care provision. However, the concept of social enterprise is not a new one, in order to provide affordable food to employees in exploitative factory conditions in Rochdale in the 1840s the social enterprise movement surfaced. Social enterprise had a resurgence and reappeared in the UK in the late 1990s after a period of decline.

Social Enterprise UK (2021) describes social enterprise as:

A social enterprise is a business that trades to tackle social problems, improve communities, people's life chances or the environment.

To fully understand the context in which an organisation operates, students must explore the political drivers and impact of social policy on the development of the placement agency or organisation. This should include an understanding of the needs analysis which led to the creation of the agency/organisation; an understanding of how the performance of the agency/organisation is measured (outcomes and outputs); an understanding of the services delivery plan (implementation strategy, monitoring processes and evaluation methods) and the current funding arrangements. Werbach (2009) suggests that the longevity of an organisation will be determined by the demand for the services it provides.

> Before my placement started, I was interviewed by the placement supervisor as if I was a new member of staff, this was common practice for this placement setting. It was important that I had some knowledge of the organisation and demonstrated that I was prepared for my placement.
>
> Umar, Health and Social Care

Through the analysis of statistical data collated by undertaking a needs assessment, the demand for services and range of provision to meet the identified need can be established (Royse et al., 2009). Need assessments may also provide evidence to justify financial investment and to support funding applications.

Students would benefit from undertaking a strengths, weaknesses, opportunities and threats (SWOT) analysis of the agency/organisation to develop a critical understanding of the work of the agency (Edwards and Best, 2020). Hayes (2010) suggests that identifying strengths, weaknesses, opportunities and threats helps provide comprehensive information about how an organisation or agency operates and identify challenges it may face. Hayes goes on to propose that the organisational context in relation to the political, economic, sociocultural environments and technological factors can be understood through completing a PEST analysis (Hayes, 2010) (Figure 5.1).

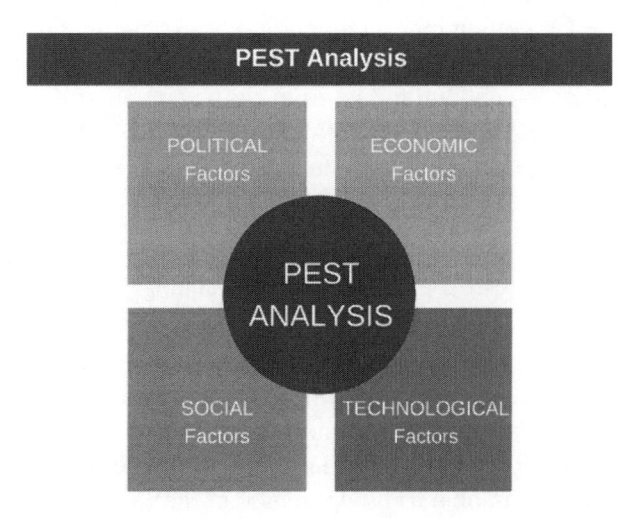

Figure 5.1 PEST analysis

Student expectations

'*all forms of learning and change start with some form of dissatisfaction or frustration*' (Schein, 1999, p 60).

It is not unusual for students to question their placement; for example, how will the organisation support their career when they have already chosen the user group they want to work with? Will they get enough relevant experience with a voluntary organisation? There are a number of reasons why experiencing different placements and dealing with these thoughts and feelings before a placement are beneficial for students. Here we will explore the benefits of the wider experiences made available and the professional growth that comes with working through the unexpected.

The health and social care sector is built on a range of services and agencies, both local and national (DoH, 2013), providing opportunities for students which expose them to the true depths of the required skills and expectations; this includes but is not limited to writing up case notes, developing funding bids and achieving the successful safeguarding of vulnerable adults and children. All the expected tasks should enable the student to advance their professional skills and meet the professional standards and competences of their chosen course (Social Work England, 2020). Statutory, private and voluntary sector agencies work alongside universities offering work experience opportunities in specific professional settings including places of worship, community halls, youth clubs, day centres, social care offices and hospitals. These placements appear very different, but all have a common expectation: to fulfil their safeguarding requirement to those who access the service provided and the wider community. These requirements set out by the government can act as a starting point and can be found at the GOV.UK website. Service delivery is set by the vision, mission and values of the organisation which will influence the main area of the placement.

It is an unsettling time for students awaiting details of the professional setting for the practice-based element of the degree study programme. Once informed, the lack of knowledge of the practice setting may increase feelings of uncertainty. This uncertainty is often experienced when students are informed of their placement in a setting which they view as different to what they hoped for. Internet research can often add to concerns due to a lack of funding for the digital representation of an organisation, bringing to mind the saying 'don't judge a book by its cover'. Smaller voluntary sector organisations will often have a limited resource pool to market themselves and students need to take this into account when investigating the identified placement setting.

As a student you will be introduced to the idea of 'resilience' and this is often discussed in line with service users, considering their resilience factors and support needs (Evans and Price, 2014). However, resilience is not specific to the service user but something that is inherent in us all. We develop our resilience through life experiences leaning on transferable skills and support to enable us to get through and overcome life's hurdles (Evans and Price, 2014). Kahneman (2011) refers to resilience as 'optimism', as it is through resilience a person is able to be optimistic in the face of their challenges.

Figure 5.2 Student expectations, opportunity and growth

To adopt our resilience when feeling uncertain about our placement we must be able to also use the skill of 'reflection' (Beesley, 2020). This is important here as a student needs to unpick some of the feelings they are experiencing and understand the processes they are going through (Butler, 2019). In some instances, a student who feels the placement is too close to their current experience should raise this; good communication skills are invaluable in these cases. However, in most instances the student will feel 'out of their depths', scared, anxious, not listened to etc (Beesley, 2020). Beesley (2020) refers to this as '*potential placement pitfall*' and the '*potential placement opportunity*' (p 11). To avoid the placement pitfall now is also a good opportunity to reflect on your motivations. Why have you chosen this pathway? Why do you want to work in the field of health and social care? Also, what experiences will broaden your skill set to become the best that you can be? Exploring these elements internally and with your academic support network will enable you to assess what you are experiencing and provide the opportunity to open you up to new experiences in an optimistic, learning and skill-enhancing way.

As a third-year student I firmly believe that the success of my placements involved me having a good understanding of what learning I could achieve from the placement setting. This included me stepping outside of my comfort zone and maturely communicating my anxieties as a way of developing my professional growth.

Kate, Youth and Community Work Student.

In Chapter 2, the concept of reflection and reflective practice is considered, and how the process supports practitioners to understand resilient methods of practice. Chapter 3 further explores professional roles and how resilience is key in being able to maintain your professional role and remain in your chosen career. This chapter also identifies what emotional resilience is and offers ideas for skill development.

How the charity sector adds value to the student experience

The Charity Commission for England and Wales sets the parameters for voluntary sector organisations and has established four core values which they must meet. These are:

Being ethical;

Having a community conscience

Providing a specialism; and

Enabling those who are most vulnerable to be heard.

(Charity Commission and Frontier Economics, 2019)

These same values underpin university health and social care colleges and schools and the study programmes they deliver including health and social care, youth work, social work and nursing programmes. These shared values support the confidence a student should have in a placement within the voluntary sector. More often, a charity will reach out to the community to become involved in volunteering with the organisation. The planned process of volunteer induction and the responsibilities a charity has to its volunteers offer evidence of its readiness to provide students with a robust professional practice placement (NCVO, 2021).

Government legislation also has its role in the outcomes a charity delivers, therefore breaking down any ideas that a charity is built on the 'good will of a few'. Instead, charities are established on the knowledge, skills and values outlined within the Charities Act 2011. This Act provides the Charity Commission for England and Wales with the guidelines to regulate charities to ensure public confidence.

The significance of the role of voluntary sector organisations and the importance of their roles is often reported within serious case reviews (SCRs). In September 2019, the NSPCC completed their findings of the role of the voluntary sector in SCRs highlighting both strengths and areas for improvement (NSPCC, 2019). The key point to take away from this is the 'need'; the needs of society are best supported through this collaborative approach between the statutory, private and voluntary sectors. What should be remembered is that the requirement to safeguard and the application of law is definitive no matter where this is applied.

I initially was not happy when I received my placement setting. It wasn't an area of work I was interested in, and I was very anxious and keen to get the placement I wanted. I talked this through with my tutor and placement coordinator. While I remained uncertain it wasn't until I started my placement that I recognised the value of the experience and reduced my anxiety. I didn't want to work with young people, but I'm now considering this as a career option.

Kirsty, Health and Social Care

When reviewing the placement a student has been offered, they should remain open to the opportunities and challenges available. A key aspect of becoming a wide-reaching professional is being able to be open to change and challenge your perspective. This is discussed by Schein (1999) in relation to Lewin's theory of change whereby students will experience 'survival anxiety' due to the impact of an unknown setting or an unexpected role. However, 'psychological safety' can be created if the student accepts how the uncertainty is affecting them and the appropriate support is in place by the university, thus *'reducing learning anxiety and … creating genuine motivation to learn and change'* (Schein, 1999, p 61).

How you adapt to your placement and make the most of the opportunities are a personal skill and a requirement within the health and social care workforce. It is the experience of the author that students will often turn to their peers, which in many cases escalates the feelings of disappointment, upset and concern before then speaking to their personal tutor or placement coordinator. Placements follow a process which often includes speaking to your placement supervisor, which is a great opportunity to ask questions and reduce learning anxieties.

Inclusive interprofessional working

You will find a dedicated chapter to interprofessional working (Chapter 10) that provides an in-depth overview into the vast aspect of work in the social care sector.

This section of the chapter relates specifically to the student's previous learning and working in the context of an agency enriching the wider learning of interprofessional working.

Interprofessional working is not just the act of working with other professionals but is the cornerstone to effective practice in safeguarding vulnerable adults and children (WHO, 2010). As noted by Thomas, Pollard and Sellman (2014, p 1), we are not only duty bound but have a *'moral obligation'* to share our practice with other professionals to holistically meet the needs of individual service users.

As a student, interprofessional learning begins in the classroom and it runs throughout the health and social care programmes of study. The WHO (2010) highlights the importance of interprofessional education and recognises how this enhances the health outcomes of services users (p 13).

A significant number of serious case reviews (SCR) have increased the need to understand the true value of interprofessional working, influencing the range of practice experiences offered through study programmes. The placement experience draws on the classroom learning, the student's independent study, the student's own skills and practice experiences to support their journey into employment.

There must be consideration of the student's responsibility to engage with their peers and seek support from their mentor to overcome any difficulties which they face in a professional environment, and/or in representing the organisation where they are completing their placement. An interesting theory to consider here is 'incremental theory'. Dweck (2000, cited Aubrey and Riley, 2019) considered learners having an incremental or entity mindset which impacts on the students 'mindset and motivation'. This theory links significantly to the students' learning experience.

> *it is not an internal quality that is fed by success ... it is a positive way of experiencing yourself when you are fully engaged and are using your abilities to the utmost in pursuit of something you value. (Dweck, 2000, p 4)*

The added value of different professional settings, whether private, statutory, or voluntary, is that they provide students with an insight into other agencies when working interprofessionally. Students can experience working with a range of people presenting with varying difficulties and support needs, often safeguarding those who are most vulnerable. There will be a diverse professional pool of people that students will meet, each with their own professional goals, experiences and professional identity, the authors experience as a manager in the voluntary sector included managing social workers, youth workers and those with lived experience within the same team.

Interprofessional practice is underpinned by government policy and guidance that will influence the professional response to working with vulnerable adults and children and outline the role of professionals and the requirement for interprofessional working. In the wide-ranging field of health and social care, those who work with children should be familiar with key legislation that has supported and enriched practice, namely Working Together to Safeguard Children (2018) guidance, underpinned by The Children Acts of 1989 and 2004, the Children and Social Work Act 2017 and the Education Act 2002 legislation (HM Government, 2018). Equally, those whose focus is working with adults should be familiar with the policy paper SD8 (2017) which outlines practice in line with the Mental Capacity Act 2005, the Care Act 2014, and the Social Services and Wellbeing Act 2014 (Office of the Public Guardian, 2017). The intention here is to emphasise that the recognition and need to work interprofessionally is not only enacted at ground level but directed through a complex matrix of legislation, governing bodies and education.

A final consideration is that which relates to inclusive interprofessional working and in the inclusion of service users. Interprofessional working does not occur effectively if the service users we hope to support are not partially or fully engaged in the process. Gray, Stroud and Chiripanyanga (2009) highlight that interprofessional learning is only a piece of the student's journey to successful collaborative working. Gray, Stroud and Chiripanyanga (2009) go on to state that the key learning from the classroom to support practice is to include '*listening to people, recognising their strengths and making a commitment to practice*'. Developing these skills will go a long way in cultivating the student's professional practice during their placement which will remain with them as they move into their chosen career. Students will develop these elements through reflective practice and supervision. Reflective practice is a skill which requires the student to critically appraise their practice and be open to constructive feedback (Beesley, 2020). Supervision provides the safe space for the student to explore their practice in a constructive and supportive environment that further enhances reflective practice and the development of the student's professional practice (Beesley, 2020).

Exposure to different agencies will introduce and/or expose students to various models of working and the experience and application of different theories within practice. Key models of working include but are not limited to the medical model, the social model and the psychosocial model; however, these are rarely stand-alone practices. It is the experience of the author that training and working with new staff and students will bring new learning and ideas into a team, and frequently enrich the team and enhance the impact of the service. This is frequently observed when students are encouraged to apply for jobs and offered work following the completion of their placement. As a student you will see that universities pride themselves on the employment statistics of graduates provided by the Higher Education Statistics Agency (HESA).

Gaining an understanding of the dominant model of practice in an organisation and how this influences practice will support the greater identification of theory to practice. Robinson, Anning and Frost (2016) explain from their research that the key model defines the starting point of practice. For example, within a medical setting the medical model would be applied, working with the presenting condition and considering need and best practice prescribing medication. Within the child and adolescent mental health service (CAMHS) setting, the medical model is supported by therapeutic interventions influenced by the outcome of the assessment. For example, children suffering with depression will be supported with theories such as systems theory, psychodynamic theory and solution-focused theory (National Institute for Health and Care Excellence, 2019).

No family or person is one-dimensional; practice requires a 360-degree and four-dimensional approach to assess need, to gain an understanding of a person's history, experiences and wishes and feelings. Work is to be in line with the organisation's policy and procedure and aim of the organisation. Interprofessional working and a good use of supervision alongside reflective practice will provide a student with the markings to work both anti-oppressively and anti-discriminatorily.

There are many theories that can be considered, with some theories that are more commonly recognised or the student feels most confident with. The practice setting will provide a platform to develop and enhance practice alongside the academic teaching. All of this is greatly influenced by what kind of worker you want to be. This is a good time to reflect on why you are stepping into the social care profession and consider what kind of practitioner you want to be.

Conclusion

As the health and social care sector continuously responds to the ever-changing landscape of delivering services against a political backdrop which sculpts how services are delivered and resourced, students need to develop an understanding of the driving forces behind organisations and agencies. In recognising the type of placement organisation, students will create a better understanding of both internal and external pressures which the organisation will be managing on a day-to-day basis. This will inevitably include funding and budget management, partnership arrangements and the legislative framework which underpins service delivery. Additionally, acquiring knowledge of where organisations and professionals fit within the jigsaw of interprofessional working will enable students to further develop links between theory and professional practice.

References

Aubrey, K and Riley, A (2019) *Understanding and Using Educational Theories*. 2nd ed. London: Sage.

Beesley, P (2020) *Making the Most of Your Social Work Placement*. London: Sage.

Beugre, C (2017) *Social Entrepreneurship: Managing the Creation of Social Value*. Oxford: Routledge.

Butler, G (2019) Reflecting on Emotion in Social Work, in Mantell, A S (ed) *Reflective Practice in Social Work*. 5th ed. London: Sage.

Care Act 2014. Available at: https://www.legislation.gov.uk/ukpga/2014/23/contents (accessed 05 May 2021).

Charities Act 2011. Available at: http://www.legislation.gov.uk/ukpga/2011/25/part/2 (accessed 05 May 2021).

Charity Commission and Frontier Economics (2019) *The Value of The Charity Sector an Overview*. Available at: https://assets.publishing.service.gov.uk/government/uploads/system/uploads/attachment_data/file/835686/Value_of_Charity_-_Oct_19_-_published.pdf (accessed 17 June 2020).

Clarke, J, Gewirtz, S and McLaughlin, E (2001) *New Managerialism New Welfare?* London: Sage.

Clay, T, Collinge, T, Piazza, R, Noble, J, Corry, D and Davis, L (2020) State of the Sector 2020. Where We Stood When the Crisis Hit. Our Research on the Big Questions Facing Charities. Available at: https___www.thinknpc.org_wp-content_uploads_2020_05_State-of-the-Sector-2020-Where-we-stood-as-the-crisis-hit-1.pdf (accessed 17 May 2021).

Cunningham, J and Cunningham, S (2017) *Social Policy and Social Work*. 2nd ed. London: Sage.

Dickinson, H and Carey, G (2016) *Managing and Leading in Inter-Agency Settings*. 2nd ed. Bristol: Policy Press.

Doherty, T and Horne, T (2014). *Managing Public Services, Implementing Change - A Thoughtful Approach*. 2nd ed. London: Taylor & Francis.

DoH (2013) The Health and Care System Explained - GOV.UK. www.gov.uk (accessed 19 July 2021).

Dweck, C. (2000) *Essays in Social Psychology, Self-Theories: Their Role in Motivation, Personality and Development*, 4. New York: Psychology Press.

Edmond, N and Price, M (2014) *Integrated Working with Children and Young People: Supporting Development from Birth to Nineteen*. London: Sage.

Edwards, D, and Best, S (2020) *The Textbook of Health and Social Care*. London: Sage.

Evans, E, and Price, M (2014) Children and Young People's Social and Emotional Development, in Edmond, N and Price, M. *Integrated Working with Children and Young People: Supporting Development from Birth to Nineteen*. London: Sage.

Field, R and Brown, K (2020) *Effective Leadership, Management & Supervision in Health and Social Care*. 3rd ed. London: Sage.

Gopee, N and Galloway, J (2017) *Leadership and Management in Healthcare*, 3rd ed. London: Sage.

Gray, R, Stroud, J and Chiripanyanga, S (2009) Inter-Professional Learning to Prepare Medical and Social Work Students for Practice with Refugees and Asylum Seekers. *Social Work Education*, 28(3):306.

Hayes, J (2010) *The Theory and Practice of Change Management*. 3rd ed. London: Palgrave Macmillan.

HM Government (2018) Working Together to Safeguard Children: A Guide to Inter-Agency Working to Safeguard and Promote the Welfare of Children. Available at: https://assets.publishing.service.gov.uk/government/uploads/system/uploads/attachment_data/file/779401/Working_Together_to_Safeguard-Children.pdf.

Hughes, L. (2012) Children with Social and Emotional Difficulties Need Support from a Range of Professionals: Preparing Professions for Integrated Working. *The International Journal of Emotional Education*, 4(2):55–56.

Kahneman, D (2011) *Thinking, Fast and Slow*. London: Penguin Group.

Laming, L (2003) The Victoria Climbie Enquiry. Available at: https://assets.publishing.service.gov.uk/government/uploads/system/uploads/attachment_data/file/273183/5730.pdf.

Learning for improved Safeguarding Practice in the Voluntary and Community Sector. https://learning.nspcc.org.uk/research-resources/2019/learning-from-inquiries-and-reports-about-safeguarding-practice.

Legislation.gov.uk (2020a) Charities Act 2007. Available at: www.legislation.gov.uk/ukpga/2011/25/part/1 (accessed 17 June 2020).

Legislation.gov.uk (2020b) Localism Act 2011. Available at: www.legislation.gov.uk/ukpga/2011/20/contents.

Local Government Association (2019) Bright Futures: Our Vision for Youth Services. Available at: www.local.gov.uk/about/campaigns/bright-futures/bright-futures-childrens-services/bright-futures-our-vision-youth-3.

Lowndes, V and Skelcher, C (1998) *The Dynamics of Multi-Organisational Partnerships: an Analysis of Changing Modes of Delivery*. Public Administration Vol. 76, 313–33. Oxford: Blackwell Publications.

Maclean, S and Harrison, R (2008) *Social Work Theory a Straightforward Guide for Practice Educators and Placement Supervisors*. 2nd ed. Staffordshire: Kirwin Maclean Associates Ltd.

Milbourne, L a (2012) From the Third Sector to the Big Society: How Changing UK Government Policies Have Eroded Third Sector Trust. *International Journal of Voluntary and Nonprofit Organizations*, 1.

Mulholland, P, Barnett, T and Woodroffe, J (2020) A Grounded Theory of Interprofessional Learning and Paramedic Care. *Journal of Interprofessional Care*, 34(1):66–75.

Murray-Davis, B, Marshall, M and Gordon, F (2011) What do Midwives think about Interprofessional Working and Learning? *Midwifery*, 27:376–81.

NCVO (n.d.) Policy and Research. Available at: www.ncvo.org.uk/policy-and-research (accessed 19 August 2019/20 October 2019).

NCVO (2021) Quality Standards. Available at: www.ncvo.org.uk//practical-support/quality-and-standards (accessed 17 May 2021).

National Institute for Health and Care Excellence (NICE) (2019) Depression in Children and Young People: Identification and Management. Available at: nice.org.uk (accessed 27 July 2021).

NSPCC (2019) Voluntary Agencies: Learning from Case Reviews. https://learning.nspcc.org.uk/media/1356/learning-from-case-reviews_voluntary-agencies.pdf (accessed 17 June 2020).

NSPCC Learning (2019a) Learning from Inquiries and Reports about Safeguarding Practice: Voluntary and Community Sector. Available at: https://learning.nspcc.org.uk/media/1872/learning-for-improved-safeguarding-practice-in-the-voluntary-and-community-sector.pdf (accessed 17 June 2020).

NSPCC Learning (2019b) Learning from Case Reviews Briefings Voluntary Agencies. Available at: https://learning.nspcc.org.uk/media/1356/learning-from-case-reviews_voluntary-agencies.pdf (accessed 17 June 2020).

Office of the Public Guardian (2017) SD8. www.gov.uk/government/publications/safeguarding-policy-protecting-vulnerable-adults/sd8-opgs-safeguarding-policy#getting-other-agencies-involved.

Ofsted (2018) Official Statistics: Serious Incident Notifications from Local Authority Children's Services 2017 to 2018: Main Findings. Available at: www.gov.uk/government/publications/serious-incident-notifications-from-local-authority-childrens-services-2017-to-2018/serious-incident-notifications-from-local-authority-childrens-services-2017-to-2018-main-findings#notifications (accessed 14 June 2020).

Osbourne, D a (1991) *Reinventing Government: How the Entrepreneurial Spirit Is Transforming Public Services*. New York: Prentice Hall.

Robinson, M and Frost, N (2016) *Developing Multi-Professional Teamwork for Integrated Children's Services*, 51–61. London: Open University Press.

Rosenfield, D, Oandasan, I and Reeves, S (2011) Perceptions versus Reality: A Qualitative Study of Students' Expectations and Experiences of Interprofessional Education. *Interprofessional Education*, 45(5):471–77

Royse, D, Staton-Tindall, M, Badger, K and Webster, J (2009) *Needs Assessment*. London: Oxford University Press.

Schein, E (1996) Kurt Lewin's Change Theory in the Field and in the Classroom: Notes Toward a Model of Managed Learning. *Systems Practice*, 9(1):27–47.

Social Enterprise UK. Available at: www.socialenterprise.org.uk (accessed 06 December 2021).

Social Work England (2020) Practice Placements Guidance - Social Work England (accessed 19 July 2021).

Thomas, T, Pollard, K and Sellman, D (2014) *Interprofessional Working in Health and Social Care: Professional Perspectives*. 2nd ed. Hampshire: Palgrave MacMillan.

Thompson, N (2015) *Understanding Social Work Preparing for Practice*. London: Palgrave MacMillan.

UK Civil Society Almanac (2019) What's The Voluntary Sector's Contribution To The Economy? Available at: https://almanac.fc.production.ncvocloud.net/impact/ (accessed 17 June 2020).

Vayrynen, S and Paksuniemi, M (2020) Translating Inclusive Values into Pedagogical Actions. *International Journal Of Inclusive Education*, 24(2):147–61.

Walsh, M, Stevens, P and Moore, S (2000) *Social Policy and Welfare*. Cheltenham: Stanley Thornes (Publishers) Ltd.

Werbach, A (2009) *Strategy for Sustainability*. Boston: Harvard Business Press.

WHO (2010) Framework for Action on Interprofessional Education & Collaborative Practice. Switzerland. Available at: https://apps.who.int/iris/bitstream/handle/10665/70185/WHO_HRH_HPN_10.3_eng.pdf?sequence=1 (accessed 17 June 2020).

WHO (2013) Interprofessional Collaborative Practice in Primary Health Care: Nursing and Midwifery Perspectives: Six Case Studies. Available at: www.who.int/hrh/resources/IPE_SixCaseStudies.pdf?ua=1 (accessed 17 June 2020).

6 Placements in challenging settings

Jackie King-Owen and Claire Ambrose

Introduction

This chapter will explore issues relating to student placements within 'challenging' settings. Arguably, all placements can offer challenges to students. However, undertaking placements within complex settings, such as secure children's homes, child adolescent and mental health services (CAMHS), hospices or working with homeless people can necessitate more detailed consideration in terms of the role, function and purpose of the placement setting. Careful consideration is needed when agreeing to undertake a placement in one of these settings although there may not be much student choice. However, despite any challenges, these settings offer a rich and dynamic learning platform where students could stretch their knowledge beyond their comfort zone (Vygotsky, 1978) and increase their compassion, understanding and overall have a positive experience.

Student placements offer the opportunity to embed learning from the classroom, using reflection and critical analysis to better understand the application of theory to practice in a safe and supported setting. Placements also encourage the student to build relational skills such as helping know how to work with others in a positive and proactive way which is helpful for future employment. This in turn leads to self-development and growth in terms of confidence building, developing negotiation and communication skills and 'softer' skills such as empathy and compassion. Building resilience and coping strategies is also vital. Students can develop their own personal style of working as well as shape their future professional identity.

Placements vary; some are working towards a professional qualification, for example, social worker or nurse, with strict criteria which must be met, and others are to fulfil hours required by a professional body such as the British Association of Counselling and Psychotherapy. Some placements are simply to give students work-based learning and experience in the field. There are diverse settings for service delivery – not just in statutory environments but increasingly in privately run establishments or contracted-out services. The third or PVI sector (private, voluntary, independent agencies) can offer different and innovative opportunities for student placements. Croisdale-Appleby (2014) identified an increase in voluntary sector placements and decrease in statutory provision, partly as a result of austerity measures from 2010 onwards. Within statutory settings, the research also identified an emphasis on procedural training within social work, spending more time on following policies and procedures and an emphasis on record keeping and monitoring service users, which is a move away from its core identity – an emphasis on the values of social justice, addressing inequality and inclusion.

There has been a move away from institutional care over the last 50 years (Goffman, 1961) but, paradoxically, an increase in specialised units or facilities offering care, containment and control (Foucault, 1977; Donzelot, 1980; Cohen, 1985). This paradigmatic shift has reinforced the impact of segregation (as opposed to integration) for some service users. These environments include CAMHS, young people's secure units, working with homeless people or within hospices with people at the end of their lives. Placements within such settings offer challenges as well as great opportunities; this chapter will consider both.

This chapter discusses:

- Self-awareness
- Strength-based approach
- Whistleblowing
- Working with children and young people who have experienced trauma
- Working with people in distress
- Working with violent behaviour
- Working with people at the end of life

Self-awareness

Placement may be emotionally challenging and require particular attention to the health and well-being of the student; this is linked to self- awareness as understanding one's own values, opinions, as well as possible triggers of past trauma. However, recognition of this is potentially cathartic and can lead to post-traumatic growth. Self-care is extremely important to avoid burnout or compassion fatigue (McCann and Pearlman, 1990) and there is also the potential for secondary or vicarious traumatisation. This may already be an issue for staff working in challenging settings, some of whom may appear detached or cynical. However, the concept of the '*wounded healer*' was identified by Jung (1963) as the means of helping others to help oneself. This can be an opportunity for personal growth and development. Similarly, Frankl (2006) recognised that suffering is a fundamental human experience and acceptance of this provides life with a profound meaning.

Nevertheless, placements can become problematic if students over-identify with the individuals' group and experience transference (Rogers, 1961) or where there may be an unconscious or conscious voyeurism into the lives of certain groups of service users. For students in a challenging setting, this may be further fuelled by the media, for example, the stigma of working with convicted sex offenders and the moral panic that this may generate. Cohen (1972) describes a moral panic as a condition, episode, person or group which may emerge as a threat to social values or interests. Chapter 9 discusses issues of self-awareness and personal insight in more detail.

Being authentic is important, stating what you may need to do and why. There is a need to avoid over-dependency, but this should be framed within a code of conduct which promotes honesty and reliability as many clients have been severely let down by professionals in the past.

> *I enjoyed my placement in India – it was a bit scary at first being away from the UK and in a different culture but I embraced it as a great learning opportunity. I am still in touch with the village school and help to fundraise to buy basic equipment.*
>
> Carole, Child, Family Health and Well-Being

They may have had several adverse childhood experiences (ACES) and have poor attachment issues (Bowlby, 1969; Howe, 1995). The need to understand the client in terms of their background and upbringing can be evidenced by ecological theory (Bronfenbrenner, 1979) and social learning theory (Bandura, 1977). When working with young people, life course theory (Elder and Giele, 2009) also helps in terms of understanding the importance of the three 'Ts' – transition, turning point and trajectory – on the young person's future life chances; for example, the negative impact of abject poverty, growing up in a 'sink' estate, exposure to domestic abuse or the loss of a parent cannot be underestimated.

Strength-based approach

Working in an anti-oppressive manner (Thompson, 2020) is essential despite the potential complexity generated by the debate of care versus control, or the professional's role of enforcer rather than enabler (anti-oppressive practice is discussed in detail in Chapter 4). This is particularly the case when working in secure settings, where the environment is based on containment and there may be limited opportunity to engage with prisoners due to the regime, with few staff and more limited resources for educational opportunities due to cutbacks in funding. Power dynamics and the damaging reputations of clients can distort creative approaches due to stigma and unconscious bias. Goffman wrote about the stigma (1963) which is reinforced in secure settings by the 'inmates' having negative histories. Becker (1963) developed this concept in relation to young offenders in the United States using labelling theory and the notion of the outsider. These factors can make working in certain environments, such as children's secure units, particularly risky and stressful.

> *I was about the same age as some of the service users and that was OK as I could relate to them, but I needed to keep reminding myself that I had to keep some professional distance and not overshare my own stuff.*
>
> Ian, Social Work

This can go spectacularly wrong resulting in physical violence and lack of confidence for the student learner, which may even hinder their wish to work in health and social care in the future. To protect against this requires robust, regular supervision and an emphasis on reflective practice. However, all students need to try to operate from a strengths-based position (Saleeby, 2006), recognising first and foremost the skills, resources and strengths of service users while adopting a '*growth mindset*' (Dwerk, 2010); this is possible by adopting an open and willing attitude and to see challenges as opportunities for learning. This approach draws on the innate capacity and potential of all individuals to develop and grow (Eichsteller and Holthoff, 2011). One approach that has this at the centre of its ethos is that of social pedagogy (Petrie, 2011); through the power of equally trusting relationships and reciprocity that involves shared learning based on mutual respect, which is the optimum strategy with any service user group. This avoids seeing service users as deficient. Instead, it espouses an empowering approach which goes beyond tokenistic consultation through participation towards full citizen control as envisaged by the concept of the ladder (Arnstein, 1969). An example of empowerment in a prison is family learning which, although not leading to control over the setting, enables the learners to take control of their own development, make connections with previous learning and plan for future joint learning with family members through utilising their strengths, experiences and knowledge and by raising confidence and self-esteem (Mackenzie, 2010). However this can conflict with concepts of power and control (Foucault, 1977), especially in relation to issues such as the role of prisons in society particularly in respect of safeguarding. The role of local authorities has, over the last 20 years, moved towards a more managerial or process-driven model (Rogowski, 2011) which often allows for limited, if any, involvement of the service user voice; thus approaches such as this have been compromised in favour of this style of working and reinforced in settings such as prisons.

Whistleblowing

An issue not often discussed in student placements is whistleblowing, that is, reporting wrongdoing by another professional. This is especially important when working with people with complex needs or facing challenging issues. Some settings are challenging due to the spontaneous and unpredictable behaviour or needs of the service users, whereas others due to prevailing ways of working or unhealthy culture. Students usually work in unfamiliar environments, hierarchies and cultures, and this could undermine a student's confidence in acting upon or reporting poor practice. Concepts such as organisational cultural norms can be challenging, particularly as the student is generally without authority, has limited power or status and needs to pass the placement. It is argued that cultural norms in organisations can be explicitly understood, for example, terminology used and ways of working with service users (Frese, 2015) and therefore students can choose whether to adapt or conform. Clarity about roles and responsibilities is necessary, especially when working in a multidisciplinary team as there may be different ways of working. Misunderstandings can arise and may impact on the effective working relationship leading to conflict.

In addition, there are informal 'rules of the game' which are particularly evident within institutions and may take time to understand within the placement setting. An example of this in prisons would be the accepted behaviour towards certain prisoners such as sex offenders. However, the research also found that social norms may reinforce staff or student behaviour and values, thereby becoming complicit in the dominant organisational culture and practices; the student becomes part of the system, and therefore part of the problem, if the organisational culture is unhealthy.

> *I found the use of restraint difficult to handle, I used supervision to challenge poor practice as it was not always handled well. I know the staff work hard in difficult circumstances, but they are there to support looked after children who, let's face it, have had a tough time growing up.*
>
> Mohammer, Youth and Community Studies

Whistleblowing can be extremely difficult for the student to initiate as well as stressful. However, it is important to do the right thing as long as the facts are correct. Observing poor or even illegal practice by colleagues may trigger the need for whistleblowing or notification under safeguarding procedures; ultimately the student may need to give evidence about other staff behaviour in an employment tribunal or criminal hearing. Robust supervision as well as an understanding of professional accountability are needed; this can be more complicated if the poor practice involves the supervisor. Such dilemmas pertain in a culture where 'we have always done it this way' is the mantra; custom and practice reinforce this as the norm and can become a barrier to positive change. Supervision is discussed in more detail in Chapter 7 and resource of self in Chapter 9.

Considering settings with children and young people

Placements such as those within young people's secure care settings try to offer holistic, therapeutic support giving safety, structure and consistency to young people who may have been without protection or boundaries in the past. Bartlett, Warner and Hales (2018) studied secure care for young people in the UK. They defined the legal frameworks under which young people can be deprived of their liberty, namely under The Mental Health Act 1983 (amended 2007) which is generally used for hospital admission for assessment (Section 2) or treatment (Section 3), and Section 25 of The Children Act 1989, which is used for secure children's hostels or via the Youth Justice System placed on remand, or serving a sentence in a children's home, secure training centre or a young offender institution (YOI).

The potential for abuse can be exacerbated in closed environments first identified by Goffman (1961) in his seminal work *Asylums*. The poor attitude of some staff to young people can give rise to questionable practice and can lead to an increase in complaints or inadequate inspection reports where these apply as some environments are unregulated (although there are moves to correct this in relation to accommodation for under 16-year-olds in the autumn of 2021). Whistleblowing or challenging poor practice may be necessary as discussed earlier. Supervision within secure care units enables students to develop good practice, exercise discretion and judgement in decision-making and develop their confidence and competence (British Association of Social Workers [BASW], 2011). Within challenging environments working with high-risk service users, it is argued that supervision is driven by checking compliance rather than positively challenging and reflecting on practice (Dustin, 2007). Students require time and encouragement within the supervision sessions to reflect on action (Schön, 1983) and learn enabling a more holistic and systemic approach when supporting people with complex needs (Reder and Duncan, 2003). Within this safe environment the examination of personal feelings prompted by the nature of the work is fundamental to effective supervision (Ingram and Smith, 2018). These issues are further explored in Chapter 7.

CAMHS is a term used for all services which work with children and young people who have difficulties with their emotional or behavioural well-being (National Health Service [NHS], 2019). CAMHS is usually made up of a multidisciplinary team consisting of psychiatrists, clinical psychologists, social workers, nurses, occupational therapists, support workers, specialist substance misuse workers, allowing an excellent opportunity for interprofessional teamwork (Tuckman, 1965). One barrier that can present in settings is that of 'craft' jargon or language (known as a restricted code) in the initial stages of placement. Students can feel that they are literally learning a new language due to the amount of diagnostic language and acronyms used. Additionally, top-down bureaucracy may result in a silo mentality with professional tribalism. Dominance of risk aversion or the medical model as opposed to the more empowering social model of disability (Barnes and Mercer, 2006) can sometimes be an issue, leading to a lack of positive risk taking and client empowerment. This may conflict with the student's value base and their wanting to make a difference.

Student placements in this multi-professional setting can be particularly stressful given the nature of the work involved with young people who are experiencing mental health issues. Over the last few years, the waiting times have increased as well as the higher thresholds required to even receive a service, resulting in children and young people presenting with much more acute mental health needs than ever, including self-harm and suicidal ideation (Bould et al., 2019). With waiting times being a significant issue in CAMHS, having waited so long for a service can be frustrating for families and some of that may present as 'being difficult', 'being angry' or 'disrespectful'. A great deal of empathy is needed as well as an understanding of how to deal with difficulties around communication and managing expectations of 'a miracle cure' to address the young person's acute mental health needs. Non-verbal body language (and sound communication) as well as interpersonal skills are needed. The SOLER model ('Sit squarely'; 'Open posture'; 'Lean towards the other'; 'Eye contact'; 'Relax') developed by Egan (1986) emphasises the importance of non-verbal communication (sometimes known as body language), which can greatly improve the effectiveness of communication between individuals. The theory explains how non-verbal communication can make an individual feel comfortable, secure and understood. Other skills students may have the opportunity to display or observe is unconditional positive regard (Rogers, 1957) when a client shares a habit or behaviour with the therapist that is self-detrimental or self-harmful, such as abusing drugs or alcohol, cutting or binge eating.

On placement, as always, students need to recognise confidentiality, its limits and to be clear about safeguarding especially in relation to self-harm or potential danger to others. This is exacerbated when working in challenging settings as there could be more serious consequences, for example, in relation to previous or potential victims of crime or extreme self-harm resulting in suicide. Also given the age differential, which may be minimal for student learners, there is a need to maintain an appropriate professional distance, a sense of identity and clear personal boundaries. Sharing experiences or over-disclosure are particularly discouraged (Brookes, 2017) as well as sharing social media. Self-disclosure is discussed in more depth in Chapter 9, 'Resource of self'.

For students working with children or young people who have been removed from their families or caregivers, consideration of a particular set of issues needs to be held in mind. For example, children often experience multiple moves within the social care system leading to disruptive relationships (especially friendships and schooling), which can lead to feelings of rejection and poor attachments. The vulnerability of the young person is often exacerbated by being placed miles from their original home and local support systems (although this may not be a negative situation given the abusive nature of some home environments and local influences). However, sharing with other young people who may be a danger to themselves or others can create a toxic mix and lead to further complications for the young person concerned. Students can utilise the 3 Ps model (Hatton, 2013) from social pedagogy to provide boundaries and a framework for creating healthy relationships in practice, while also sharing this model with the young person so they can establish relationships on a more stable and positive level with clear boundaries.

Debriefing in challenging settings, that is, continuous on the job support, is vital as some of the disclosures may be distressing, for example, suicidal ideation or details of childhood sexual abuse. Students need strong, regular, formal supervision in a safe, private space in order to explore emotional issues such as the impact of a student's own historical trauma in order to avoid a serious impact on the student's own health and well-being. This promotes effective supervision through encouraging critical reflection and analysis of practice. This approach sets out clear risk assessment categories (worries, strength, safety, goals and next steps) for the student on placement. Furthermore, Kadushin's

(1992) three-pronged supervision model of management, education and support provides a useful framework for ensuring that placement objectives, performance management and learning are promoted as part of supervision. Joining a 'community of practice' (Lave and Wenger 1991, cited by Farnsworth, Kleanthous and Wenger-Trayner, 2016) with staff or other students can be an empowering, cathartic and reassuring process where anonymised experiences and their emotional impact can be discussed within a safe and supportive environment.

Challenging settings add an additional layer of complexity to building relationships and listening to the voice of young people, since young people can experience changes in staff or relocation which hampers the development of stable, safe and reciprocal relationships. An additional challenge for students on placement is relationship building and trust; often the young people concerned have experienced a huge turnover of staff in their short lives, which when added to the frequency of moves within care settings can lead to increased insecurity and low self-esteem. It is important to avoid over-dependency and handle transitions as well as planning an exit strategy when ending the relationship with a service user or leaving the placement setting (Doel and Best, 2008). Placements are short in terms of time but the impact of the student on the young person can have a longer lasting effect; acknowledgement of this and feedback from the young person can be invaluable to the learning opportunity.

Structural issues in settings with children and families

Understanding some of the underlying structural factors and theoretical approaches influencing delivery in children's services is essential. Since the 1960s, individual pathology has emerged as the most common explanation for anti-social behaviour rather than a more sociological analysis based on external factors, social policy and the changing welfare state (Burney, 2009). This model has been particularly evident due to the influence of neoliberalism and the individualist agenda promoted during the Thatcher era (1979–90) and has continued in some form since. Foucault (1977) described the social welfare system as being regulated by the social control of deviant populations. Donzelot (1980) also described the idea of policing families. This is referred to as the 'tutelary complex' which is a system of institutions that are meant to keep the child within the family based on agreed norms defining success. State institutions are part of this, including schools, social work and the judiciary. Cohen (1985) sees social work service delivery as part of a subtle process of control dispersed through multi agencies. McCarthy (2011) claims that early intervention may identify families at risk of future offending, but this has now been reduced due to the deliberate austerity agenda from 2010 to the present day (Alston, 2018), resulting in the reduction of early help to families. With the closure of Sure Start projects, the focus of service delivery now is mostly available only when families are in crisis. McCarthy (2011) also argues that this approach is rooted in middle-class values (portrayed by professionals) and the inevitable clash based on cultural prejudice.

Unconscious bias also needs to be recognised as this involves reinforcing stereotypes and prejudice (Bellack, 2015).

There are also issues around the marketisation of social care, meaning that commercial care is motivated by profit and may not represent value for money or be up to an agreed standard (Ord, 2011). There is a mismatch between the needs of young people and the suitability of placements when often young people are placed there due to 'its availability' or relatively cheaper cost to the local authority. Poorly trained or inexperienced, often temporary, unqualified staff can lead to different views and behaviour in relation to care quality which in turn leads to difficulties in trust, communication and inconsistent care delivery.

Considering placements within homelessness organisations

Homelessness organisations can offer rich learning opportunities for students on placement. There is a regional variation in terms of availability of services to homeless people, and this presents as a postcode lottery with cities providing more services due to sheer numbers, networks and demand. However, rough sleeping is still prevalent with an increase in street homelessness (Ministry of Housing, Communities & Local Government [MHCLG], 2018). There are also hidden homeless people who may live in unsuitable, unsafe, temporary accommodation or who are '*sofa surfing*' (Fitzpatrick et al., 2018). Homeless people often have other presenting problems apart from lack of accommodation, including poor mental health, drug dependency and alcohol misuse, or for ex-service personnel, post- traumatic stress disorder. Lack of money, an address or employment makes these problems more acute. Bail hostels may involve working with violent or sex offenders; this can present a moral dilemma to student learners. There may be concern about the social mix within the hostel, lone working and thus a personal risk assessment will need to be undertaken. If a student has had their own previous experience of homelessness or being in a refuge, this may trigger past trauma. There may be conflict in terms of a student's own values, for example, working with sex offenders. Working in a chaotic environment of, for example, a bail hostel may impact on the student in terms of fear of frequent or spontaneous violence as well as unpredictable or anti-social behaviour. Student learners will need to have an awareness of the impact of both illegal and prescribed drugs, be resilient and be able to work in a fast-flowing, chaotic situation sometimes involving 'thinking in action' (Schon, 1983) in order to deal with difficult situations. How students cope with this will help shape their ongoing professional identity; maintaining a positive work-life balance as well as acting with utmost integrity are key assets. Clear boundaries are essential to avoid conflict, over-dependency, potential abuse of power or compassion fatigue.

In the age of austerity, homelessness has become more prevalent and complicated as 'joined up' solutions are less readily available, not least because of the shortage of social housing, as well as reduced resources for support needs and independent advocacy (Alston, 2018). Changes in benefits, such as the introduction of universal credit, have left many people worse off, and some people have become homeless by being evicted due to cuts in housing benefit. Once in rent arrears, it is more difficult to be rehoused, despite The Homelessness Reduction Act (2017). Local authorities have complained that their resources are being overstretched and that they are often only able to offer information rather than more practical help. Student learners working with homeless people will need to understand housing rights as well as tenants' responsibilities. This can impact on the placement experience as students find themselves having to navigate complex systems that can often not support clients adequately, leading to a sense of helplessness and futility. However, adopting a person-centred approach when working with homeless people can help; using Sanderson's (n.d.) person-centred planning toolkit can help students better understand the person and is a practical way to capture information that feeds into support planning, as well as to improve communication and relationships.

Placements within hospices

Dealing with end-of-life care can be particularly draining both emotionally and spiritually. Working with death and the dying speaks to one's own mortality as well as triggers memories of loved ones who may have died. It may not be suitable for someone who has been recently bereaved or has unresolved grief. The work around bereavement by Kubler-Ross (1972) in relation to the five stages of grief – denial, anger, bargaining, depression and acceptance – can help with some understanding of the key issues, but it may not be a linear experience, more of a curve as in the dual process model (Stroebe and Schut, 1999). Thus, other bereavement models such as Worden's (1991) Tasks of Mourning or Weller's (2015) Gates of Grief offer different perspectives which can be helpful to the student on placement when reflecting in supervision. This application of theory to real experiences with the dying can form part of the placement assessed written work, giving a further opportunity for reflection and synthesis.

Careful preparation for a hospice placement is required such as reflecting on your reasons for opting for the placement. Self-care is vital, but Mannix (2017) is keen to stress that working in hospices can be joyful, empowering and life affirming; narratives illustrate this with numerous acts of kindness and growth during the final days. Dealing with endings in a real sense requires resilience, kindness and compassion. Students may also find a variety of differing views on death or issues such as assisted suicide from both colleagues and clients, which may challenge their own religious or ethical views. Students may be responsible for finding out key information for clients on extremely sensitive issues, signposting to other agencies or making things happen by helping the service user realise their 'bucket list'. They may even assist in helping others plan their own funeral.

Conclusion

This chapter has discussed some of the themes when working in challenging environments such as emotional distress, working with those who have experienced trauma, display violence or unpredictable behaviour and working with those about to die. However, although this can appear daunting, placements for students are all about learning and what these settings provide are massive opportunities to stretch and challenge one's own expectations, preconceived judgements and thinking about people we work with. Placements should not be about repeating previous experiences or coasting comfortably; they need to be rich, diverse and enable professional and personal growth. Vygotsky (1978) reminds us to stretch and challenge ourselves as lifelong learners and as part of our continuing professional development.

References

Alston, P (2018) *Statement on Visit to the United Kingdom, by Professor Philip Alston, United Nations Special Rapporteur on Extreme Poverty and Human Rights*. Available at: https://ohchr.org/Documents/Issues/Poverty/EOM_GB 16 Nov2018.pdf (accessed 28 November 2018).

Arnstein, S (1969) Ladder of Citizen Participation. *Journal of the American Planning Association*, l35(4):216–24.

Bandura, A (1977) *Social Learning Theory*. Englewood Cliffs: Prentice Hall.

Barnes, C and Mercer, G (2006) *Independent Futures*. Bristol: Polity Press.

Bartlett, A, Warner, L, and Hales, H (2018) *Young People's Secure Care: Professionals' and Parent's Views of Its Purpose, Placements and Practice*. London: St George's University of London.

Becker, H. (1963) *Outsiders: Studies in the Sociology of Deviance*. New York: The Free Press of Glencoe.

Bellack, J. (2015) Unconscious Bias: An Obstacle to Cultural Competence. *Journal of Nursing Education*, 54(9):563–64.

Bould, H, Mars, B, Moran, P, Biddle, L and Gunnell, D (2019) Rising Suicide Rates among Adolescents in England and Wales. *The Lancet*, 394(10193):116–17. DOI:https://doi.org/10.1016/S0140-6736(19)31102-.

Bowlby, J (1969) *Attachment and Loss*. New York: Basic Books.

The British Association of Social Workers (2011) *UK Supervision Policy*. Available at https://www.basw.co.uk/system/files/resources/basw_73346-6_0.pdf (accessed 20 September 2020).

Bronfenbrenner, U (1979) *The Ecology of Human Development*. Boston: Harvard University Press.

Brookes, J (2017) *A Wounded Healer*. Available at: https://lostincare.co.uk/2017/01/04/a-wounded-healer/ (accessed 30 September 2021).

Burney, E (2009) *Making People Behave: Anti-Social Behaviour, Politics and Policy*. 2nd ed. Cullompton: Willan Publishers.

The Children Act (1989) S.25. Available at: https://www.legislation.gov.uk/ukpga/1989/41/section/25 (accessed 30 September 2021). London: HMSO.

Cohen, S (1972) *Folk Devils and Moral Panics*. London: MacGibbon and Kee.

Cohen, S (1985) *Visions of Social Control: Crime, Punishment and Classification*. Polity Press: Cambridge.

Croisdale-Appleby, D (2014) *Re-visioning Social Work Education: An Independent Review*. Available at: https://assets.publishing.service.gov.uk/government/uploads/system/uploads/attachment_data/file/285788/DCA_Accessible.pdf (accessed 30 September 2021).

Doel, M and Best, L (2008) *Experiencing Social Work and Learning From Service Users*. London: Sage.

Donzelot, J (1980) *The Policing of Families: Welfare versus the State*. London: Hutchinson University Library.

Dustin, D (2007) *The McDonaldization of Social Work*. Aldershot: Ashgate.

Dwerk, C (2010) Mindsets and Equitable Education. *Principal Leadership*, 10(5):26–29.

Egan, G (1986) *The Skilled Helper: A Systematic Approach to Effective Helping*. 3rd ed. Belmont: Brooks Cole.

Eichstellar, G and Holthoff, S, Conceptual Foundations of Social Pedagogy: A Transnational Perspective from Germany. in Cameron, C and Moss, P (eds) *Social Pedagogy and Working with Children and Young People: Where Care and Education Meet*, 33–52. London: Jessica Kingsley.

Elder, G H, Jr and Giele, J Z (2009) Life Course Studies: An Evolving Field, in Elder, G H, Jr and Giele, J Z (eds) *The Craft of Life Course Research*. New York: The Guilford Press.

Farnsworth, V, Kleanthous, I and Wenger-Trayner, E (2016) Communities of Practice as a Social Theory of Learning: A Conversation with Etienne Wenger. *British Journal of Educational Studies*, 64(2):139–60. DOI:10.1080/00071005.2015.1133799.

Fitzpatrick, S, Pawson, H, Bramley, G, Wilcox, S, Watts, B and Wood, J (2018) *The Homelessness Monitor: England 2018*. London: Crisis.

Foucault, M (1977) *Discipline and Punish: The Birth of the Prison*. London: Penguin.

Frankl, V (2006) *Man's Search for Meaning*. Boston: Beacon Press.

Frese, M (2015) Cultural Practices, Morms, and Values. *Journal of Cross-Cultural Psychology*, 46(10):1327–30. DOI:10.1177/0022022115600267.

Goffman, E (1961) *Asylums: Essays on the Social Situation of Mental Patients and Other Inmates*. New York: Doubleday.

Goffman, E (1963) *Stigma: Notes on the Management of a Spoiled Identity*. London: Penguin

Hatton, K (2013) *Social Pedagogy in the UK, Theory and Practice*. Dorset: Russell House.

Homelessness Reduction Act 2017. S.10 Available at: https://www.legislation.gov.uk/ukpga/2017/13/contents (accessed 1 October 2021).

Howe, D (1995) *Attachment Theory for Social Work Practice*. London: Palgrave Macmillan.

Ingram, R and Smith, M (2018) *Relationship-Based Practice: Emergent Themes in Social Work Literature*. Available at https://www.iriss.org.uk/sites/default/files/2018-01/insights-41_1.pdf. (accessed 20 September 2020).

Jung, C G (1963) *Memories, Dreams, Reflections*. New York: Pantheon Books.

Kadushin, A (1992) *Supervision in Social Work*. 3rd ed. New York: Columbia University Press.

Kormanski, C (2008) Leadership Strategies for Managing Conflict. *The Journal for Specialist in Group Work*, 7(2):112–18. https://doi.org/10.1080/01933928208411708.

Kubler-Ross, E (1972) On Death and Dying. *The Journal of the American Medical Association*, 221(2):174–79.

Mackenzie, J (2010) *Family Learning: Engaging with Parents*. Edinburgh: Dunedin Academic.

Mannix, K (2017) *With the End in Mind: How to Live and Die Well*. Croydon: William Collins.

McCann, I L and Pearlman, L A (1990) Vicarious Traumatization: A Framework for Understanding the Psychological Effects of Working with Victims. *Journal of Traumatic Stress* (3):131–49.

McCarthy, D J (2011) Classing Early Interventions: Social Class, Occupational Moralities and Criminalisation. *Critical Social Policy*, 31(4):495–516.

The Mental Health Act (1983) S.2 Available at: https://www.legislation.gov.uk/ukpga/1983/20/contents (accessed 1 October 2021).

The Ministry of Housing, Communities and Local Government (2018) *Rough Sleeping Statistics Autumn 2018, England*. Available at: https://www.gov.uk/government/statistics/rough-sleeping-in-england-autumn-2018 (accessed 20 September 2020).

NHS (2019) *Child and Adolescent Mental Health Services*. Available at: https://www.nhs.uk/using-the-nhs/nhs-services/mental-health-services/child-and-adolescent-mental-health-services-camhs/ (accessed 20 September 2019).

Ord, J (2011) *Critical Issues in Youth Work Management*. Abingdon: Routledge.

Petrie, P (2011) *Communication Skills for Working with Children and Young People: Introducing Social Pedagogy*. 3rd ed. London: Jessica Kingsley Publishers.

Reder, P and Duncan, S (2003) Understanding Communication in Child Protection Networks. *Child Abuse Review*, 12(2):82–100. DOI:10.1002/car.787.

Rogers, C R (1957) The Necessary and Sufficient Conditions of Therapeutic Personality Change. *Journal of Consulting Psychology*, 21(2):95–103. https://doi.org/10.1037/h0045357.

Rogers, C R (1961) *On Becoming a Person: A Therapist's View of Psychotherapy*. Boston: Houghton Mifflin.

Rogowski, S (2011) Managers, Managerialism and Social Work with Children and Families: The Deformation of a Profession? *Practice: Social Work In Action*, 23(3):157–67. https://doi.org/10.1080/09503153.2011.569970.

Saleeby, D (ed) (2006) *The Strengths Perspectives in Social Work Practice*. 4th ed. Boston: Allyn and Bacon.

Sanderson, H (n.d.) Person-Centred Thinking Tools. Available at: http://helensandersonassociates.co.uk/person-centred-practice/person-centred-thinking-tools/ (accessed 1 October 2021).

Schön, D (1983) *The Reflexive Practitioner: How Professionals Think in Action*. New York: Basic Books.

Stroebe, M and Schut, H (1999) The Dual Process Model of Coping with Bereavement: Rationale and Description. *Death Studies*, 23:197–224.

Thompson, N (2020) *Anti-Discriminatory Practice*. 7th ed. Basingstoke: Palgrave Macmillan.

Tuckman, B W (1965) Developmental Sequence in Small Groups. *Psychological Bulletin*, 63:384–99.

Vygotsky, L S (1978) *Mind in Society: The Development of Higher Psychological Processes*. London: Harvard University Press.

Weller, F (2015) *The Wild Edge of Sorrow: Rituals of Renewal and the Sacred Work of Grief*. Berkeley: North Atlantic Books.

Worden, J W (1991) *Grief Counselling and Grief Therapy: A Handbook for the Mental Health Practitioner*. 2nd ed. London: Routledge.

7 Managing your placement and supervision

Diana Conroy, Nigel Down and Helen Morgan

Introduction

The focus of this chapter will be to explore supervision and support as a means of enabling student learning and to build student resilience. This will be discussed keeping potential organisational drivers for supervision – such as managerialism – in mind. The chapter will explore the working agreement between student, practice agencies and the university, considering the challenges of personal development, pastoral care and workload management, while also considering the perceived power dynamics that can exist between the student and supervisor. Supervision is defined as a formal process and relationship between workers (usually one that is a manager oversees the other) to review workload, monitor performance and standards, and identify knowledge, skills and learning opportunities (Skills for Care, 2020). However, there is an expectation that students will take joint responsibility for their learning, requiring them to seek out supervision and support, showing initiative and commitment. This chapter will discuss some of these issues, including the focus of supervision, which can impact on the student's performance.

Sometimes in placements, issues such as challenging situations, differing priorities and role confusion can occur. This chapter will cover and critique the different mechanisms that can be utilised to manage difficulties in professional practice placement settings. A number of supervision models will be examined, providing students with insights to encourage open and safe debate, as well as devise concrete strategies for developing and maintaining healthy working relationships. Professional bodies, including the Nursing & Midwifery Council (NMC) (2018), state that supervision is a process between the student, educational institution, practice learning partner and practice supervision, enabling '*students to learn and safely achieve proficiency and autonomy*' (p 6). This chapter will also draw on reflective theory as a tool for improving practice and relations, building understanding of formal and informal agency structures, while emphasising the importance of the student fully understanding their role and remit within the context of their placement agency.

This chapter discusses:

- Expectations of supervision
- Managing difficulties
- Managing your supervisor
- Models of supervision
- Outcomes from supervision

Expectations of supervision

Students enter placement with an expectation of receiving supervisor guidance and support. However, the supervisory role is one that is also balanced against a requirement to manage student workload and performance, including meeting specific standards if the course is linked to a profession, such as social work, where students are required to demonstrate competence in a range of areas (Social Work England, 2021). This can lead to conflict, potentially affecting the working dynamic between the supervisor and supervisee, particularly where good practice is in question on either side, or where there are differences in perspectives and expectations about roles and responsibilities. In essence, the supervisory relationship between the placement supervisor and student may rely on the balance between providing appropriate support and fostering an appropriate level of autonomy, including serving three functions named by Inskipp and Proctor (1993): formative, normative and restorative. This model suggests that a formative function enables students to change and grow on both personal and professional levels, develop insight, link theory to practice and build new understanding in a range of ways. The normative function acknowledges that students operate within an organisation and its norms, including its policies and practices. As with the formative function, the goal is to support students to develop their practice, but also be mindful of their professional responsibilities. The restorative function of supervision in this model is geared towards helping students reflect on their work and its emotional responses and content, with the supervisor supporting the student to explore some of the more challenging feelings related to working with clients.

However, if too much support is given – such as being given prescriptive knowledge that does not allow the student to understand or question practice, or being overly directed and controlled – then students may feel that they have no ownership of their professional practice experience, leading to disempowerment. Conversely, too little support may make the student feel anxious, abandoned and unable to make decisions.

There is also an expectation from students that supervisors will perform their duties with a high level of professionalism, reflecting sound professional values, ethics and anti-oppressive practice, and that the university will support students if difficulties arise. However, the reality and experience for students is often quite different. The consequence can result in misunderstandings, conflict, resentment and tension, leaving students in a state of despair and/or fear about their career path and possible adverse placement assessment outcomes. Light, Cox and Calkins (2011) note, '*Supervision involves a constant interaction between the supervisor and the student and since this is a one-to-one relationship, crude stereotypes of each other can destroy deeper learning*' (p 156). While this primarily refers to supervision in education, the issue they highlight is an important one; supervision is an intimate relationship and one that is fragile if the two people involved do not take time to build it. Rothwell et al. (2021) note that one of the key enablers of effective supervision is an open, supportive and safe environment and a positive and trusting relationship between supervisor and supervisee. Furthermore, regular meetings that are not rushed to give time both for the relationship to develop and for reflection and feedback to take place are vital.

Practically, there is therefore a need for a clear understanding on all sides of both agency and university organisational policies, processes and procedures and how they interlink. Consideration about other factors influencing supervisor/supervisee dynamics, such as personality, gender, age and culture, can also have a profound impact on the relationship (Thompson, 2016). Nevertheless, there are also the influences of the wider sociopolitical environment, such as the climate of austerity and a reduction in resources, which place services and agencies under pressure. Whether students are placed within statutory, voluntary or private sector arrangements does not necessarily reduce the managerial expectation for staff, with students also required to show they can perform and meet identified learning outcomes and service targets. Hence, the dilemma of desiring quality service standards and provision weighed against the reducing availability of enough resources to deliver can put pressure on students as well as qualified workers, reflecting the overall growth of managerialism, with its emphasis on accountability and performance management, which can mean that the style of supervision is one of ensuring compliance, practice audit and task completion (Wonnacott, 2012).

One of the most important parts of preparing for a placement is identifying what skills you want to develop when you are on placement. I used a number of tools to help me with this process and reflect on my current skills and areas I wanted to enhance.
Michael, Health and Social Care

Managing difficulties

Many students have professional practice or work experience placements as an integral element of their programme of study and consider the placement as an exciting opportunity to gain or further develop knowledge, skills and experience. Practice placements can offer the chance to foster the important and valuable skill set required for a chosen career, and often the greatest learning experience is gained from the most demanding encounter (Rose, 2011). However, challenging experiences during practice placements can potentially present a barrier to learning. Universities have a responsibility to prepare students adequately for placement, including building emotional resilience so students are properly equipped (see Chapter 3 for more on resilience). Yet, some courses have been fiercely criticised for failing in this duty of care (Narey, 2014).

There has been more and more emphasis across the health and social care sector on producing graduating students who possess a range of recognisable graduate attributes, alongside an array of industry-specific skills and relevant knowledge. While this is arguably a useful goal, there also needs to be an acknowledgement of the balance that is required in recognising the student as a learner, underpinned by a clear understanding that students will develop at differing rates. Nevertheless, employability is now a critical part of the learning experience, with traditional liberal humanist perspectives of the university that were concerned with teaching and learning having to incorporate skills and behaviours for the labour market, due to the increasing challenges from wider sociopolitical and economic influences, such as government agendas (Cheng et al., 2021). Student supervision, therefore, should be more than the supervisor being available to talk about the work in relation to the job in hand, but also provide the student with a platform to explore and contextualise their learning.

Most placement settings commonly involve both internal and external stakeholders who will inevitably hold differing priorities; an example of which would be a manager being an internal stakeholder and a client being an external stakeholder. The client may be an individual in the community who wants a particular care agency or package, which the agency may or may not be able to provide. Students may also experience a tension between expectations of their course and university, the placement setting and relevant stakeholders (Marshall, 2018), such as a student being required to demonstrate certain competencies in client practice, but the placement being unable to support these either due to factors such as being unable to offer the opportunity due to resources or staffing. One of the best ways to ensure an effective educational experience is to have clear expectations, and roles and responsibilities of the student during the placement. This should ideally involve developing a joint understanding of the potential risks which may pose a threat to providing a high-quality learning experience, such as staff turnover where a supervisor leaves part-way through a placement. Differing university structures will identify specific roles to manage the overall delivery of professional practice placements, each with different terminology which helps identify those roles and responsibilities. The key term which describes the main point of contact is the placement supervisor. If a student is worried about their placement, then initial concerns should be directly raised with the placement supervisor; this could be undertaken informally in the first instance, or if the student feels the concern is more serious, through the process of formal supervision. However, where this is not possible or the concerns are about that point of contact, and/or are serious, then taking the issue to the university tutor can be the preferred course of action. Preparation for practice should also have included what to do in the face of difficulties and with policies and procedures for measures such as whistleblowing clearly communicated (Social Work England, 2021). Whistleblowing is covered in more detail in Chapter 6, 'Challenging settings'.

Managing your supervisor

The overall purpose of a professional practice placement should be to enable the student to have the experience of working in a contemporary workplace setting relevant to their chosen profession, which contributes to the development of autonomous and self-directed practitioners (NMC, 2018). Light, Cox and Calkins (2011) suggest that supervisors will have expectations for students to embrace their practice experience, with the supervisory relationship providing a useful teaching arena and place to build confidence and competence. The placement should provide a period of supported and guided practice, underpinned by a safety net which allows the student to make mistakes and learn from a broad range of practice experiences. The role of the placement supervisor is crucial in facilitating the learning process and enabling the student to undertake an effective process of reflection on their working practice during the placement. The function of supervision is to support the student to acquire the relevant knowledge, skills and values (Skills for Care, 2020). However, as Rotherwell et al. (2021) note, issues such as organisational pressures and the workload of the supervisor can impact on the relationship. Furthermore, the work environment is arguably becoming more stressful, with the complexities of client need growing, with clients reflecting the increasingly convoluted world and politicised and turbulent environment, one which supervisors have to deal with on a day-to-day basis (Hood, 2018).

The formal supervision process during the placement should assist in consolidating the student's learning while providing the necessary support for the student to make sense of any issues which may impact on their emotional welfare. A student supported in reflection and exploration of issues, incidents and practice examples will enhance the overall learning process of the placement experience, with the emotional impact of the work also explored so the student can build self-awareness (Rose, 2011). Schon (1983) states that the process of reflection is a process by which students can begin to engage in a personal journey that results in lifelong learning. Parker-Rees et al. (2010) describe reflection as:

> Taking the opportunity to think about the work that we are doing, either as we are doing it or after we have done it, attempting to draw the lesson we can learn from it in terms of how that work has impacted upon us and others and how it made or makes us feel about ourselves.
>
> (p 146)

It is therefore crucial that supervision incorporates reflection and students need to feel empowered enough to ask for this element from the supervisor.

The formal supervision process is generally a planned meeting involving the placement supervisor and student. However, what is not often acknowledged in the relationship is the power differentials, with the term 'supervisor' implying that there is an expert in the relationship, who instructs and guides, and as Westergaard (2017) offers, needs to be a relationship where the supervisor is responsible to and not for the student. Students also need to take responsibility for their supervision and learning in placement. Furthermore, the interpersonal relationship may also contain power dynamics, such as those resulting from individual characteristics such as gender or race. Subtle power dynamics can play out in what is arguably a therapeutic relationship such as stereotyping, objectification or othering (Turner, 2021). The most effective supervisors, therefore, will be aware of their authority and power in relation to the student and their characteristics. This means that the supervisor also needs high levels of self-awareness and understanding of each of these areas to create a working relationship with the student where power is acknowledged and not inadvertently abused. Ideally, frequent periodic supervision sessions should be scheduled in line with university guidance for specific programmes which should include the regularity, time and agenda during the placement period. The importance of supervision should be stressed by the student to supervisor, emphasising the worth to learning and personal and professional development that can arise from the process.

Models of supervision

The most common model of supervision in the field of health and social care is what is known as clinical supervision: an experienced professional supporting and guiding the practice of a less experienced professional (Snowdon et al., 2020), in this case, the supervisor and student. However, it is important to recognise that there is not one model that will fit every student (Attard et al., 2010). The seven-eyed process model, suggested by Hawkins and Shohet (2012), incorporates both relational and systemic perspectives to examine the relationship not only between the work and client but between the worker and supervisor, and how the wider system impacts on those relationships. Figure 7.1 illustrates an example of this using a nurse who works with a family.

An effective facilitator is one who makes sure students are fully aware of not only what is going on between student and clients, but also their relationship and the impact of wider forces on it, such as organisational change, managerialism and policy.

The supported reflection and exploration of issues, incidents, relationships and practice examples will enhance the overall learning process of the placement experience. Reflection is considered an important tool for health and social care practitioners, and it is mentioned in various professional codes of practice and recognised as part of continuing professional development (CPD) and included in the 'Code of Conduct for Healthcare Support Workers and Adult Social Care Workers in England' (Skills for Care, 2013). It is considered crucial as it provides the practitioner not only the chance to review their practice, but the learning from this review should be used to influence future practice and consequently change it. However, there are dangers that, initially, when this skill is being developed, it may lead to an individual ruminating on a day's activity with students falling into self-criticism. Good practice would indicate that the process of reflection should be given a time limit, and the supervisor then helps the student to process any negative feelings in order for them to be able to put them to one side after the session. Driscoll (2006) describes supervision as

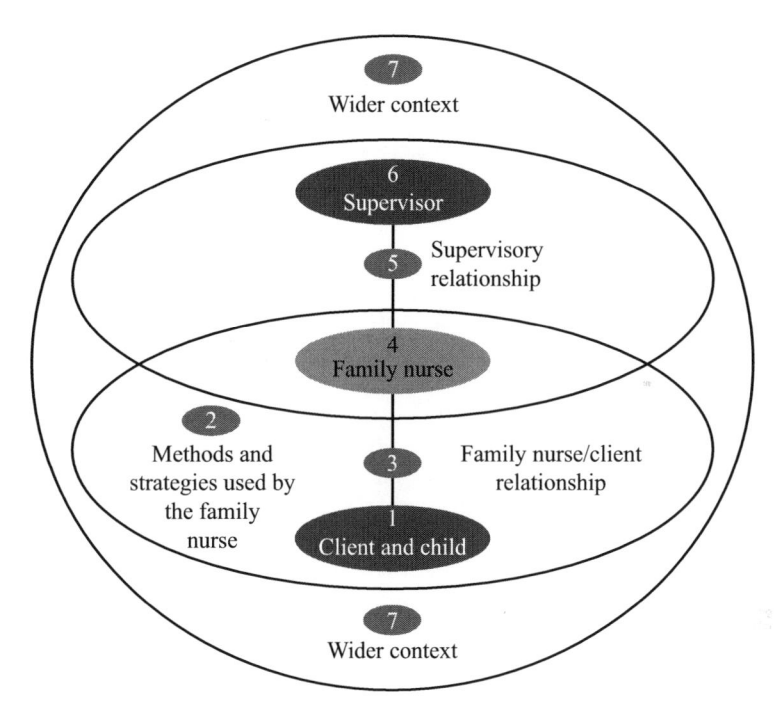

Figure 7.1 *The Hawkins and Shohet model, adapted by Andrews (2020)*

a supported process of guided reflection, using the following model, which is comprised of three components.

- What? – being the description of the event.
- So what? – which is an analysis of the event.
- Now what? – which is the proposed actions following an event.

This model encourages the student to consider what happened, how they reacted, as well as how other people reacted. The second component explores feelings, their own at the time as well as post events, alongside the feelings of others. The third component encourages reflection on the implications of the event as well as how practice may be changed going forward. However, this model is led by an event, incident or specific issue rather than an overview of a workday or work practice in general. Nevertheless, it is a useful, structured reflective tool to use in supervision sessions.

The climate of constant change across the wider landscape of health and social care services dictates that reflective practice be a paramount feature for professionals throughout the disciplines, and thus needs to be a component of good supervision. The often-complex work environment and ever-changing context of provision demand that practitioners utilise strategies which benefit their professional development, as well as seeking better outcomes for service users. Price (2004, p 18) states that *'For reflection to become a transferable skill that is used in practice, practitioners need to learn how to combine this skill with critical thinking'*, and goes on to explore the motives and benefits of reflective practice for practitioners: to develop an understanding of one's motivation, perceptions, attitudes, values and feelings associated with work; to provide an inward-facing view of situations arising within practice and to challenge notions, emotions and actions; and explore different approaches to practice situations. Reflection is viewed as an integral element of professional development for both professionals in training and for experienced practitioners, and as a way of recognising the connectivity between theory and professional practice.

The value of reflective practice is widely supported by the belief that it is more than just living through the experience that leads to learning, and that the fundamental element is the process of reflection. Experiences gained through professional practice placements offer alternative methods of education, as opposed to traditional approaches which often include the conventional transfer of knowledge delivered in formal learning environments. Placements can often be one of the most significant forms of professional development, where students can enhance their praxis within the context of their occupation.

Arguably, reflection can help focus away from organisational, political and societal factors which may influence our practice and concentrates us on our personal response. Bold (2011) states that effective reflection involves *'looking at oneself in relation to the impact one has on others'*, while Giddens (2017) describes the reflective process as confirming the relationship between understanding the knowledge we have and its influence on our actions. Through a formal process of reflection students are able to consider the societal role of the agency, their function during placement and the impact of the placement experience on their learning. Kolb (1984) developed his cyclical theory of reflection as a method of learning which consists of active experimentation, having a concrete experience, undertaking reflective observation and abstract conceptualisation, resulting in experiential learning. Therefore, students will not learn from their experience and complete the learning cycle if they fail to sufficiently reflect. Robb (2007) sums this up nicely:

> *The aim of reflection is not to ascertain 'the truth' about a situation or experience, but it can offer an opportunity to make sense of experiences, whether they are positive, negative or just plain puzzling, and to inform practice.*
>
> (p 79)

The Kadushin model (1985) was developed primarily for use with social work and describes three functions as being necessary to social work supervision, but these functions can be adapted to provide a holistic framework for the student and supervisor in other disciplines. The functions are identified as educational, supportive and administrative, and are represented as three interconnecting areas which directly relate to and complement each other. The three functions overlap and are not necessarily of equal size or importance, but they do provide a useful structure.

1. The educational function is focused on the development and understanding of knowledge and skills, such as clinical skills in nursing.

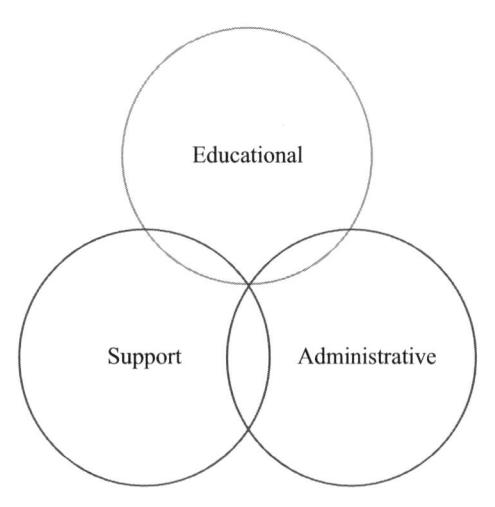

Figure 7.2 The Kadushin model (1985)

2. The supportive function gives consideration to the nature of the work and helps identify interventions to support students with issues like stress.

3. The administrative function is related to the law, relevant legal and ethical frameworks as well as specific codes of conduct important to the field.

The model is shown in Figure 7.2:

> *To get the most out of supervision I found it was really important to prepare for the meeting. Spending time thinking about the day-to-day operation and my development in terms of the support I needed, the general administrative tasks I needed to complete and what I was learning and needed to learn was essential.*
>
> Chloe, Counselling and Psychotherapy

A solution-focused model offers a different approach as it involves an outcome-focused process as opposed to problem-solving; it rests on considering what skills, strengths and assets a student already has, and valuing and *'privileging the supervisee's knowledge'* (p 213), rather than seeing the supervisor as an expert (Ratner, George and Iveson, 2012). This assumes that the supervisee (student) has the answers and it is simply the role of the supervisor to ask useful questions to uncover these, with the focus being on developing strategies to move forward and of mutual respect. Some of the ideas and techniques used as part of solution-based brief therapy are applied to the supervisor–supervisee relationship such as the preferred future, looking for exceptions (when the problem does not occur), the use of scales to measure progress, constructive feedback and follow-up tasks (George, 1999). Together these techniques encourage and support the supervisee and supervisor to work together to find solutions and take this forward to enhance and develop practice.

The integrative developmental model (Stoltenberg and McNeill, 2010) identifies four stages that supervisees and supervisors work through.

Level 1 Self-centred – the student is concerned about their lack of experience and knowledge.

Level 2 Client-centred – the student is at the stage of confidence versus lack of confidence.

Level 3 Process-centred – as professional confidence grows, the student depends less on the supervisor.

Level 4 Process-in-context-centred – the student is demonstrating the skills that they have developed.

This model acknowledges that the student's learning journey is a developmental one and the student will demonstrate skills, competencies and behaviours that reflect each level. However, Salvador (2016) observes that this model has been criticised as vague and simplistic; each student will have their own pace and way of growing and learning in different areas, so overgeneralising can be unhelpful and affect a student's confidence. Arguably, a good supervisor will use a model that is tailored to the individual student and avoid a one-size-fits-all approach of practice which can be mechanistic and oppressive (Thompson, 2016). Furthermore, there is not one model that will fit every practice placement. However, models of supervision are generally believed to provide a framework for support for both the supervisee and supervisor to work together to reflect on practice, deal with concerns and change, develop or enhance practice and allow practising professionals to develop professional skills (Butterworth, Bishop and Carson, 1992).

Outcomes from supervision

Many students may have clearly defined expectations of what they imagine they will glean from the student–supervisor relationship, specifically in terms of the support and guidance they will receive throughout the placement experience. A study by Malin (2000) concluded that nurses' clinical supervision has two major themes: giving advice and support and improving accountability. However, due to the general day-to-day pressures of work, some expectations may be unrealistic. Alongside their usual work responsibilities, placement supervisors will balance the time they spend supporting the student and the requirements of their own job role. As a result, the amount of autonomy which students are allowed will depend on a number of factors: the type of placement, the perceived risk to service users, the perceived risk to the credibility of the organisation, the observed professionalism of the student and an understanding of the student's competence at the time (Social Work England, 2021). At the outset of the placement, agreement should be sought around the type of tasks which students will be involved in and what the placement setting expects as a result of students undertaking these tasks, clarifying the student roles and responsibilities during the placement. The supervisor may view the performance of the student on their ability to effectively manage their allocated workload while maintaining an appropriate level of professional performance. The supervisor may also perceive their role as being one that not only motivates students but encourages them to acquire knowledge beyond what they need to pass assessments and placement (Elen et al., 2007).

It is important for students and placement agencies to fully understand each of their role and remit during the practice placement experience and to appreciate the position of the student as a practitioner in training. The nature of the placement setting can present challenges for both the student and the placement agency regarding the experiences which the student is able to obtain. Students studying at Level 4 (first year of university) should expect to have a different emphasis on their placement experiences than those in their last year, studying at Level 6, with more autonomy and self-direction anticipated with Level 6 study. Furthermore, the expectations of the placement agency should be comparable with the standard of competence, skills and knowledge expected at each stage of the university programme. A comprehensive understanding of the anticipated learning outcomes for the practice-based module will help nurture realistic expectations of the student and the placement setting and find common ground in identifying suitable tasks and responsibilities while still offering a meaningful practice experience for the student. Clear outcomes for both supervision and placement should be established at the start.

Understanding the learning outcome for the placement module is vitally important, as it will directly link to the module assessment. This may mean that you have to demonstrate the learning outcome in your practice throughout your time on placement.

Phoebe, Counselling and Psychotherapy

Conclusion

This chapter has examined a range of different perspectives in relation to supervision in placement. Undertaking practice placements can provide students with a vast array of opportunities for professional development and provide experiences which enable students to make the links between theory and practice. However, it is clear that time spent developing the relationship between the students and the supervisor can be pivotal to realising the learning taking place and supporting the student through this journey. Challenging and difficult situations can invariably present themselves to students at any point in placement, but being clear on their role, remit and expectations with a supervisor from the start can help them navigate this.

Placement offers opportunity to grow and reflect, and the supervision process presents a formal place for this to be explored in detail, using a variety of models. However, there is no doubt that wider forces also play a sometimes unseen but important role in the relationship such as the demands of the agency, professional practice placement requirements or individual differences such as age, class or gender. What is clear is that the supervision relationship can be one that supports students to develop as a practitioner, consolidate learning and link theory to practice. Placements can be the source of tremendous confidence building for students, and they also have the responsibility to ensure that they make the most of supervision to both build on their strengths and identify areas for development.

References

Andrews, L (2020) *The Vital Role Clinical Supervision Plays in the FNP Programme*. Available at: https://fnp.nhs.uk/blogs/the-vital-role-clinical-supervision-plays-in-the-fnp-programme/ (accessed 24 November 2021).

Attard, A, Di Lorio, E, Geven, K and Santa, R (2010) *Student-Centered Learning – Toolkit for Students, Staff and Higher Education Institutions*. Brussels: European Students Union.

Bold, C (2011) *Supporting Learning and Teaching*. London: Routledge.

Butterworth, C, Bishop, V and Carson, J (1992) First Steps Towards Evaluating Clinical Supervision in Nursing and Health Visiting: Theory, Policy and Practice Developments. *Journal of Clinical Nursing*, 5:127–32.

Cheng, M, Adekola, O, Albia, J and Cai, S (2021) Employability in Higher Education: A Review of Key Stakeholders' Perspectives. *Higher Education Evaluation and Development*. https://doi.org/10.1108/HEED-03-2021-0025.

Driscoll, J (2006) *Practicing Clinical Supervision: A Reflective Approach*. London: Harcourt.

Elen, J, Clarebout, G, Leonard, R and Lowyck, J (2007) Student-Centered and Teacher-Centered Learning Environments: What Students Think. *Teaching in Higher Education*, 12(1): 105–17.

George, E (1999) *Problem to Solution*. London: BT Press.

Giddens, A (2017) *Sociology*. 8th ed. Cambridge: Polity Press.

Hawkins, P and Shohet, R (2012) *Supervision in the Helping Professions (Supervision in Context)*. Maidenhead: Open University Press.

Hood, R (2018) *Complexity in Social Work*. London: Sage.

Inskipp, F and Proctor, B (1993) *The Art, Craft & Tasks of Counselling Supervision Part 1: Making the Most of Supervision*. Twickenham: Cascade Publications.

Kadushin, A (1985) *Supervision in Social Work*. New York: University Press.

Kolb, D A (1984) *Experimental Learning: Experience as the Source of Learning and Development*. Englewood Cliffs: Prentice Hall.

Light, C, Cox, R and Calkins, S (2011) *Learning and Teaching in Higher Education: The Reflective Professional*. London:Sage.

Malin, N A (2000) Evaluating Clinical Supervision in Community Homes and Teams Serving Adults with Learning Disabilities. *Journal of Advanced Nursing*, 31(3):548–57.

Marshall S J (2018) Internal and External Stakeholders in Higher Education, in *Shaping the University of the Future*. Singapore: Springer. https://doi.org/10.1007/978-981-10-7620-6_4.

Narey, M (2014) *Making the Education of Social Workers Consistently Effective: Report of Sir Martin Narey's Independent Review of the Education of Children's Social Workers*. Available at: https://dera.ioe.ac.uk/19338/1/Social_worker_education_report.pdf (accessed 18 November 2021).

Nursing & Midwifery Council (2018) *Realising Professionalism: Standards for Education & Training. Part 2: Standards for Supervision & Assessment*. Available at: www.nmc.org.uk/globalassets/sitedocuments/standards-of-proficiency/standards-for-student-supervision-and-assessment/student-supervision-assessment.pdf (accessed 23 November 2021).

Parker-Rees, R, Leeson, C, Savage, J and Willian, J (2010) *Early Childhood Studies*. Exeter: Learning Matters Ltd.

Price, A (2004) Encouraging Reflective and Critical Thinking in Practice. *Nursing Standard*, 18.

Ratner, H, George, E and Iveson, C (2012) *Solution Focused Brief Therapy: 100 Key Points & Techniques*. Hove: Routledge.

Robb, M (2007) *Youth in Context: Frameworks, Settings and Encounters*. London: Sage.

Rose, C (2011). *Self Awareness and Personal Development*. Macmillan International Higher Education.

Rothwell, C, Kehoe, A, Farook, S F and Illing, J (2021) Enablers and Barriers to Effective Clinical Supervision in the Workplace: A Rapid Evidence Review. *BMJ Open*, 11(9):e052929. https://doi.org/10.1136/bmjopen-2021-052929.

Salvador, J T (2016) Integrated Development Model (IMD): A Systematic Review and Reflection. *European Scientific Journal, ESJ*, 12(19):244. https://doi.org/10.19044/esj.2016.v12n19p244.

Schon, D (1983) *Teaching in the Lifelong Learning Sector*. Maidenhead: Open University Press/McGraw-Hill Education.

Skills for Care (2013) Code of Conduct for Healthcare Support Workers and Adult Social Care Workers in England.

Skills for Care (2020) *Effective Supervision: A Practical Guide for Adult Social Care Managers and Supervisors*. Available at: www.skillsforcare.org.uk/Documents/Learning-and-development/Effective-supervision/Effective-supervison-in-adult-social-care-Summary.pdf (accessed 23 November 2021).

Snowdon, D A, Sargent, M, Williams, C M, Maloney, S, Caspers, K and Taylor, N F (2020) Effective Clinical Supervision of Allied Health Professionals: A Mixed Methods Study. *BMC Health Services Research*, 20:2. https://doi.org/10.1186/s12913-019-4873-8.

Social Work England (2021) *Guidance on Practice Placements*. Available at: www.socialworkengland.org.uk/standards/practice-placements-guidance/#supervision (accessed 23 November 2021).

Stoltenber, C D and McNeill, B w (2010) *IDM Supervision: An Integrative Developmental Model for Supervising Counselors and Therapists*. 3rd ed. New York: Routledge.

Thompson, N (2016) *Anti-discriminatory Practice*. 6th ed. Basingstoke: Palgrave MacMillan.

Turner, D (2021) *Intersections of Privilege and Otherness in Counselling & Psychotherapy*. Oxon: Routledge.

Westergaard, J (2017) *An Introduction to Helping Skills*. London: Sage.

Wonnacott, J (2012) *Mastering Social Work Supervision*. London: Jessica Kinsley Publishers.

8 Technology and digital literacy

Valerie Fletcher, Tom Matthews and John Hills

Introduction

This chapter will explore diverse issues relating to the impact technology has on professional practitioners and organisations and understanding this in relation to the settings in which students are placed as part of their courses. Different elements and models of digital literacy skills will be explored in detail in relation to how these relate to student placements, including critical thinking, planning and evaluation. Bronfenbrenner's (1974) model considers how the family and social environment affects child development, and has been expanded into a wide range of topics to gain an understanding of the relationship between an individual, their environment and variables. This model uses categorised systems, namely the microsystem (the immediate environment, such as peer, school, work and family); the mesosystem (the interaction between these systems); the exosystem (extended family, friends, neighbours, community); the macrosystem (wider society, political ideas and culture within these systems), and the chronosystem (changes occurring over life generally). This chapter uses this model as a framework to explore digital literacy on placement. However, other models are applied, and ideas and concepts will be linked to wider political, economic, social and legal issues, such as data protection. While many students go on placement as part of their courses, there may be differences in the levels of experience and skills in relation to life in general, theory relating to practice, digital literacy capabilities and work environments. These elements are discussed and theorised while suggesting ideas for students to develop these skills further.

The chapter will cover:

- The individual student
- Ethical/legal responsibilities
- Interacting with technology

- Employability
- The exosystem: technology in placement
- Agile working
- The macro/chronosystem

The individual student

There can be a fine line between the use of information technology (IT) by individual students for social purposes and for studies. While a student is an individual, they also exist as part of a social system, which Bronfenbrenner (1974) called the microsystem. Examples include the individuals a student lives and spends time with, and the places they study and work. Many of these interactions can be seen; however, in addition, Vélez-Agosto et al. (2017) discuss how human development also takes place within cultural systems, which are the reality of the person but perhaps harder to see. These may be shaped by local and distant communities and social institutions, constantly changing within that context through political policies, laws and regulations. The student interacts within different contexts with their own cultural values and practices, making each experience unique to that individual and, in turn, the individual has an impact upon the different environments they engage with.

Ethical/legal responsibilities

The use of IT on placement presents many questions for a student. The student has additional ethical responsibilities while using IT, particularly in health and social care positions, such as keeping case notes up to date in a social work team, keeping client notes in counselling or accurate patient notes in a hospital. Privacy, confidentiality and data protection factors all come into play (British Psychological Society, 2020); for instance, who has access to the meetings' links, could the interaction be recorded and who is in the room with the participant or professional? Accessibility of this mode of communication for both students and the colleagues they work with is also an area of dilemma. An example may be in relation to a student having the space and privacy to talk via an online format, having available access to digital technology and the space to concentrate and engage away from the demands of day-to-day life. In the field of counselling and psychotherapy, the British Association of Counselling and Psychotherapy (BACP, 2019) stresses, '*absolute security in the digital world does not exist*' (p 6), so decisions need to be considered carefully. BACP (2019) state this involves ensuring reasonable steps are taken to ensure security for the client, for example, providing adequate password protection and using encryption methods, avoiding chances of a person being overheard by someone who the client has not given consent for, using private Wi-Fi channels and ensuring computer history cannot be searched and/or deleted. Other professions also have individual guidance set out by their respective professional bodies.

Pelden and Banham (2020) discuss the lack of uniformity between professional standards of accreditation bodies and the emerging demands and expectations of the community and practices being served. An example being healthcare appointments being moved online in the light of Covid-19, and professional bodies lagging behind the real situation. The student could find themselves with an ethical dilemma regarding conflict between the organisation's rules/ethics, their own ethics and the ethics of their regulatory body. In situations of ethical dilemmas, the student is advised to make effective use of supervision (Reid and Westergaard, 2013). Students can therefore talk this through with their allocated supervisors and are encouraged to plan to ensure privacy is enabled.

Selected policies and safeguarding documents relevant to this point are at the end of the chapter.

Working with risk

The important notion of risk while working online needs to be addressed. In many ways, assessing risk online should be undertaken in a similar way to the face-to-face equivalent. There is, however, increased importance for discussions between students, tutors and supervisors to prepare for this, as working remotely may make accessing colleague support in these moments more difficult than being placed within an office or clinic environment. Discussions need to take place regarding any concerns about working remotely, with students prepared by having, for instance, an available list of who to contact (supervisor, safeguarding lead etc) if risk is identified and ways that different situations may be handled. Specific questions may be what to do if someone ceases a call following a disclosure of risk, or how we share support information with people as we cannot directly hand them the information (British Psychological Society, 2020). Assessing risk may feel more difficult when working either on the telephone or video platforms, as it is harder to observe certain aspects of the interaction (Social Care Institute for Excellence [SCIE], 2020). It may be that to prepare for this, students ask to be made aware of specific questions, relevant to their role on placement, to ask regarding risk, to ensure important information is gathered (SCIE, 2020). This may focus upon ensuring that as much information as needed is gathered, with clear descriptions, and that these are appropriately documented. This will be supported through students feeling familiar with expectations and guidelines set by the placement organisation, as well as being aware of relevant policies, laws and procedures.

It may sound obvious (and not very exciting) but making sure you know what the rules and policies are around digital technology, note keeping etc is really important. It is the best way to do things right, and it's much better to know this before than to find out afterwards (trust me).

Sam, Counselling and Psychotherapy

I've used video and phone counselling. Video has technological issues with signal. I wish I had had previous explanations of what would happen if Zoom or connection failed, I planned to do this in the Zoom session, yet the connection was so bad I couldn't even get to that point. Because the internet had gone down, I couldn't even find the number to call to tell anyone.

Sandra, Counselling and Psychotherapy

Technology and accessibility

A question emerges as to what extent digital technology may promote inclusivity; for example, some people who identify as having disability may find technology facilitates access, while for others the same technology may be a barrier. Inclusivity must be a priority, with an appreciation of multi-layered intersectionality being required (Rivera, 2016). Crenshaw (1989) coined the term 'intersectionality' to describe how issues such as race, religion, gender and sexuality can overlap and intersect, affecting how an individual experiences the world, and this experience can be different depending on the issue, not just the sum of the parts. In practice this means that technology should not be seen as a 'one-size-fits-all' addition to our working lives. Like all interactions, some will require adaptations in order for technology to be able to improve and add to opportunities available through placement. Thus, a consideration is how accessible technology is to everyone involved, with the idea of a 'reasonable adjustment' not solely relating to placements and learning within a physical setting. This may be informed through the education setting and placement setting working together to ensure a fair and successful placement opportunity is arranged. Armstrong and Armstrong (2005) and Graham and Slee (2008) refer to inclusion models being more like regulatory models than facilitators for equality, and accessibility can also relate to a student on placement who may feel isolated or held back professionally depending on their individual need.

Using technology on placement may allow students to feel connected, involved and capable of influencing their placement experience or it could place them in a more vulnerable position of surveillance (Foucault, 1977), where they have their lives recorded in '*big data*' (Bloomberg, 2020, p 191) and they must fit into the structure. Technology can broaden the horizon of the student and open accessibility, connectivity and doors; this will depend on variables such as the student, the placement and the client group they are working with, as well as the type of organisation.

Work out how your placement uses tech and ask questions about how this is going, and the things that have been easy and hard so you can think about what may be useful. Don't be worried in speaking up if you have an idea, it may not work out, but it is helpful just to share the idea as no one else may have thought of it.

Becky, Counselling and Psychotherapy

The microsystem: where placement and students meet

When starting a placement, a student joins a team, which will have its own way of doing things and a team culture which the student joins with. An interaction begins between the individual, team and environment in which they are located (Bronfenbrenner, 1977). A student's microsystem is proposed by Bronfenbrenner (1979) to be the immediate environment in which a person is located and so can engage in face-to-face interaction. The relationship between the person and this setting is proposed to be part of a two-way interaction (Bronfenbrenner and Ceci, 1994), meaning students impact upon placement, but crucially play an active role in this interaction (Bronfenbrenner and Evans, 2000) and they can also have impact upon placement during their time there.

The concept of digital technology is ever changing and has arguably changed the way students learn, including on placements (Hamilton, Rosenberg and Akcaoglu, 2016; Siemens, 2005); the use of such may, however, be complex and placements will vary in the level to which technology has been incorporated. Placements are often located within complex organisational and social structures, understood as macro and exosystems (Bronfenbrenner, 1974). By understanding the team and organisation's relationship with technology, opportunities within a placement to develop and utilise this may emerge. While the 'digitisation' of organisations such as the NHS is nationally supported (Honeymoon, Dunn and McKenna, 2016), the adoption of technology in clinical settings is often driven locally, with there being a limited experience of 'push' from overseeing organisations such as the government or NHS overall (Llewellyn et al., 2015). This 'bottom-up approach', while disadvantageous in terms of equity of access for people using services across the country, suggests potential for influence at a microsystem level between students and their placement setting. This positions students as a force of change, with fresh ideas and resources which may prove valuable to placement settings (Orrell, 2018; Zegwaard and Rowe, 2019). As a student you may adapt to the circumstances presented (within ethical and legal constraints) and perhaps utilise the technology platform to advantage.

The SAMR model (Puentedura, 2014) explores the complex and different ways technology can be utilised, mapping technology application onto four levels: Substitution, Augmentation, Modification and Redefinition.

It is proposed that when technology is utilised to modify or redefine practice (the upper two stages of the model), this underpins a transformation of practice (Puentedura, 2014). More commonly, however, placements may have a relationship with technology in which it has been developed in place of pre-existing processes, such as a move from a paper-based to computerised note keeping system. An example of SAMR in practice could be two colleagues working together to create and deliver a training session. A substation would be to copy the notes from their planning conversation onto some slides. In this regard, a redefinition would be to use online videos and resources to communicate the concepts they wish to present. Further redefinition would be to utilise technology during

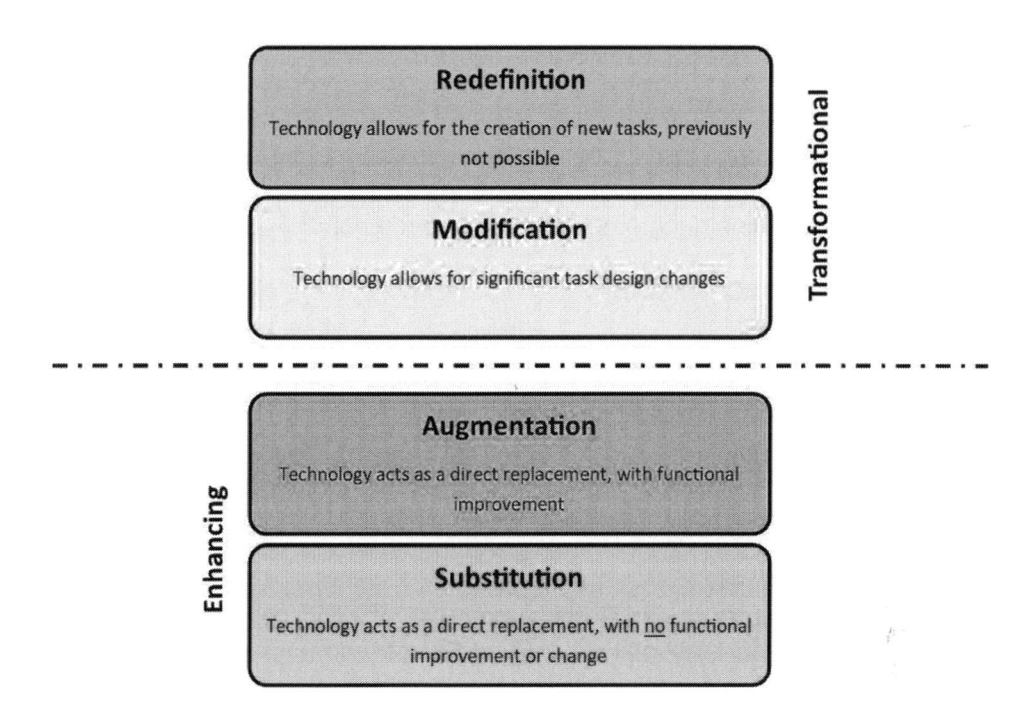

```
                    ┌─────────────────────────────────┐
                    │          Redefinition           │
                    │ Technology allows for the       │  T
                    │ creation of new tasks,          │  r
                    │ previously not possible         │  a
                    └─────────────────────────────────┘  n
                    ┌─────────────────────────────────┐  s
                    │          Modification           │  f
                    │ Technology allows for           │  o
                    │ significant task design changes │  r
                    └─────────────────────────────────┘  m
```

Figure 8.1 SAMR model (based upon Puentedura, 2014)

the training so that participants can contribute to the training through using their own digital devices. Such opportunities are ever expanding and could include a sketchpad/ comment board on the screen or a quiz in which each participant provides their answers. While the SAMR (Puentedura, 2014) model may oversimplify the complex and multi-layered ways in which technology may be utilised and interacted with (Hamilton, Rosenberg and Akcaoglu, 2016), it may provide structure when considering to what level a placement is utilising technology, applying the model in a context-specific way, as well as understanding barriers in considering technology use.

Within a placement, colleagues may vary in their confidence and familiarity with technology, a term that could be understood as digital literacy (Gilster, 1997), which is defined as the ability to process and deal with information from varying digital sources and being literate in the digital age. This is less about understanding specific tasks and more about having a confidence with digital ideas generally (Bawden, 2008). Many students entering placement could view themselves as a 'digital native': a person who has been immersed in technology their whole life (Bennett, Maton and Kervin, 2008). This term is used to distinguish from those who have had to immigrate into a digital world (Prensky, 2001). A student familiar with technology, perhaps 'digitally native' (Prensky, 2009), may experience navigating digital systems within placement as 'clunky' or difficult based upon their intuitive approach to technology.

However, while some students may feel native in a digital world, not all students entering placement feel this way. They may be located within a team and contribute to the team as a person with abilities in technology (Bennett, Maton and Kervin, 2008; Cornelli, Kominek and Ljungqvist, 2012). Thus, understanding the team's relationship with digital technology, and the role it plays in their functioning, may be an important part of understanding the placement environment more fully and getting maximum benefit from this. Later in this chapter, consideration is given to the impact of Covid-19 on the integration of technology within placements, but it is apparent based upon the idea of a 'digital native' that certain students and placements may have incorporated these practices with lesser and greater ease.

Agile working

Agile working refers to the practice of having flexibility in the places in which a person can work, including away from an office environment. This often includes no longer having a consistent desk or physical location within an office, commonly known as 'hot desking'. Both arrangements have become increasingly common in recent years, including in services such as the NHS and social care (Millward, Haslam and Postmes, 2007; Jeyasingham, 2019) and so are likely to be a feature of many placements.

The practice of agile working can have positives, largely enabled by digital technology, such offering greater flexibility and convenience around how we do our work (Jeyasingham, 2019). Concerns around the practices of agile working have been raised, however, such as a possible experience of 'dislocation' and a reduction in feelings of belonging and identification within a team (Albert, Ashforth and Dutton, 2000; Millward, Haslam and Postmes, 2007). To try to overcome this, greater importance may be placed on digital means of communication in relation to face-to-face contact to create a sense of cohesiveness between team members (Millward, Haslam and Postmes, 2007). Examples may include extra emails and video-based communications; however, the digital migrant placement student may experience this as even more challenging and even more remote. Thus, consideration of the means in which communication and connection can be forged may be central in setting up a placement, based upon open dialogue with supervisors and team members about how the team utilise technology as part of their agile working. This may also include consideration of areas in which you could support the student to develop this further, suggesting alternative ways of working or communicating using technology to find solutions and develop practice (Cornelli, Kominek and Ljungqvist, 2012).

The exosystem: the digital divide and the empowerment of service users

Placements are situated within the exosystem (Bronfenbrenner, 1989; O'Neill, 2015). The exosystem may be thought of as the community level of an organisation that students and clients operate within and are indirectly influenced by.

In health and social care placements, students may become acutely aware that work with clients does not happen within a vacuum, but is clearly influenced by wider social determinants including wealth inequality, job insecurity, disempowerment at work, poor housing, failing local services, exposure to crime, discrimination and social alienation. There is now a substantial body of evidence that outcomes across a range of measures including life expectancy, heart disease, obesity, smoking, depression and psychosis are highly associated with our position in social hierarchies (Wilkinson and Pickett, 2011), or what Marmot (2015) described as the '*social gradient*'.

Given therefore the measurable influences of the exosystem over outcomes, the influence of the digital environment, including digital poverty or the digital divide, also needs to be considered (Maceviciute and Wilson, 2018; Bach, Wolfson and Crowell, 2018; Acquavita et al., 2019). The digital divide is a consequence of variable access to the technology and resources of the digital age, meaning that different people have different degrees of access to and competency within the digital environment (Hilbert, 2011; Maceviciute and Wilson, 2018). The Covid-19 pandemic and the subsequent shift of many health services and wider psychosocial support towards virtual settings exacerbated the health disparities which may be attributed to digital inequality (Early and Hernandez, 2021; Clare, 2021). For instance, evidence emerged of an association between lower broadband access and reduced vaccination rates given the online nature of the appointment booking systems (Early and Hernandez, 2021).

Internet access is increasingly understood as a necessary factor in social and economic inclusion (Bach, Wolfson and Crowell, 2018). However, there are clear inequalities with respect to broadband access, with reduced connection and speeds available to single-parent families, low-income households, in rural areas and across age, racial and gender divides. Furthermore, lack of digital literacy is observed to limit social inclusion, for instance, in refugee populations (Maceviciute and Wilson, 2018). Those who fall on the wrong side of the digital divide may have fewer opportunities to seek work, or indeed to work from home, heightening social exclusion and alienation further.

When working with clients virtually on placement, the device they are using may be influenced by their socioeconomic status, with more disadvantaged groups in society, as reflected in income, education or ethnicity, more likely to be dependent on their smartphone (Bach, Wolfson and Crowell, 2018; Acquavita et al., 2019; Early and Hernandez, 2021). The additional challenges presented in establishing connection with service users in virtual space mean it may be harder again for patients and clients to read the subtleties of our non-verbal communications – for instance, body language or tone of voice – as projected through a mobile device rather than a full screen. Other social determinants may compound digital inequalities, such as cramped housing conditions meaning reduced access to privacy during phone or online consultations. There is an increased likelihood of 'meeting' the service user's family members; children may be present in the online consultation if the service user does not have access to adequate childcare facilities.

Practitioners too may experience the uptake of digital technology and remote working in the delivery of services as a double-edged sword, with impacts beyond their working life. Remote working may be experienced as an increase of managerial control into workers' private spaces, the so-called flexploitation phenomenon (Miele and Tirabenu, 2020). Furthermore, for students as well as colleagues and the client group they work with, the boundaries between home and work life may become increasingly blurred with work expanding into what might traditionally have been thought of as non-productive (free) time, and thus making it a struggle to switch off. There are indications that remote working can not only interfere with family life but moreover exacerbate more traditional gender inequalities with mothers struggling to balance work and family commitments, while fathers devoting more of their time to work. Furthermore, the colonisation of work into private spaces and free time has also been associated with the neglect of social lives and hobbies (Cannito and Scavarda, 2020). However, use of technology, especially the provision of telehealth and online services, can also be considered to mitigate against some of the physical barriers – such as distance or time – which may have traditionally limited access to services for people from less advantaged circumstances (Hanley and Wyatt, 2020). The traditional power differentials associated with healthcare between practitioner and service user may be re-shaped using technology. For example, there was evidence in a recent systematic review of higher education students' access to talking therapies online that clients felt the online medium gave them greater access to steer the conversation and to work at their own desired pace. In addition, it was observed that some students were storing written exchanges with their therapist online to revisit at a later juncture, which the authors credit with fostering the client's own sense of agency, in turn associated with better therapeutic outcomes (Hanley and Wyatt, 2020). More generally, the expansion of information technology may be seen to empower individuals from marginalised groups, not least through the sharing of information directly relating to their health, or participation in society, or indeed through greater connectivity – the capacity to discover and meet with potential collaborators at geographical distance (Bach, Wolfson and Crowell, 2018).

The macrosystem and the chronosystem: the big wide world and how it changes over time

Unlike the other levels, the macrosystem is made up of parts and influences which a student does not directly interact with. This level reflects the societal and cultural influences upon them, though the model suggests that these parts will set and influence the places in which a person does directly interact (Bronfenbrenner, 1977). An example would be the law which states a child is anyone under the age of 18 years, which in turn influences the age group of people which a student interacts with on a placement with children.

In 2020, the world experienced the Covid-19 pandemic, a global health crisis. Technology emerged, based on the developments of the previous decades, as a tool to maintain and protect core clinical and educational services (Ting et al., 2020). The importance of technology has been both to provide health, social care and educational services, and to communicate, such as the increased use of video-based communication platforms (Vargo et al., 2021). The use of technology as a means of fulfilling the placement requirement has become increasingly important particularly with the unprecedented Covid-19 virus, which dramatically shifted the placement landscape (Pelden and Banham, 2020). New systems and procedures were standardised to enable students to continue with their placements, and universities and governing bodies had to quickly adapt policies.

The long-term impact on the integration of technology into health and social care settings is yet to be seen. What appears clear, however, is that the experience of Covid has developed new patterns and processes in which technology is placed at the forefront of clinical services. In some settings, this will have been used to substitute face-to-face clinical services until a time when services can resume; in others, the patterns of embedding technology may have modified and redefined how support and services will be delivered in future (Puentedura, 2014).

In relation to the chronosystem, the part of Bronfenbrenner's (1992) model that incorporated the notion of time to acknowledge the change of environments, such as major events and transitions, Covid-19 symbolises such an event. As development is a forward-moving process, it will not be an event which will be removed from individual, cultural, societal and organisational memory. Organisational memory refers to the information from an organisation's history which is used to make decisions at the current time (Walsh and Ungson, 1991). Students entering placements in the years to come may be entering a new placement territory with Covid-19 as part of its sociological history and memory, the impact of which is yet to be known or navigated. In addition, not only are there changes in the placement environment, Davidson (2020) suggests that the legacy is also at the individual level with Covid's legacy leading to *'different students, different needs'* (p 92). It may be that these experiences lead to large and noticeable changes, or that the impact will be less obvious; however, Covid-19 is likely to leave a lasting trace in relation to the use of technology as part of placement (Daniel, 2020). Placements may, therefore, be a setting in which there is an energy and drive for incorporating technological ideas and advancements into clinical practice, or one in which there is a tiredness to the idea of depending upon technology within services. A starting point for placement students may, therefore, be to locate the placement context in their technological journey. For example, does the team communicate using video-based technology? Is there an option for virtual meetings and appointments for those you work with? Or is there an online shared platform where useful information and tools can be shared? Alternatively, does the team tend to function using more traditional communication methods, such as whiteboards, face-to-face meetings and a physical folder of resources?

Conclusion

This chapter has discussed some of the different elements and challenges that technology presents to the individual and their environment, including wider factors such as social determinants of health and the recent pandemic. The experience of the Covid-19 pandemic has seen the development of new patterns and processes in which technology is placed at the forefront of clinical services; however, the digitisation of our workplaces was increasing even before that. Students need to consider their own digitised identity in relation to their experience, knowledge and background. With universities continually introducing IT into the curriculum and deliberately incorporating this in the learning outcomes of a course, technology can present a significant challenge within the placement experience.

The incorporation of technology will continue to impact on students and their experience of placement, influencing experience and opportunities at multiple levels. Bronfenbrenner's (1974) theory provides a structure to conceptualise the impact of these systems on students' experiences. Not only shining a light on these influences, but also highlighting opportunities of influence for the student due to the interactions being theorised as being bidirectional (going in both directions: student to placement and placement to student). On commencing placement, a student brings with them a range of insights and experiences, including their experiences of digital technology and the digital world. It remains essential, however, to hold in mind the context in which technology is being used on every placement, and the social, economic and legal inequalities which can be illuminated by digital technology use. Through understanding the different types of influence and the ways technology may help or hinder a placement, a student is best able to take advantage of digital technology on each of their placements.

Safeguarding resources

Department for Education (2020) *Working Together to Safeguard Children*. Available at: www.gov.uk/government/publications/working-together-to-safeguard-children–2 (accessed 28 June 2021).

Department for Education (2021) *Safeguarding and Remote Education during Coronavirus (Covid-19)*. Available at: www.gov.uk/guidance/safeguarding-and-remote-education-during-coronavirus-covid-19 (accessed 28 June 2021).

Office of the Public Guardian (2020) *Safeguarding Policy: Protecting Vulnerable Adults*. Available at: www.gov.uk/government/publications/safeguarding-policy-protecting-vulnerable-adults (accessed 28 June 2021).

References

Acquavita, S P, Krummel, D A, Talks, A, Cobb, A and McClure, E (2019) Assessing the Digital Divide Among Low-Income Perinatal Women: Opportunities for Provision of Health Information and Counselling. *Telemedicine and e-Health*, 25(1):48–54.

Albert, S, Ashforth, B E and Dutton, J E (2000) Organizational Identity and Identification: Charting New Waters and Building New Bridges. *Academy of Management Review*, 25(1):13–17.

Armstrong, P and Armstrong, H (2005) Public and Private: Implications for Care Work. *The Sociological Review*, 53(2):167–87. DOI:10.1111/j.1467-954X.2005.00579.x.

Bach, A J, Wolfson, T and Crowell, J K (2018) Poverty, Literacy, and Social Transformation: An Interdisciplinary Exploration of the Digital Divide. *Journal of Media Literacy Education,* 10(1):22–41.

Bawden, D (2008) Origins and Concepts of Digital Literacy, in Lankshear, C and Knobel, M (ed) *Digital literacies: Concepts, Policies and Practices*, 17–32. Oxford: Peter Lang.

Bennett, S, Maton, K and Kervin, L (2008) 'The digital native' Debate: A Critical Review of the Evidence. *British Journal of Educational Technology*, 39(5):775–86.

Bloomberg, J (2020) *Organization Theory: Management and Leadership Analysis*. London: Sage.

British Association for Counselling & Psychotherapy (2019) *Good Practice in Action 047 Fact Sheet Working Online in the Counselling Professions*. Lutterworth: BACP.

British Psychological Society (2020) *Effective Therapy via Video: Top Tips*. Available at: www.bps.org.uk/sites/www.bps.org.uk/files/Policy/Policy%20-%20Files/Effective%20therapy%20via%20video%20-%20top%20tips.pdf (accessed 25 May 2021).

Bronfenbrenner, U (1974) Developmental Research, Public Policy, and the Ecology of Childhood. *Child Development*, 45(1):1–5.

Bronfenbrenner, U (1977) Toward an Experimental Ecology of Human Development. *American Psychologist*, 32(7):513–31.

Bronfenbrenner, U (1979) *The Ecology of Human Development: Experiments by Nature and Design*. Cambridge: Harvard University Press.

Bronfenbrenner, U (1989) Ecology of the Family as a Context for Human Development: Research Perspectives. *Developmental Psychology*, 22(6):723–42.

Bronfenbrenner, U (1992) Ecological Systems Theory, in Vasta, R (ed) *Six Theories of Child Development: Revised Formulations and Current Issues*, 187–249. London: Jessica Kingsley.

Bronfenbrenner, U and Ceci, S J (1994) Nature-Nurture Reconceptualized in Developmental Perspective: A Bioecological Model. *Psychological Review*, 101(4):568–86.

Bronfenbrenner, U and Evans, G W (2000) Developmental Science in the 21st Century: Emerging Questions, Theoretical Models, Research Designs and Empirical Findings. *Social Development*, 9(1):115–25.

Cannito, M and Scavarda, A (2020) Childcare and Remote Work during the Covid-19 Pandemic: Ideal Worker Model, Parenthood and Gender Inequalities in Italy. *Italian Sociological Review*, 10(3S):801–20.

Clare, C A (2021) Telehealth and the Digital Divide as a Social Determinant of Health during the Covid-19 Pandemic. *Network Modeling Analysis in Health Informatics and Bioinformatics*, 10(26):1–3.

Cornelli, F, Kominek, Z and Ljungqvist, A (2012) Monitoring Managers: Does it Matter? *The Journal of Finance*, 68(20):431–81.

Crenshaw, K (1989) Demarginalizing the Intersection of Race and Sex: A Black Feminist Critique of Antidiscrimination Doctrine, Feminist Theory and Antiracist Politics. *University of Chicago Legal Forum* (8):139–67. Available at: https://philpapers.org/archive/CREDTI.pdf?ncid=txtlnkusaolp00000603.

Daniel, J (2020) Education and the Covid-19 Pandemic. *Prospects*, 49(1):91–96.

Davidson, P M (2020) Nursing Homes & Covid-19: We can and Should do Better. *Journal of Clinical Nursing*, 29(Issue 15–16):2758–59.

Early, J and Hernandez, A (2021) Digital Disenfranchisement and Covid-19: Broadband Internet access as a Social Determinant of Health. *Health Promotion Practice*. Available at: https://journals.sagepub.com/doi/10.1177/15248399211014490 (accessed 25 May 2021).

Foucault, M (1977) *Discipline and Punishment*. London: Tavistock.

Graham, L J and Slee, R (2008) An Illusory Interiority: Interrogating the Discourse/s of Inclusion. *Educational Philosophy and Theory*, 40(2):277–93.

Gilster, P (1997) *Digital Literacy*. New York: Wiley Computer Publishing.

Hamilton, E R, Rosenberg, J M and Akcaoglu, M (2016) The Substitution Augmentation Modification Redefinition (SAMR) Model: A Critical Review and Suggestions for Its Use. *TechTrends*, 60(5):433–41.

Hanley, T and Wyatt, C (2020) A Systematic Review of Higher Education Students' Experiences of Engaging with Online Therapy. *Counselling and Psychotherapy Research*, 21. DOI:10.1002/capr.12371.

Honeyman, M, Dunn, P and McKenna, H (2016) *A Digital NHS: An Introduction to the Digital Agenda and Plans for Implementation*. Available from: www.kingsfund.org.uk/publications/digital-nhs (accessed 21 May 2021).

Hilbert, M (2011) The End Justifies the Definition: The Manifold Outlooks on the Digital Divide and their Practical Usefulness for Policy-Making. *Telecommunications Policy*, 35(8):715–36.

Jeyasingham, D (2019) Seeking Solitude and Distance from Others: Children's Social Workers' Agile Working Practices and Experiences Beyond the Office. *The British Journal of Social Work*, 49(3):559–76.

Llewellyn, S, Procter, R, Harvey, G, Maniatopoulos, G and Boyd, A (2015) *Facilitating Technology Adoption in the NHS: Negotiating the Organisational and Policy Context – a Qualitative Study*. Available at: https://europepmc.org/article/NBK/nbk259891 (accessed 20 May 2021).

Lynch, M (2018) Digital Learning Theories and Models that All Educators Should Know. *The Edvocate*. Available at: www.theedadvocate.org/digital-learning-theories-and-models-that-all-educators-should-know/ (accessed 21 May 2021).

Maceviciute, E and Wilson, T D (2018) Digital Means for Reducing Digital Inequality: Literature Review. *Informing Science: The International Journal of an Emerging Transdiscipline*, (21):269–87.

Marmot, M (2015) *The Health Gap*. London: Bloomsbury Publishing.

Miele, F and Tirabeni, L (2020) Digital Technologies and Power Dynamics in the Organization: A Conceptual Review of Remote Working and Wearable Technologies at Work. *Sociology Compass*, 14(6):e12795.

Millward, L J, Haslam, S A and Postmes, T (2007) Putting Employees in their Place: The Impact of Hot Desking on Organizational and Team Identification. *Organization Science*, 18(4):547–59.

O'Neill, B (2015). Ecological Perspectives and Children's Use of the Internet: Exploring Micro to Macro Level Analysis. *Estonian Journal of Education*, 3(2):32–53.

Orrell, J (2018) Work Integrated Learning: Why Is It Increasing and Who Benefits? *The Conversation*. Available at: https://theconversation.com/work-integrated-learning-why-is-it-increasing-and-who_benefits-93642 (accessed 15 May 2021).

Pelden, S and Banham, V (2020) Counselling Placements Caught up in the Mismatch of Standards and Realities: Lessons from Covid-19. *Journal of University Teaching and Learning Practice*, 17(4):1–8.

Prensky, M (2001) Digital Natives, Digital Immigrants Part 2: Do they Really Think Differently? *On the Horizon*, 9(6):1–6.

Prensky, M (2009) H. Sapiens Digital: From Digital Immigrants and Digital Natives to Digital Wisdom. *Innovate: Journal of Online Education*, 5(3). Available at: https://nsuworks.nova.edu/innovatee/vol5/iss3/1/ (accessed 5 May 2021).

Puentedura, R (2014) *Building Transformation: An Introduction to the SAMR Model*. Available at: www.hippasus.com/rrpweblog/archives/2014/08/22/BuildingTransformation_AnIntroductionToSAMR.pdf (accessed 14 May 2021).

Reid, H and Westergaard, J (2013) *Effective Supervision for Counsellors*. London: Sage.

Rivera, D P (2016) Revealing Hidden Intersections of Gender Identity, Sexual Orientation, Race, and Ethnicity, in Case, K A (ed) *Intersectional Pedagogy*, 172–93. London: Routledge.

Siemens, G (2005) Connectivism: A Learning Theory for the Digital Age. *International Journal of Instructional Technology & Distance Learning*, 2:3–10.

Social Care Institute for Excellence (2020) *Risk Identification and Virtual Interventions for Social Workers*. Available from: www.scie.org.uk/care-providers/coronavirus-covid-19/social-workers/risk-identification (accessed 27 September 2021).

Ting, D S W, Carin, L, Dzau, V and Wong, T Y (2020) Digital Technology and Covid-19. *Nature Medicine*, 26:459–61. DOI:10.1038/s41591-020-0824-5.

Vargo, D, Zhu, L, Benwell, B and Yan, Z (2021) Digital Technology use during Covid-19 Pandemic: A Rapid Review. *Human Behavior and Emerging Technologies*, 3(1):13–24.

Vélez-Agosto, N M, Soto-Crespo, J G, Vizcarrondo-Oppenheimer, M, Vega-Molina, S and García Coll, C (2017) Bronfenbrenner's Bioecological Theory Revision: Moving Culture from the Macro into the Micro. *Perspectives on Psychological Science*, 12(5):900–10.

Walsh, J P and Ungson, G R (1991) Organizational Memory. *Academy of Management Review*, 16(1):57–91.

Wilkinson, R G and Pickett, K (2011) *The Spirit Level: Why Greater Equality Makes Societies Stronger*. New York: Bloomsbury.

Zegwaard, K E and Rowe, A D (2019) Research-Informed Curriculum and Advancing Innovative Practices in Work-Integrated Learning. *International Journal of Work-Integrated Learning*, 20(4):323–34.

9 Resource of self

Diana Conroy

Introduction

Students undertaking placement must realise and work with their own sense of 'self'. To do this well, it is necessary to recognise and reflect upon one's own internal aspects of self – such as personality and relatability, as well as external aspects that affect the self, such as organisational structure and influence of others. A wider understanding of one's own self, application of appropriate theory and a skill set of reflective practice can enable students to be resilient practitioners on placement.

This chapter will debate the theoretical context of self, and how this is applied, along with a discussion on psychotherapeutic concepts such as transference, countertransference, complexes and reactions. The chapter deals with the concepts of empathy and compassion, examining how self-compassion can be utilised to enable personal and professional growth while on placement.

This chapter discusses:

- What is the 'self'?
- The Johari window: a model for improving self-awareness
- Ideas that assist in comprehending the more hidden dynamics that occur in relationships
- Empathy including tolerating vulnerability and self-disclosure
- Reflective practice: recognising 'the shadow'
- Self-compassion for students on placement

What is the self?

The one thing students always bring to placement is themselves or, rather, their self – all the things that make them unique: a personal history, collection of experiences, characteristics and personality. There is no escaping the fact that on placement students have to 'show up' as they are. It does not matter that the bus was late, it was raining, the baby would not settle last night or an argument was had with a partner; the professional mask goes on and the day must start. However, a student on placement cannot pretend that they are an automaton, programmed just to carry out professional tasks; they are people as well as professionals, dealing with clients, colleagues and supervisors who are also people with lives and issues, and this is the beauty and complexity of human relationships (Jacobs, 2006). In this sense, there is a personal self and a professional self, and the balance between them is a delicate one, requiring students to learn to manage the demands and tensions this creates (Thompson, 2016).

Internal factors

As Trevithick (2017) notes, terms such as 'use of self' in practice are problematic, with multiple definitions and understandings, and there is limited clarification as to what self is and how these fit in with concepts such as the 'professional self'. Nevertheless, while there is no general agreement on what 'self' is between professionals and perspectives, what is accepted is that all practitioners have their own beliefs, attitudes, values and biases, both conscious and unconscious, that impact practice to a lesser or greater degree (Gladwell, 2005). Yalom (2003) observes that professionals are also 'fellow travellers' in practice, meaning that client, colleague and manager in placement are all in the mire of life experiencing the joys, pleasures, doubts, disillusionment and hopelessness that come with everyday life. Furthermore, there are often large portions of our personal and professional journey where ambiguity is rife, we are unsure and lost, plagued by fear, doubt, disappointment or grief, wandering around trying to make sense of life while having to try to support or enable others to do the same (Hollis, 1996). In placement, the student practitioner often uses their knowledge, skills and attributes to help clients, and therefore needs to know the effect and impact they have on others both positively and negatively (Thompson, 2015). Kaushik (2017) suggests that 'conscious use of self' is the mechanism by which practitioners intentionally draw on their professional training along with these other factors to facilitate change. Although it is often impossible to gauge the impact on others, a practitioner's self-awareness is the cornerstone to conscious practice.

External factors

However, it is not just internal factors such as our knowledge or skills that influence use of self, there are external ones too. Organisations, for example, play an integral role as well.

Most businesses know that the key to their success is their employees and maximising their potential, and this can be challenged when organisational change occurs. Change and stress are directly related, and this impacts on the use of self; it can cause anxiety and influence a student's ability to learn and engage meaningfully, particularly if they have difficulties embracing what Dwerk (2010) describes as a *'growth mindset'*, which is an openness and willingness to learn, an attitude that views problems as challenges and being able to rise to the occasion and bounce back after setbacks (be resilient). Resilience is discussed in detail in Chapter 3 of this book.

In the caring professions, change is a regular occurrence: government funded and statutory services are squeezed tighter, and the voluntary sector lives under the constant uncertainty of applying for contracts and bidding for funding. This leads to *'role overload (too many tasks given), role ambiguity (not knowing what the job expectations are) and role boundary (caught between conflicting job demands)'* (Tan, 2005, p 25; see also Chapter 13). These issues can be a challenge for students on placement, as they are also subject to the changes that occur and may find their mentors leave or the service they are in loses its funding. These external factors can lead to a student feeling lost or unsupported which can impact on their own abilities, knowledge and resources. For example, the ability to be compassionate and empathic can be hindered by stress caused by organisational mismanagement or change.

Personality

Research indicates that worker personality plays a key role in client interventions (Edwards and Bess, 1998; Kaushik, 2017). There are multiple definitions about what personality is, but Allport's description is that *'a dynamic organisation, inside the person ... systems that create the person's characteristic patterns of behaviour, thoughts, and feelings'* (1961, p 11). This suggests that there are both changeable and more fixed elements that make up our identity. To explore personalities and traits, there are a plethora of tests that could be undertaken, including Cattell's 16 PF (personality factors), the 'big 5' personality traits questionnaire and Myers-Briggs among them. However, the old ideas that personality was fixed have been replaced by new research that suggests that *'important and meaningful'* (p 286) changes can occur (Boyce, Wood and Powdthavee, 2013). Students therefore should not be disheartened if they discover something about themselves (that they did not know) that they find unpalatable or surprising when completing tests (this is demonstrated by Johari's window later in the chapter). Gladwell (2005), for example, a black academic, discovered his own unconscious bias towards black men when completing Harvard's Implicit Attribution Test. As Jacob (2006) suggests, the key is to be able to confront disturbing or uncomfortable elements of ourselves to change them.

Previously in life my natural curiosity had been labelled as 'nosiness' an attribute that during placement I was determined to not display, as the negative connotations of the word had begun to resonate, and I too began to see only the negative in my curiosity. Allowing the label to take over I refused to ask the burning questions and found it extremely difficult to explore my caseloads fully, until one day I finally confided in my practice educator. She taught me to embrace my curiosity and gave it the new label and positive attribute of 'professional curiosity' and in doing so allowed me to embrace the strengths of my personality.

Kate, Social Work

Attachment

As well as personality characteristics, understanding how we bond and relate to other individuals is a critical aspect of placement in helping professions. Bowlby's (1977) theory of attachment described the link between social environment and psychological development, and further research has widely acknowledged that an individual's pattern of bonding with others has a strong bearing on how they form and maintain relationships, including in the workplace. All helping professions require students on placement to build relationships with others and this can be assisted by understanding attachment patterns. There are four main types of attachment (secure, insecure anxious, insecure avoidant, disorganised), and it is useful for students to have an idea of their own attachment type. A student who understands their own attachment pattern will be able to counteract and compensate if they discover their pattern is not secure. Students may be unduly wary of others or find that they become entangled or enmeshed with clients; these are indicators of insecure patterns (Bowlby, 1977). Clients will also have their own attachment patterns just as workers do. For example, adults with a more anxious attachment have a stronger need to be liked and recognised for their contributions, compared to those with a secure attachment. Moreover, individuals with a secure attachment pattern tend to have a greater ability to reflect and mentalise, making them more resilient (Howe, 2011). While some relationships in the workplace are of short duration, there are others that last years and are often characterised by closeness and intimacy. A carer, for example, may be the only person who has ever assisted a client with personal care, or a therapist the only one who has knowledge of a client's history of sexual abuse. By the very nature of the contact with a service, a client may be at their most vulnerable, and it is in distress that attachment styles are at their most prominent (Howe et al., 1999).

Self-awareness

Freud compared the mind to an iceberg, suggesting that only a small portion of its tip is visible and in our conscious control, with the major portion of the mind unconscious and therefore difficult to access (Green, 2019). However, while this may be the case, there are models and approaches, some of which are already widely used in the helping professions,

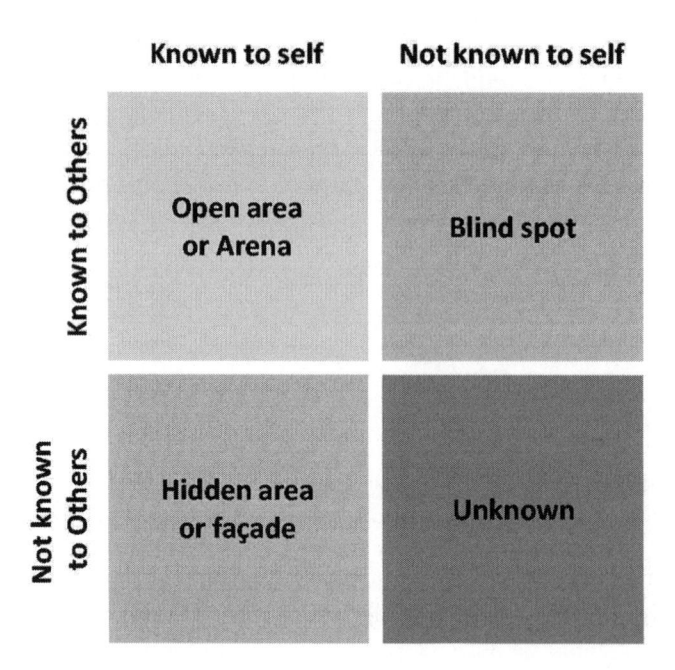

Figure 9.1 The Johari window model

such as reflective practice, that can enable students to become more insightful of self (Bolton, 2012). Nevertheless, as Rose (2011) observes, self-awareness is only possible if there is a willingness to grow and develop, and this can be a difficult and ongoing task that is often avoided because of the discomfort it can cause.

When considering how to understand the self, one of the most useful techniques that enable this is the Johari window. This model was developed by Luft and Ingham in 1955 ('Johari' being a combination of their first names) to examine the four aspects of self in relation to our knowledge and to others.

The model has four quadrants that explain how to understand different aspects of the self:

1. Known to others, known to self is the 'open' part of our personality – what we and others know and clearly see about us.

2. Known to others, not known to self are our 'blind spots' – things that are clear to those around us, but we miss.

3. Not known to others, known to self – the hidden areas that we do not choose to share with others, but we know about.

4. Not known to others, not known to self – this could be considered what is unconscious in us, to both ourselves and others.

Understanding the windowpanes can help explain why it is sometimes troublesome unpicking our own and others' reactions and behaviours, some of which may be far beyond awareness. When thinking about why students think or do what they do, Rose (2011) suggests honestly examining through asking difficult questions of the self and others to identify their blind spots or where unconscious material is playing out.

While training in some helping professions covers issues such as the unconscious and defence mechanisms, these concepts are not universally included, and some of the common processes such as transference and projection are not always understood. Kivlighan (1995, cited in Parth et al., 2017) suggests that transference and its partner, countertransference, are key to understanding self, and having some knowledge of psychotherapeutic concepts that manifest in relationships can be useful to understand relationship dynamics. Students on placement who have a basic understanding of these, which are discussed shortly, will be able to build better relationships with colleagues, supervisors and clients, as they will be able to recognise and understand some of the more subtle dynamics in play and the complexities of different relationships. Freud began discussing the idea of transference in 1888 and it evolved into the concept widely understood today as:

> *a tendency in which representational aspects of important and formative relationships (such as with parents and siblings) can be both consciously experienced and/or unconsciously ascribed to other relationships.*
>
> (p 391)

What this means for students on placement is that they might unconsciously expect a client or colleague to behave or treat them in a certain way. For example, a student who had a critical teacher at school might then expect their mentor to be the same because they are in a position of authority, or the mentor might remind the student of that person from the past. Countertransference then is that person responding in the same fashion (ie the mentor becoming that critical teacher). While this might sound bizarre to comprehend, there is considerable evidence that this occurs on a frequent basis (Levy and Scala, 2012).

Complexes

Jung (1965) spoke about complexes as both conscious and unconscious forces in our lives. Complexes are often hard to identify as they are not tangible, but can be described as group of perceptions, memories, emotions and the like that relate to an idea or theme (hence terms such as 'father or daddy complex' that have entered our mainstream language). Imagine you have a ball that is made of Velcro for each of the major issues that you come across in your life. As you go along, every time something happens around that issue, it sticks to that ball. As you can imagine, the more things that happen, and the more negative things that occur, the bigger the ball gets with all the sticky issues. An example of a 'father complex' in a student's personal life playing out at placement was that of student social worker John. John had a difficult relationship with his dominant father, meaning that he had ideas about how men behave, and he showed responses to males that he was unaware of. This came to light when he was unable to challenge male colleagues or clients and instead of speaking up he shrank away and agreed with everything that clients asked of him, even when this was not realistic. John's supervisor pointed this out to him, and they were able to explore why this was occurring by looking at John's relationships with other men. Thus, one of the sticky issues on John's 'father' ball (complex) got smaller. But as Hollis (1996) wryly observes, it is not that we have complexes, the issue is if our complexes have us. This suggests whether we are aware or not, the phenomena are playing out. Complexes that are attached to themes such as money, power or mother undoubtedly influence how we view a situation and relate to others and underestimating or lacking understanding of the power of these can be disastrous for us personally and professionally. Complexes are always present, whether we are aware of them or not. To manage these unseen forces, questioning, reflection and self-honesty are needed to identify and try to counteract them.

Another key indicator that a complex is at work is the depth of the response to an issue. Often if this is disproportionate and heated, a complex is at work, and it is the task to look beyond the obvious and question what lies beneath (Hollis, 1996). For example, Susan, a nursing student who had a placement in acute care, found it difficult to deal with and care for patients who had injured themselves when drunk, treating them coldly and complaining heatedly to colleagues about them wasting time and resources. When she examined the issue with her mentor, who had heard her repeatedly speaking about these clients negatively, it turned out that Susan's own father was an alcoholic, and the unresolved anger that she had towards him was unconsciously being played out with these patients. Thus, students must come to understand what their 'buttons' and 'triggers' are to ensure that these do not cloud judgement or compromise professionalism.

However, undertaking this is no easy task. Jung (1965) spoke of building an understanding of what he named as 'the shadow', which is literally our 'dark side', whereas the poet Robert Frost aptly puts, the '*Something we were withholding made us weak / Until we found it was ourselves*'. In placement, students are often under scrutiny and pressure to perform, to demonstrate the best and most competent parts of themselves, so our weaknesses and inferiority may be even much less on show than usual. Nevertheless, recognising and taking responsibility for shortcomings means being honest and setting aside regular development time to do this. Encountering the shadow can sometimes be in the form of acknowledging unsettling responses that arise, acting against one's own moral code or saying one thing and doing another. It is easier to blame others, bury the issue and continue with business as usual, but as Hollis (2007) rightly puts, '*What is not made conscious will continue to haunt our lives – and the world … our quality of life if a direct function of the level of awareness we bring to our daily choices*' (p 5). Blindly carrying can make one pay a high price both personally and professionally.

> *I would advise students to use their supervision sessions as your safe space. Placement can at times become overwhelming and the shift from studying to being out in practice can be a difficult adjustment. However, allowing the professional who is undertaking your supervision to understand your troubles or concerns often results in the problem being broken down and therefore becomes less daunting. Bear in mind that unless a person knows you well, they may not be able to see the internal struggles that you have.*
>
> Cheryl, Social Work

However, it is argued that everyone has 'Shadow' tendencies (Hollis, 2010). For example, students going in placement may well get their first taste of professional power; clients may seek advice, look for reassurance or confide their deepest fears, and this will often activate issues around the power complex. It is not unusual to see some professionals in highly responsible positions have what is known as a 'God complex' where they feel their opinion/approach is wholly right and are unwilling to listen or consider anything outside this, or others who take pleasure using their position and misuse authority. However, part of using self as a resource is to acknowledge these are at play, watch out for when they emerge and take steps to counteract them. Reflective practice, eliciting feedback and supervision can all be helpful mechanisms to explore the issue.

One example of reflective practice could be keeping a reflective journal or diary, where we think about our day, what went well and what we would like to do differently next time, which is a practical way to try to harness insights. In his influential work on shame, Bradshaw (1991) suggests that we keep an *'Over-reaction Diary'* to identify when we were upset, what was happening, who was around and what was said. Getting to truly know ourselves takes time, dedication, courage and commitment, and it relies on the individual doing the work and others being honest when giving feedback but can be helped through *'tuning in'* (p 4) to the effect that we have on others (Thompson, 2015). On placement, this could be achieved by exploring reactions with peers or colleagues as a sounding board or using time in supervision for this purpose. Supervision is covered in detail in Chapter 7 of this book. However, this can also be achieved by using some of the tools of the helping profession trades such as empathy, to which this chapter now turns.

Empathy

Moss (2017) notes that empathy is the ability to see a situation from another's perspective and differs from sympathy in that it is interactive and relational; it is trying to get to know the real experience and feelings that accompany this so it can be understood where the other person is coming from and, as the popular metaphor goes, 'walk in their shoes'. As well as encouraging another to share their inner worlds, this also means practitioners opening up to receive this, which can feel emotionally risky. Questions like 'what if I cannot handle what my client wants to share' or 'what if I say the wrong thing' can torment, and this anxiety can prevent real and meaningful connections with others (Yalom, 2003). Accepting humanity and fallibility is key, as is committing to doing better when one falls short. As poet Maya Angelou said: 'Do your best until you know better. When you know better, do better'.

Recognising the humanity in another is critical to empathy as it breaks down the barriers between professionals and clients. It acknowledges that we are not perfect and can fail and potentially stops power from being misused. Furthermore, research has consistently shown that the more empathic our care, the better and more effective it is (Howe, 2013). However, this also means sometimes dropping the professional mask and revealing more humanness to clients, but this can be difficult as it calls for bravery. Brown (2012) states that to receive honest communication from the people around us requires courage and determination, as emotional exposure can often mean feeling vulnerable. Yet, it is the willingness to engage in this that cuts through fear and disconnection, and being game to enter this fragile emotional state is one of the factors of deep connections. Indeed, being able to tolerate feeling vulnerable is a requirement for any relationship to be truly meaningful. In placement, students can be anxious, and it is sometimes very difficult to admit to a client that they do not know something, or to ask a mentor to help, particularly when the inner, critical voice might be saying 'you should know'. Brown also argues that letting go of our tendencies to try to be perfect or right is key to humanising the workplace to ensure that '*creativity, innovation and learning*' are ignited (2012, p 184). However, Brown also acknowledges that this process of entering the arena of vulnerability is far from easy. However, it is being able to tolerate vulnerability that is one of the keys to both knowing self and using self.

In placement, students often have a considerable amount of life experience to draw upon, and this also brings up the question of how much of this to share in practice. Potentially, this can be a resource of self that is drawn upon but should be approached with some caution. Yalom (2003) gives arguments both for and against disclosing personal information to clients, noting that this issue is highly controversial and caution is advised, and that what must be borne in mind is that while clients are protected by confidentiality, practitioners are not. For example, when working in a team, it is likely that the client may work with more than one practitioner at a time or over the course of the team's intervention. On placement, students are often working with multiple professionals with a client. For example, a student may feel happy about talking about their family life, but a client may then expect this level of openness from other team members too, who may not be equally happy to share personal information. Therefore, advice is not to reveal any information that students would not be happy to have out in the public arena, and they should clearly record what they have told a client and why. There may be times, and clients, where the relationship calls for appropriate self-disclosure. For students considering this, it is best to reflect what the purpose of revealing personal information would be, reflecting with a colleague or supervisor to gauge if it is wise to proceed and what the possible ramifications might be.

My advice using the skills of empathy and self-disclosure as a combination can enrich the therapeutic relationship. Disclosure does not have to come from the status of sharing past experiences or feelings. Some disclosure can be in the present. You may find it appropriate to disclose how a client material has made you feel. For example, a client who has achieved a particular goal, you may feel excited, overjoyed or pleased for them. However, caution should be taken when sharing of your feelings about the client's material, does it add value to the client material and/or the therapeutic relationship?

Ria, Counselling

Reflection

Reflection is a critical skill that can be used to understand how to use the self in placement; we must become skilled and familiar with questioning our own responses, assumptions and prejudices. Chapter 2 of this book is dedicated to understanding reflection in detail, but to put it briefly, Schon (1983) identified two types of reflection that are useful to be familiar with: reflection-in-action and reflection-on-action. Reflection-in-action is described as the way people think and theorise about practice while they are doing it and is often unintentional; whereas reflection-on-action is an intentional, conscious process and involves purposely exploring experience and thinking about what has happened after it has taken place. This is to retrospectively interpret and analyse the situation so new knowledge and perspectives can emerge from it. Undertaking reflection and thinking about the different aspects of the Johari window can help deepen the process, and this can be further enhanced when doing this with another individual in placement such as a colleague or mentor, who can help recognise the blind spots that may be holding development back (Luft and Ingram, 1955).

Bolton (2010) advises the reflective writing to be considered as a '*through-the-mirror*' (p 69) approach that requires both reflection and reflexivity, where one is invited to enter a world where nothing is certain, the certain cannot be taken for granted and perspectives changed through understanding the stories that we tell ourselves and others. In contrast to reflection, reflexivity goes further and is thinking about the bigger picture and wider implications for what a student has learnt by reflecting, such as the impact of their attitudes or values. For example, a student might identify from reflecting that they treated a client of a certain gender differently. Reflexivity would be to explore what the meaning of this is, how this affects the student's attitudes of gender overall and what this might mean for other judgements or assumptions the student might be making for that gender or other characteristics a client has. However, this also requires openness to learning and invitation to participate; no one can do this on our behalf – we must be the ones that take the ultimate personal responsibility of entering this place where our attitudes, beliefs and assumptions are (more often than not) shattered. It can be easier for students on placement to avoid deeper reflection and shy away from the surprise, anxiety and uncertainty that this creates, thereby reflecting on a more superficial level by examining actions without looking at the driving factors behind them. Questions about 'why I did what I did' need to be asked in supervision, with an exploration as to the different explanations behind it. Sometimes behaviour can be a mixture of different drives, motivations and beliefs, and no matter how well intentioned can be influenced by other factors such as unconscious bias (Fiarman, 2016), so using supervision and trusted peers or colleagues as a sounding board is essential.

After undertaking deep reflection, it is helpful to also hear what the inner critic has to say, but caution is needed; it may not always be constructive and could be something negative along the lines of 'you're rubbish at this', 'you're pathetic', 'nothing you do goes right' or scripts of a similar nature. Peterson (2018) advises to ignore the internal critic, who is often unfavourably comparing oneself to others, and *compare yourself to who you were yesterday, not who someone else is today*' (p 85). Self-compassion is key to avoid the traps of negative self-talk and harsh critics, and personal condemnation should be avoided (Gilbert, 2013). Being kind and compassionate to the self is sometimes harder to achieve than self-criticism and acknowledging deficits due to the sensitivity of our minds to focus more intensely on the unpleasant aspects of life. The term 'negativity bias' is well known in psychology to describe the tendency to focus on the negative, and the inner critic reflects this, with negative information having a stronger impact than the positive (Ito et al., 1998). This means students are susceptible to catastrophising problems or overlooking strengths in favour of everything that went wrong in a day. Using reflective practice means evaluating what went well, as well as what could be different, and good supervision support will enable this. However, Gilbert's (2010) work on the negativity bias has identified that this is not anyone's fault; our minds are made tricky by biology and evolution that has programmed us to scan the environment and look for threats. Furthermore, the threat system and subsequent feelings of anxiety are easily activated by modern life. This is further compounded by brains that have evolved to be able to plan and think, meaning that they can also ruminate and go over unpleasant scenarios that have occurred or are anticipated again and again, causing a great deal of emotional distress. Gilbert (2010) found that negativity, anxiety and threat are calmed when soothing systems are activated. Turning on the soothing system by practising self-compassion in the form of mindfulness, breathing or other exercises can help. Students can often neglect self-care in a rush to complete work, impress superiors or even manage everyday life. Student mental health is a serious issue, with research indicating that one-third of students sought professional help for psychological issues, and 21% have a current mental health diagnosis (Hubble and Bolton, 2019). These issues follow students also to placement. Effective resource of self also means making sure that students replenish these, bringing to mind the old adage, 'you can't pour from an empty cup'.

Self-compassion

A lot has been written about the need for compassion in the caring professions, and the seeming lack of it in the NHS has been highlighted several times, most notably in the

Francis Report in 2013 following the inquiry into failings in care in Mid-Staffordshire NHS Foundation Trust. The report summarised there was a deficit in compassion in a range of professionals, leading to the NHS bringing in the aspirational 6 Cs value model (care, compassion, competence, communication, courage and commitment). However, counter to this is the knowledge that compassion fatigue and burnout is common in the caring professions, and students are likely to witness under-resourced, overworked and stressed professionals when in placement. Placement is real life and students are often exposed to the same emotionally intense situations as their qualified colleagues (Butler, Carello and Maguin, 2017).

So, while compassion is rightly emphasised as the crucial quality it is, we need to ensure that self-compassion is not overlooked either. Neff (2015) states that self-compassion entails three main components, each of which has a positive and negative pole that represents compassionate versus uncompassionate behaviour, these are: self-kindness versus self-judgment; a sense of common humanity versus isolation; and mindfulness versus over-identification. It is a combination of these various components that represents a self-compassionate frame of mind. In placement, it is important to be aware of our frailty, and other peoples', to build our self-compassion. It's more likely to be developed if there is a conscious attempt to do so, knowing it is part of our ongoing journey, a large part of which will be lost in what Hollis (1996) describes as the dismal places of doubt, fear, loneliness and despair. As well as compassion for clients, self-compassion practices can therefore be an important element of a successful placement, including watching out for the judgemental inner critic, reaching out to others and being aware of what we are thinking or feeling instead of being caught up in either or both.

Conclusion

Using the self as a resource means a commitment to continuously question our opinions, attitudes and motives (Thompson, 2016), for how we can truly 'use' ourselves if we are not aware of who we are and what we stand for? Fundamentally, what separates a good practitioner from a poor one is dedication and commitment to growing knowledge of the self, with all the surprises and shocks this can present. It is the willingness to step out of comfort zones and confront what might be some of the unpalatable aspects of personality. Self- knowledge around different aspects of the personality, how one relates to others are critical and these can be built up in a range of ways. This chapter has touched upon some of the key models and theories such as the Johari window, transference, countertransference, complexes and the shadow, as well as useful approaches to foster empathy, compassion and self-compassion. Attachment theory has been considered as key knowledge to build that influences relationships with others. However, it is important not to get lost in the quagmire of what is 'wrong' but focus on what is also 'right and good' – the positive aspects of personality, skills, assets and strengths – of which students in placement have many.

References

Allport, G (1961) *Pattern and Growth in Personality*. New York: Holt, Rinehart & Winston.

Bolton, G (2010) *Reflective Practice: Writing & Professional Development*. 3rd ed. London: Sage.

Bowlby, J (1977) The Making and Breaking of Affectional Bonds: Aetiology and Psychopathology in the Light of Attachment Theory. *British Journal of Psychiatry*, 130:201–10.

Boyce, C J, Wood, A M and Powdthavee, N (2013) Is Personality Fixed? Personality Changes as Much as 'Variable' Economic Factors and More Strongly Predicts Changes to Life Satisfaction. *Social Indicators Research*, 111:287–305. DOI:10.1007/s11205-012-0006-z.

Bradshaw, J (1991) Taming the Shameful Inner Voice, in Zweig, C and Adams, J (eds) *Meeting the Shadow: The Hidden Power of the Dark Side of Human Nature*. New York: Tarcher/Putnam.

Brown, B (2012) *Daring Greatly: How the Courage to Be Vulnerable Transforms the Way We Live, Love, Parent, and Lead*. London: Penguin Books.

Butler, L D, Carello, J and Maguin, E (2017) Trauma, Stress, and Self-Care in Clinical Training: Predictors of Burnout, Decline in Health Status, Secondary Traumatic Stress Symptoms, and Compassion Satisfaction. *Psychological Trauma: Theory, Research, Practice, and Policy*, 9(4):416–24.

Dwerk, C (2010) Mindsets & Equitable Education. *Principal Leadership*, 10(5):26–29.

Edwards, J K and Bess, J M (1998) Developing Effectiveness in the Therapeutic Use of Self. *Clinical Social Work Journal*, 26(Issue 1):89–105; 26:89. DOI:10.1023/A:1022801713242.

Gilbert, P (2010). *Compassion Focused Therapy: The CBT Distinctive Features Series*. London: Routledge.

Gilbert, P (2013) *The Compassionate Mind*. London: Robinson

Gladwell, M (2005) *Blink: The Power of Thinking without Thinking*. London: Penguin Group.

Green, C D (2019) Where did Freud's Iceberg Metaphor of Mind Come From? *History of Psychology*, 22(4):369–72.

Hollis, J (1996) *Swamplands of the Soul: New Life in Dismal Places*. Toronto: Inner City Books.

Hollis, J (2007) *Why Good People Do Bad Things: Understanding Our Darker Selves*. London: Penguin Books.

Hollis, J (2010) *What Matters Most: Living a More Considered Life*. London: Penguin Books Let.

Howe, D (2011) *Attachment across the Life Course: A Brief Introduction*. Basingstoke: Palgrave Macmillan.

Howe, D (2013) *Empathy: What It Is and Why It Matters*. Hampshire: Palgrave Macmillan.

Howe, D, Brandon, M, Hinings, D and Schofield, G (1999) *Attachment Theory, Child Maltreatment and Family Support: A Practice & Assessment Model*. Basingstoke: Palgrave Macmillan.

Ito, T A, Larsen, J T, Smith, N K and Cacioppo, J T (1998). Negative Information Weighs More Heavily on the Brain: The Negativity Bias in Evaluative Categorizations. *Journal of Personality and Social Psychology*, 75(4):887–900. http://dx.doi.org/10.1037/0022-3514.75.4.887.

Jacobs, M (2006) *The Presenting Past: The Core of Psychodynamic Counselling and Therapy*. 3rd ed. Maidenhead: Open University Press.

Jung, C G (1965) *Memories, Dreams and Reflections*. Oxford: Benediction Classics.

Kaushik, A (2017) Use of Self in Social Work: Rhetoric or Reality. *Journal of Social work Values and Ethics*, 14(1):1–21.

Levy, K N and Scala, J (2012) Transference, Transference Interpretations, and Transference-Focused Psychotherapies. *Psychotherapy*, 49(3):391–403. DOI:10.1037/a0029371.

Luft, J and Ingham, H (1955) The Johari Window, a Graphic Model of Interpersonal Awareness, in *Proceedings of the Western Training Laboratory in Group Development*. Los Angeles: UCLA.

Moss, B (2017) *Communication Skills in Health & Social Care*. London: Sage.

Neff, K (2015) The Self-Compassion Scale is a Valid and Theoretically Coherent Measure of Self-Compassion. *Mindfulness*. DOI:10.1007/s12671-015-0479-3.

Parth, K, Datz, F, Seidman, C and Löffler-Stastka, H (2017). Transference and Countertransference: A Review, 2(81):167–211. DOI:10.1521/bumc.2017.81.2.167.

Peterson, J (2018) *12 Rules for Life: An Antidote to Chaos*. London: Penguin Books.

Rose, C (2011). *Self Awareness and Personal Development*. Macmillan International Higher Education.

Schon, D A (1983) *The Reflective Practitioner: How Professionals Think in Action*. Reprint, Aldershot: Ashgate Publishing Limited, 1995.

Tan, N T (2005) Maximising Human Resource Potential in the Midst of Organisational Change. *Singapore Management Review*, 27(2):25–35.

Thompson, N (2015) *People Skills*. 4th en. London: Palgrave MacMillan.

Thompson, N (2016) *Anti-discriminatory Practice*. 6th ed. Basingstoke: Palgrave MacMillan.

Trevithick, P (2017) The 'Self' and 'Use of Self' in Social Work: A Contribution to the Development of a Coherent Theoretical Framework. *The British Journal of Social Work*, 48(Issue 7):1836–54. https://doi.org/10.1093/bjsw/bcx133.

Whitfield, C (1993) *Boundaries and Relationships: Knowing, Protecting and Enjoying the Self*. Deerfield Beach: Health Communications Inc.

Yalom, I (2003) *The Gift of Therapy*. London: Harper Collins.

Part 3
Advanced skills

10 Interprofessional learning and working

Jodie Low, Liz Eate and Fran Fuller

Introduction

Interprofessional working is not a new phenomenon, having been discussed in many spheres of health and social care and beyond. Much of the research and writings associated with interprofessional working within health and social care have occurred following a significant event such as a child being seriously injured or a vulnerable adult dying (Baldwin, 1996); however, it does not rest solely in the field of safeguarding. This has been very much evident in the interprofessional working around the Covid-19 pandemic bringing people together to problem solve across sectors such as business, politics, media, community services and emergency services through local resilience forums (Cabinet Office, 2013). Students will experience interprofessional working during their placement experience, which may be in different guises such as community safety responses, children's safeguarding, integrated care planning or in meeting special educational needs. This chapter will provide some guidance and insight to maximise learning.

This chapter will cover:

- Definitions of interprofessional learning and working
- Agenda clashes
- Knowledge of other professions
- Communication and information sharing
- Teamwork
- Professionals' meetings
- Technology
- Resourcing

Definitions of interprofessional learning and working

To consider this chapter in the context of professional learning it is important to clarify and identify a working interpretation of the words 'interprofessional' and 'interprofessional learning' as opposed to 'interprofessional working'. The concept of interprofessional working emerged in the 1960s when mainly health professionals attending one-off workshops to focus on collaborative working (Barr and Coyle, 2013). This was surprising given that findings from child death enquiries as far back as 1945 had suggested there was a lack of information sharing between professionals, which led to poor communication and a distinct lack of interprofessional working (Reder, Duncan and Gray, 1993).

The definitions of interprofessional learning, interprofessional working or interprofessional education all share common themes and largely go uncontested (Hammick, Olckers and Campion-Smith, 2009). The Centre for the Advancement of Interprofessional Education (CAIPE) defines *interprofessional education* as:

> *When two or more professions learn with, from and about each other to improve collaboration and the quality of care.*
>
> (CAIPE, 2002)

Freeth et al. (2005) then argues that *interprofessional learning* can be determined as:

> *Learning arising from interaction between members (or students) of two or more professions. This maybe a product of interprofessional education or happen spontaneously in the workplace or in education settings.*
>
> (p xv)

For students, learning interprofessionally could be through lectures, training or in the workplace; such discussions help foster understanding and better communication, which in turn can challenge assumptions about professional roles and responsibilities. However, interprofessional learning could also present barriers for students as some may come with preconceived ideas as to what their and others' professional identities are. The challenges experienced in interprofessional learning are mirrored in interprofessional working. For example, although in practice students are delivering towards the same goal around a common theme, the different professional approaches may present barriers which can prevent students of different professions from working or learning together (Peckover and Golding, 2017). This is inevitable to some degree as health and social care organisations have their own histories, cultures and agendas which often present barriers to working together.

Despite legislation and policy citing the importance of interprofessional working, it seems that there are still failings by agencies in effectively working together (National Society for Prevention of Cruelty to Children, 2021). In university too, interprofessional learning and working for students is seen as crucial to improve care outcomes (Atwal, 2018; Kozlowska et al., 2018; Taylor, Whiting and Sharland, 2008); however, while this learning experience is now built into the curriculum of many health and social care courses, it can be limited and teaching and learning usually happen independently on each course.

Overcoming barriers to effective interprofessional working

For students, it can be difficult to analyse, engage and develop interprofessional experiences without prior experience. Students should familiarise themselves with the possible range of barriers and ways of overcoming these through professional working. Students should develop their awareness of potential agenda clashes, the knowledge or lack of knowledge between professions, challenges with communication and resourcing. The following sections of this chapter discuss these areas and propose methods to overcome them. Students can reflect on how the following propositions could be applied to interprofessional learning environments as interprofessional learning seeks to break down barriers and offers solutions to enable students to learn and work together (Peckover and Golding, 2017). This chapter now explores and responds to several key issues with interprofessional learning.

Agenda clashes

In spite of social policies such as Working Together to Safeguard Children (Department for Education, 2018) advocating interprofessional working and learning, different services are still given separate responsibilities and regulations instead of being treated as one body of interprofessional workers. For example, there is growing research that demands young people with offending behaviour are recognised as 'children first'; Case and Browning (2021) set out four tenets underpinning this principle which focuses on the developmental needs of children and 'pro-social identity' using a rights- and strengths-based approach. This is highlighted in the growing concern for child criminal exploitation protected through modern slavery legislation (Sturrock and Holmes, 2015), yet our policing practices fail to recognise this with an outdated focus on female victims and sexual exploitation (Bryant and Bryant, 2019). This can potentially create disciplinary 'silos' where workers are encouraged to remain apart from other professions.

Hood, Gillespie and Davies (2016) suggest that agencies also tend to work in isolation because of ingrained cultural systems, which form barriers to interprofessional working with agencies wanting to protect their own professional identities, knowledge base and standing (Hudson, 2007), making workers feel 'territorial' about their profession. This territorialism should, however, not be reduced to an understanding of professional arrogance; professions have evolved over generations, developing their best practice on historical lessons learnt, research and evaluation. The dilution of professionalism through interprofessional working must be considered, planned and celebratory of professional practice. For example, a community nurse being managed by a youth worker could accelerate the community approach of the nurse and develop strategic understanding of health, but it could also negate the complexity of medical needs. The power of the youth work line manager could shift the focus of the nurse to social and community engagement. Both aspects of the professional discussion are valid but the interplay of power dynamics between supervisor and supervisee could pollute the professional response (Carpenter et al., 2015). For students, this could be a very real experience whereby their mentor or line manager may not be of the same profession or qualification. The power dynamic is further complicated depending on how the organisation values and supports the student. Therefore, the student should maximise the professional supervision process and university teaching to unpick their experiences (see Chapter 7).

The different models of working, such as the medical versus social model (Pilgrim and Rogers, 2005), can also create issues for health and social care professionals working together. For example, in mental health, the medical model tends to focus on the individual who faces the issue, such as in depression where medication is prescribed to balance certain chemicals in the brain; diagnosis of the individual's problem and treatment are applied to resolve the issue. A social model approach focuses on the relationships, interactions and dynamics with others, in communities or society. The intervention to resolve the issue from this perspective looks outside of the individual, to factors such as poverty, housing, social support and access to healthcare, benefits, etc. Aside from the potential clash in models between individual professionals, the medical model remains a source of power in the sector with the social model being seen as potentially lesser (Pilgrim and Rogers, 2005). For students, familiarisation of these models enables them to focus critical thinking and discussion of their experiences within these models, enabling accuracy in understanding interprofessional interactions. Therefore, setting a sound platform for effective and progressive collaborative working. Considering the conflicting models of working, it could be considered that there is potential for a clash of professional values, but this can be overcome by keeping the service user at the centre of all decisions by students and professionals, maintaining a desire to improve health and wellbeing for all, a common goal.

Agenda clashes can be resolved by using conflict resolution approaches such as those described by Danesh and Danesh (2002) and Smith, Vernard Harrington and Neck (2000); techniques such as finding a shared meaning through common goals, connection, education and celebrating the strengths of diverse approaches enable respect and support an interprofessional team to find connection and collaboration. Students are often in a unique position of objectivity to facilitate discussions; professionals will expect critical analysis of experiences and therefore a student can offer this to develop working practice.

Without knowing what has worked well before or knowing the history of other professions you can fall into a trap of professional disrespect. You might be trying to work things out using the stereotype of that professional. Step back and do your research on what works and why.

Genna, Masters, Youth Work, Health and Community Development

Knowledge of other professionals

Peckover and Golding (2017) consider that although professionals know their own roles and responsibilities, there may be a lack of understanding of other professions. This ignorance of other professions can impede the ability to find a common goal and collaborative communication, not only between the different agencies but also with service users (Hood, Gillespie and Davies, 2016). Granheim, Shaw and Mansah (2018) suggest that to reduce communication barriers and increase knowledge of other professions, it is important that students are exposed to other professions in their learning environment to learn from each other. Students should take every opportunity to ask questions, engage in discussions and absorb the insights of others. Having knowledge of other roles and responsibilities will create the glue needed to work together as an interprofessional team (Kozlowska et al., 2018). Roles should be clear; students should take action to facilitate and contribute to making the integrated working group successful for the service user. Again, roles should be discussed and agreed along with expectations at the start of the working together.

Communication and information sharing

Information sharing is commonly cited as a barrier to interprofessional working. Legislation underpins the General Data Protection Regulation (The Data Protection Act, 2018), and individual's 'right to privacy' under Article 8 of The Human Rights Act (1998) must be respected. However, in relation to Human Rights, this is what is called a 'qualified right' meaning that it can be interfered with if it is in the interests of the wider community or to protect other people's rights. A confident and informative conversation with other services or professionals to enable them to understand the nuances of sharing information can overcome this; knowledge of organisational policy is crucial. Thompson (2020) outlines the importance of naming the resistance to sharing information and advises to use open dialogue and debate to achieve a robust joint conclusion. Knowing organisational policy, it is argued, informs a common language and understanding of the principles woven into practice. For example, the NHS generally uses The Caldicott Principles (UK Caldicott Guardian Council, 2020), meaning that consent should be sought and information sharing should be justified, necessary and proportionate. Students can enhance good interprofessional working by acknowledging principles and finding shared ground.

It is essential to set up confidentiality and data sharing agreement with service users at the start of contact or intervention and to see the service user as the key driver in their care and support. A student can strive for this by actively practising personalisation (Social Care Institute for Excellence [SCIE], 2011) and participation (Badham and Wade, 2005), and therefore can promote the consent for information sharing with the service user in control. Personalisation places the service user at the centre of their own care planning; this approach sees the service user as expert in their experience and lead in decision-making and control in their care. Participation takes this a step further by aiming to embed a service user's voice in shaping services and affecting social change on issues they are concerned with.

When working interprofessionally, students may start to appreciate the challenges of language, different acronyms, terms and concepts that become part of the discussions and often part of the norm in professional discussions. For many years practitioners have grappled with the notion of establishing a common language and continue discussing how it can be made not only common, but understandable for professionals and for the users of the services alike. Examples of this can be identified in initiatives such as the Common Assessment Framework (Holmes et al., 2012), Thresholds and Pathways (Department for Education, 2018) and Personalisation (SCIE, 2011). Students have a fundamental role in asking for terms to be explained and keeping professionals aware of ensuring that discussions are accessible.

Thompson (2020) proposes a detailed breakdown of communication and language emphasising the need for clarity, avoiding jargon, 'think[ing] first' to avoid misunderstandings, avoid wasted time, promoting self-confidence, and earning the respect and confidence of others.

If you don't know the acronyms, the language that people talk, it leaves you unable to contribute to discussions and to make things happen for the people you work with. Always ask people to explain or have a trusted person you can go to and ask after a meeting.
Genna, Masters, Youth Work, Health and Community Development

This approach emphasises assertiveness, with a focus on promoting relationships, authenticity and respect through Jakubowski's (1977, cited in Thompson, 2020, p 38) *'Tenets for Assertive Philosophy'*. It is argued that by becoming assertive we promote authenticity and integrity when underpinned by *'unconditional positive regard'* (Rogers, 1961, cited in Thompson, 2020, p 39). Observation of others and self-reflection should be practised by students to develop these skills, acknowledging positionality – how differences in power and status affect access and experiences in society.

When working with a focus on individuals, sharing information for most cases will be based on consent; the person whose information is being shared must have provided informed consent to share this, unless there is serious risk to self, others or criminal activity (UK Caldicott Guardian Council, 2020; Department for Education, 2018); but depending on the circumstances, consent may have to be breached. Alongside this, there are a raft of principles and ethics to be considered (sometimes distinct to a profession) as to what is appropriate to share or not; these should initially inform a student's decision-making to share but also should be discussed with the individual. For example, if a young person is associating with others who may have a high profile of offending behaviours, there is an ethical dilemma as to whether to share this information with the police. Teams such as police have a sophisticated intelligence system which is a tool for meeting public interest (Ministry of Defence, 2009) that can often contradict the right to privacy. Consequently, information sharing around individuals can be debatable, controversial and contested depending on the professionals in the group. For the individuals themselves, they may give consent to share with some and not others; there may be some elements of the information they are comfortable sharing and others not. Therefore, they must be partners in the process and be informed on implications of sharing to give informed consent (Selinger, 2009).

Good information sharing will stay focused on respect, the relationship and trust of the service user. Kina (2018) argues that trusted relationships that enable change go through three stages: initial resistance, establishment of relationship and the transformative relationship. Consent and transparency are central themes to achieve effective relationships and trust; consequently, students and practitioners should consider consent and clarity at every stage of interprofessional working to enable continued transformational relationships with service users. Trust builds through being informed, being heard and having a say. Therefore, frequent communication on what information to share and with whom is essential at every point.

When working with vulnerable people who are at risk of harm, although there is no requirement for consent if risks are significant enough to have to take action to protect a client or others, in order to maintain the transformational relationship the service user should stay informed and a partner in the process. Similarly, when information sharing is being decided based on the premise of public interest, that is, is it proportionate and necessary to share information in the interest of community safety (Crime and Disorder Act, 1998), maintaining the relationship still needs to shape practice. This is challenging and requires being assertive, authentic and transparent with service users; in such cases, good supervision and planning communication with colleagues will help increase a student's confidence.

Students should be aware of the core difference for interprofessional working focused on individuals in comparison to focus on the community; it is essential for students to recognise this element of practice to adhere to their principles, values and legislation (The Data Protection Act, 2018; General Data Protection Regulation and people's human 'right to privacy' under Article 8 of The Human Rights Act, 1998). Many health and social care practices are moving to a contextual or sociological way of working to address health inequalities, disadvantaged communities and community safety; therefore, targeted interprofessional working is seeing a move to a focus on the community.

Interprofessional working at a community or strategic level is very different as it is not constrained by the legislation around information ownership. Information of spaces, places, trends, issues and service success come with a shared goal and shared ownership; so there is, therefore, less procedures in place for information sharing. However, it is not entirely straightforward; the sensitivities may play out through professional agendas, community stereotyping, organisational reputation, strategic communication policies and quality assurance (Firmin et al., 2021). This is of growing relevance to students as the context and sociological understanding of practice is changing the way we understand individual needs and the risks individuals and communities may face. This is evident through the research and influence of the Contextual Safeguarding Network (Safer Young Lives Research Centre, 2020). Nevertheless, information sharing must follow a process and may be guided by a sharing agreement (Firmin et al., 2021). These agreements are as with any group; the ground rules to transparently set expectations and ways of working so should be signed and considered fully before engaging in work together. Students should seek out such agreements and be informed on the policy and expectations within their role when working at a community or strategic level. Policy and expectations may be set by the university and/or the organisation they are practising at.

Teamwork

Primarily, good teamwork sits at the heart of interprofessional working. Consider the systems theory of groups (Ludwig von Bertalanffy, 1968 cited in Greene and Schriver, 2017) that argues groups have patterns of behaviour and rituals to create norms and smoother functioning; an example is sitting in the same seats with the same people – this helps to create equilibrium. A stronger team can be created by developing an interprofessional group through enhancing the dynamics and functioning. This includes an investigation into the power dynamics, roles and enablers within a group. An interprofessional group is no different from a group of service users, so it is helpful to be observant and responsive to the group dynamics. When approaching a setting, consider the behaviour patterns and how they affect teamwork, and which need reinforcing or challenging. Students can support reflections on group behaviour and barriers to working with the interprofessional group and in supervision. There may be others in the room who are not as well-equipped to facilitate and develop group functioning. Therefore, making use of network theory (Gilchrist, 2000) which suggests identifying the nodes (relationships), the strength of connections and their patterns enables analysis and understanding of a group. Applying network theory supports students to exemplify their inclusive values, by ensuring actions support individual significance for each of the group members by supporting the group functioning. This can be achieved by mapping out with a supervisor, or a lead in the interprofessional group, reflections on the relationships and connections.

Furthermore, students need to be open to explore the context of the team and the driving force behind the purpose of the interprofessional group. A community safety-led agenda may not look, feel and play out in a similar manner to an early help support agenda. McKinsey's 7s model (Waterman, Peters and Phillips, 1980) is a good starting point to analyse an interprofessional group, by exploring the hard elements (strategy, structure and systems) alongside the soft elements (values, skills, style and staff). For example, an interprofessional group working on child exploitation may be using strategies and systems developed to respond through a trauma-informed approach (Levenson, 2017) meaning the behaviours are recognised as communication of mental health needs and responses should account for the trauma behind the behaviour. Therefore, the soft elements of the interprofessional group may be dominated by skills, style and values of the social work, youth work and health professionals. In comparison, an interprofessional group working on tackling violence may be underpinned by an enforcement agenda, increasing stop and search, surveillance through enacting powers of civil law (Home Office, 2020).

By using McKinsey's model (Waterman, Peters and Phillips, 1980) and analysing the interprofessional group interactions exploring hard and soft elements may enable students to locate their role in the group. Engaging in discussions with group members, preparing well for meetings and actively supporting the flow of discussions in the group will accelerate this.

> *Teamwork can be beneficial yet challenging, it is effective in bringing different talents to the table, however, this can be a source of conflict and barrier; this is especially true when there is a lack of clear roles and responsibilities. Ensure that you consciously reflect on how you contribute towards interpersonal working in such a way that positively contributes and promotes positive inter-partnership working practice.*
>
> Lolo, Youth and Community Leadership

Professional meetings

French and Raven (1960, cited in Maclean and Harrison, 2015) suggest that people arriving first in a group hold a level of 'informational power'; they have knowledge of interactions, conversations and who people are before the formal group interaction takes place. This is the perfect opportunity for students to build 'relational power' through developing professional relationships by introducing people, making connections and presenting their professional self (Friar and Eddleston, 2007; Smith, Vernard Harrington and Neck, 2000; Strype et al., 2014). This mode of power enables trust, credibility and professional legitimacy.

Time before the formal meeting starts is invaluable in creating conversation and shared meaning on topics external to work. It can develop relationships, reinforce respect and enhance the connection between people by showing and modelling concern for people, by what Northouse (2015) proposes as *'consideration behaviour'* (p 111) – behaviour that is mindful and thoughtful of others. Personal connection can diffuse negativity if there is a need to challenge others in the professional discussion; practitioners and students can personalise conflict which becomes detrimental to the functioning and impact of the multi-agency group (Strype et al., 2014). Increasing positivity by having an external or personal shared meaning, discussion can move to the personal discussion again after the meeting to create balance in the exchange and relationship; thus, role modelling the ability to stay professional and objective. A useful reflection is provided by Petrie (2011) in their summary of practice through the *'head, heart, and hand'*. The 'heart' in practice being our ethics, beliefs and values, the 'hand' being the practical day-to-day activity with clients and the 'head' being reflective practice bringing structured, purposeful and educated interactions with people (see further discussion on reflection in Chapter 2).

This approach embeds this in discussion of communication and the messages we convey through appropriate balance of the 'three Ps' – the 'professional, personal and private' self that brings authenticity to the trusted relationship. This is achieved by being able to use professional skills, with our personal commitment and having accurate management of our private boundaries and is often managed through trusted, accurate supervision (see supervision in Chapter 7).

Meetings are places to come to discuss, negotiate and agree on actions; thus, preparation is key. Healy and Rodriquez, (2020) argue good preparation will give confidence and level the power dynamic between professions. Preparation can include discussing the agenda items with colleagues, agreeing what outcome is being sought and what information is needed from others attending. Students can check what the expectation for contribution is and ensure information and evidence is to hand to back up dialogue and negotiations. The initial action usually in a meeting is for introduction that includes a short summary of roles (Friar and Eddleston, 2007). This process indicates who is in the room and who discussion can be directed to; everyone will need to know name, role and reason for attending the meeting. With new interprofessional groups, effective practice is to note individuals' names and roles, and use individual's name to hold their attention and relay respect. When in discussions, identifying the connections with colleagues enables memorable and meaningful exchanges, thus enhancing relationships and fundamentally a stronger network (Friar and Eddleston, 2007). Exchanges which are thoughtful and attempt to stay relevant and on track build on this, as well as acknowledging gaps in knowledge; this gives honesty to professional relationships. Following up actions between meetings is an opportunity to demonstrate integrity, maintain and build the interprofessional functioning.

Technology

Chapter 8 covers technology specifically, but in the context of interprofessional working, technology can create efficiencies and enhance communication in interprofessional practice. Digital and technological literacy and competency is now a core skill (Perron et al., 2010). Technology is an aid and is likely to be successful if the platform and foundations of interprofessional working are already effectively embedded (Goodwin, 2017; Syväjärvi et al., 2005). Students should reflect on their digital capabilities and challenge traditional practice; the use of video conferencing, cloud stored records or group messaging efficiently replaces the tradition of face-to-face meetings, which can delay progress updates. It should also be considered whether the service user should have access to these spaces. This could enhance understanding of their supporting services, relieve stress by increasing service user control and provide an alternative method of communication and involvement. Furthermore, in the wake of the Covid-19 pandemic, online meetings can enhance accessibility, and for some service users this may be a less hostile platform to meet professionals (Glauner, Plugmann and Lerzynski, 2021).

Resourcing

Funding and resourcing are a consistent issue across delivery of health and social care services (Kozlowska et al., 2018). Support provided by every service is permeated with thresholds, eligibility criteria and scales of priority and rationing. For example, in the NHS, some medication and surgical procedures that patients want are not available due to cost or efficacy. Commonly, students recognise a sense of 'firefighting' rather than engaging in the work that creates long-term change, or preventative impact, thus creating a dissatisfaction, reflecting feelings of being overworked, undervalued and ineffective in the workforce (Unison, 2018). This is a catalyst for cyclical issues of staff retention and shortages (Sander et al., 2010; Unison, 2018). With a period of austerity lasting since its announcement by the coalition government in June 2010, now exaggerated by the Covid-19 pandemic, there has been a year-on-year cut to some budgets, which has impacted on services' ability to function, perpetuating the demand of services and the desirability to join the sector. It has been evident that interprofessional working is a long-term solution to this, but also a short-term challenge of time and capacity. Students will be able to get a sense of the different issues that organisations face, but it is useful also to have a broader understanding of these wider factors. Regardless, it is clear from research such as Carney et al.'s (2019) observation that interprofessional working brings tangible benefits to patient care through overlapping care and recognition of the limits, complementary interventions and support across professions.

Interprofessional working requires a time commitment and needs to be viewed as part of the everyday work of the practitioner and students, rather than additional to workloads. As future leaders and managers, students should be aware that strategic leaders and managers need to structurally embed interprofessional working into their workforce to overcome the time commitment barrier. This is similar to networking being an undervalued practice; it is often a lesser priority, although there is a clear case for the benefits of effective networking (Friar and Eddleston, 2007). Interprofessional working provides multi-layered sustainability as well as meeting service user needs; it can provide the framework for networking and achieving real change for people. Therefore, accountability for interprofessional working needs to be written into policies and procedures, with named accountability and authority alongside toolkits to enable effective working together (Kozlowska et al., 2018). Students at a practice level, through supervision, can acknowledge this and challenge the expectation on commitment and time to be set out as early as possible with a realistic agreement as to what this would entail.

Conclusion

Interprofessional working is widely agreed as the way forward for progressive and effective service delivery which is evident through the current integrated care systems proposed in The Health and Social Care Bill (2021) and policy in children's safeguarding (Department of Health, 2018). Disciplinary 'silos' are counter-productive (Carney et al., 2019). This chapter has highlighted best practice in transferring the common core skills of working with service users to develop the same respectful trusted relationships with colleagues across professions. The challenge is not in the complex notions of working together; it is in applying core values and principles to colleagues and partners. Being conscious of the agenda clashes and power dynamics provides an objective understanding of the foundation for building interprofessional relationships. This involves using good communication, principled information sharing and harnessing an appropriate balance of the 'three Ps' (Thompson, 2020; Petrie, 2011) to create a functioning, dynamic community of practice. This is the bedrock of supporting people, challenging oppression and structural barriers through a collective and diverse group to achieve the best for our communities.

References

Atwal, A (2018) Interprofessional Learning Interventions: Championing a Lost Cause? *Evidence Based Nursing*, 21(2). http://dx.doi.org/10.1136/eb-2018-102888.

Badham, B and Wade, H (2005) *Hear by Right: Standards for the Active Involvement of Children and Young People*. London: The National Youth Agency/Local Government Association.

Baldwin, D W C (1996) Some Historical Notes on Interdisciplinary and Interprofessional Education and Practice in Health Care in the USA. *Journal of Interprofessional Care*, 10(2):173–87.

Barr, H and Coyle, J (2013) Introducing Interprofessional Education, in Loftus, S, Gerzina, T, Higgs, J, Smith, M and Duffy, E (eds) *Educating Health Professionals: Practice, Education, Work and Society*. Rotterdam: Sense Publishers. https://doi.org/10.1007/978-94-6209-353-9_16.

Bryant, R and Bryant, S (eds) (2019) *Handbook for Policing Students*. Oxford: Oxford University Press.

Cabinet Office (2013) *Local Resilience Forums: Contact Details*. Available at: www.gov.uk/guidance/local-resilience-forums-contact-details#history (accessed: 31 May 2021).

Carney, P A, Thayer, E K, Palmer, R, Galper, A B, Zierler, B and Eiff, M P (2019) The Benefits of Interprofessional Learning and Teamwork in Primary Care Ambulatory Training Settings. *Journal of Interprofessional Education & Practice*, 15:119–26.

Carpenter, J, Webb, C, Bostock, L and Coomber, C (2015) Effective Supervision in Social Work and Social Care. *Social Care Institute for Excellence. Research Briefing 43*. Available at: https://southwark.proceduresonline.com/pdfs/scie_effective.pdf (accessed 31 May 2021).

Case, S and Browning, A (2021) *Child First Justice: The Research Evidence Base*. Available at: https://repository.lboro.ac.uk/articles/report/Child_First_Justice_the_research_evidence-base_Full_report_/14152040 (accessed 18 August 2021).

Centre for the Advancement of Interprofessional Education (CAIPE) (2002) *Interprofessional Education—A Definition*. Available at: https://www.caipe.org/aboutus (accessed 08 December 2021).

Danesh, H and Danesh, R (2002) A Consultative Conflict – Resolution Model: Beyond Alternative Dispute Resolution. *International Journal of Peace Studies*, 7(2):17–33.

The Data Protection Act (2018) *The Data Protection Act*. London: HMSO.

Department for Education (2018) *Working Together to Safeguard Children: A Guide to Inter-agency Working to Safeguard and Promote the Welfare of Children*. Available at: https://assets.publishing.service.gov.uk/government/uploads/system/uploads/attachment_data/file/942454/Working_together_to_safeguard_children_inter_agency_guidance.pdf (accessed 28 June 2021).

Firmin, C, Lloyd, J, Manitser, M, Peace, D, Walker, J and Wroe, L (2021) *Contextual Safeguarding System Review Guidance*. Available at: www.csnetwork.org.uk/en/resources/practice-guides-and-resources/toolkits/system-review-toolkit (accessed 31 May 2021).

Freeth, D, Reeves, S, Koppel, I, Hammick, M and Barr, H (2005) Evaluating Interprofessional Education: A Self-Help Guide. *Higher Education Academy: Health Sciences and Practice*. Available at: www.caipe.org/resources/publications/freeth-d-reeves-s-koppel-i-hammick-m-barr-h-2005-evaluating-interprofessional-education-self-help-guide-higher-education-academy-health-sciences-practice (accessed 31 May 2021).

Friar, J H and Eddleston, K A (2007) Making Connections for Success: A Networking Exercise. *Journal of Management Education*, 31(1):104–27.

Gilchrist, A (2000) The Well-Connected Community: Networking to the 'edge of chaos'. *Community Development Journal*, 35(3):264–75.

Glauner, P, Plugmann, P and Lerzynski, G (2021) Covid-19 as a Driver for Digital Transformation in Healthcare. *Digialization in Healthcare*, 93–102.

Goodwin, N (2017) How Important is Information and Communication Technology in Enabling Interprofessional Collaboration?. *Journal of Health Services Research & Policy*, 22(4):202–03.

Granheim, B M, Shaw, J M and Mansah, M (2018) The Use of Interprofessional Learning and Simulation in Undergraduate Nursing Programs to Address Interprofessional Communication and Collaboration: An Integrative Review of the Literature. *Nurse Education Today*, 62:118–27.

Greene, R R and Schriver, J (2017) *Human Behaviour and the Social Environment: Social Work with Families*. London: Routledge.

Hammick, M, Olckers, L and Campion-Smith, C (2009) Learning in Interprofessional Teams: AMEE Guide no 38. *Medical Teacher*, 31(1):1–12.

Holmes, L, McDermid, S, Padley, M and Soper, J (2012) *Exploration of the Costs and Impact of the Common Assessment Framework*. Available at: https://assets.publishing.service.gov.uk/government/uploads/system/uploads/attachment_data/file/184025/DFE-RR210.pdf (accessed 08 December 2021).

Home Office (2020) *Violence Reduction Unit Interim Guidance*. Available at: https://assets.publishing.service.gov.uk/government/uploads/system/uploads/attachment_data/file/876380/12VRU_Interim_Guidance_FINAL__003_2732020.pdf (accessed 23 September 2021).

Hood, R, Gillespie, J and Davies, J (2016) A Conceptual Review of Interprofessional Expertise in Child Safeguarding. *Journal of Interprofessional Care*, 30(4):1–6.

Hudson, P T W (2007). Implementing a Safety Culture in a Major Multi-national. *Safety Science*, 45:697–722.

The Human Rights Act 1998 (SI 1998/42). London: HMSO.

Kina, D (2018) Relationship Centrality in Work with Young People with Experience of Violence, in Alldred, P, Cullen, F and Edwards, K, *The Sage Handbook of Youth Work Practice*. London: Sage.

Kozlowska, O, Alistair, A, Lumb, A, Garry, D, Tan, C and Rustam Rea, D (2018) Barriers and Facilitators to Integrating Primary and Specialist Healthcare in the United Kingdom: A Narrative Literature Review. *Future Healthcare Journal*, 5(1):64–80.

Legislation.gov.uk. (2015) *Crime and Disorder Act 1998*. [online] Available at: http://www.legislation.gov.uk/ukpga/1998/37/contents (accessed 08 December 2021).

Levenson, J (2017) Trauma-Informed Social Work Practice. *Social Work*, 62(2):105–13.

Maclean, S and Harrison, R (2015) *Theory and Practice: A Straightforward Guide for Social Work Students*. 3rd ed. Staffordshire: Kirwan Maclean Associates Ltd.

Ministry of Defence (2009) *The Public Interest Test*. [online] Available at: https://assets.publishing.service.gov.uk/government/uploads/system/uploads/attachment_data/file/16835/E420090701MOD_FOI_Guidance_Note.pdf.

National Society for the Protection of Cruelty to Children (2021) *Recently Published Case Reviews*. Available at https://learning.nspcc.org.uk/case-reviews/recently-published-case-reviews (accessed 26 June 2021).

Northouse, P G (2015) *Introduction to Leadership: Concepts and Practice*. London: Sage.

Peckover, S and Golding, B (2017) Domestic Abuse and Safeguarding Children: Critical Issues for Multiagency Work. *Child Abuse Review*, 26:40–50.

Perron, B E, Taylor, H O, Glass, J E and Margerum-Leys, J (2010). Information and Communication Technologies in Social Work. *Advances in Social Work*, 11(2):67–81.

Petrie, P (2011) *Communication Skills for Working with Children & Young People: An Introduction to Social Pedagogy*. 3rd ed. London: Jessica Kingsley Publishing.

Pilgrim, D and Rogers, A (2005), The Troubled Relationship between Psychiatry and Sociology. *International Journal of Social Psychiatry*, 51(3):228–41.

Reder, P, Duncan, S and Gray, M (1993) A New Look at Child Abuse Tragedies. *Child Abuse Review*, 2(2):89–100.

Safer Young Lives Research Centre (2020) *What Is Contextual Safeguarding?* Available at: www.csnetwork.org.uk/en/about/what-is-contextual-safeguarding (accessed 18 August 2021).

Sander, P, Stevenson, K, King, M and Coates, D (2010) University Student's Expectations of Teaching. *Studies in Higher Education*, 25(3):309–23.

Selinger, C P (2009) The Right to Consent: Is It Absolute? *British Journal of Medical Practitioners*. [online] Available at: www.bjmp.org/content/right-consent-it-absolute#:~:text=While%20no%20one%20can%20consent.

Smith, W J, Vernard Harrington, K and Neck, C P (2000) Resolving Conflict with Humor in a Diversity Context. *Journal of Managerial Psychology*, 15(6):606–25. https://doi.org/10.1108/02683940010346743.

Social Care Institute for Excellence (2011) *Personalisation: Implications of the Equality Act 2010*. Available at: www.scie.org.uk/personalisation/introduction/equality-act-2010.

Strype, J, Gundhus, H I, Egge, M and Ødegård, A (2014) Perceptions of Interprofessional Collaboration. *Professions and Professionalism*, 4(3):806.

Sturrock, R and Holmes, L (2015) *Running the Risks: The Links between Gang Involvement and Young People Going Missing.* Available at: www.oscb.org.uk/wp-content/uploads/2019/04/Catch22-Running-The-Risks.pdf (accessed 18 August 2021).

Syväjärvi, A, Stenvall, J, Harisalo, R and Jurvansuu, H (2005) The Impact of Information Technology on Human Capacity, Interprofessional Practice and Management. *Problems and Perspectives in Management*, (1):82–95.

Taylor, I, Whiting, E and Sharland, R (2008) Building Capacity for the Children's Workforce: Findings from the Knowledge Review of Higher Education Response. *Learning in Health and Social Care*, 7(4):184–97.

Thistlethwaite, J (2012) Interprofessiobnal Education: A Review of Context, Learning and Research Agenda. *Medical Education*, 46(1):58–70.

Thompson, N (2020) *Anti-discriminatory Practice*. 7th ed. Basingstoke: Palgrave Macmillan.

Unison. (2018) *The Government Must Turn Back the Tide on NHS Nursing Shortages, Says UNISON.* Available at: www.unison.org.uk/news/article/2018/01/government-must-turn-back-tide-nhs-nursing-shortages-says-unison/ (accessed 08 December 2021).

UK Caldicott Guardian Council (2020) *The Eight Caldicott Principles.* Available at: www.ukcgc.uk/manual/principles (accessed18 August 2021).

Waterman, R H, Peters, T J and Phillips, J R (1980) Structure Is Not Organisation. *Business Horizons*, 23(3):14–26.

11 Involving others
Vita Snowden and Gavin Jinks

Introduction

This chapter contains two distinct sections written by different authors. Both sections explore meaningful ways for the student to involve others to improve the quality of their placement. The first section focuses on how students and placement settings can learn from the untapped expertise of family carers. The section builds on exploratory theory to suggest how students can actively involve carers while on placement. The second section explores how to ensure students obtain meaningful feedback about their practice from people who access their services. It critiques methods of obtaining feedback which lack validity. It goes on to suggest practical ways in which students might use the feedback received to reflect on how they have learnt and what they have learnt.

The 'Student advice' section will help to identify carers and their contributions within the context of the placement and connect those carers and colleagues to each other and/or to further support. This will lead to better outcomes for the person with care and support needs and for the carer involved. It also enables the student and placement to recognise and learn from carer contributions.

Section one – the untapped expertise of family carers

Students are likely to meet unpaid/family carers while on placement within a health and social care setting. Carers may be indirectly involved in the student's placement or not at all (Haugland, Hysing and Sivertsen, 2020). Alternatively, carers may play a central part within the setting, but their role is unseen or viewed as secondary (Hammond and McLean, 2009). Students may encounter this pattern of invisibility from both practitioners and carers themselves. By acknowledging carers' contributions, students can play a pivotal part in changing the perspective of both practitioners and carers while on placement, leading to improved practice and benefit to all.

Unpaid/family carers often do not relate to the word 'carer' (Burton, 2008; Henderson and Forbat, 2002; National Development for Inclusion [NDTi], 2019a). They might see themselves as 'just' someone's relative, partner or friend (Burton, 2008; NDTi, 2019b). Professionals, with a 'person-centred' lens at the forefront of their minds, will often overlook carers too (Jones, 2015; Manthorpe et al., 2020; NDTi, 2019a; McKimm and Phillips, 2009). Consequently, students on placement can play a key role in identifying unpaid/family carers and linking those carers to community activities and ensuring that they are 'equal expert partners' alongside professionals (Musson, 2017; NDTi, 2019b). Several theories are useful in explaining how carers significantly contribute to meeting the needs of loved ones by working together with others. Burton (2008) argues that the concept of 'carer' has been constructed to have negative connotations, for example, he suggests, '"burden" and "restricted" are key words throughout the debate' (p 494).

However, this research proposes that negative associations with the word 'carer' do not reflect the perceptions carers have of themselves. An exclusive focus on the needs of carers, rather than their contributions, means it is difficult to escape a 'deficit' model (Teater, 2014). A 'deficit' model is where practitioners only consider what is wrong in a situation. Students have an opportunity to proactively learn from carers by recognising their contributions.

Theories can be applied to the different types of contributions carers make. For example, the 'equal expert partner' concept lends itself to a strength-based approach (Saleebey, 1996) where the carer is using their assets to support someone they love. By drawing on asset-based and strength-based theories (Maclean and Harrison, 2015; Payne, 2014), a more holistic picture emerges. Some might argue that the co-user of services is about co-dependency (eg attachment theory [Bowlby, 1969]) applied to adults (Maclean and Harrison, 2015), but the reality is that many carers and their loved ones are in symbiotic relationships where they look after each other (Carers UK, 2019b).

To illustrate the extent that carers provide multiple contributions in supporting others, those contributions are separated out in Figure 11.1. Each type of contribution is explicit. The same person could make all, or nearly all, the contributions listed. The purpose of the table is not to identify and describe unique characteristics of different types of carers, but rather demonstrate the multiple ways carers contribute to our health and social care system. UK carers are estimated to save the state £132 billion a year – close to the cost of a second NHS (Yeandle and Butler, 2015). Students on placement can be aware that an unpaid/family carer not only exists but may be contributing in a range of ways (perhaps unnoticed by others within the placement organisation). The student will be in a strong position to ask questions that lead to the carer's contribution being learnt about within the work of the placement.

Carers value independent peer support groups (NDTi, 2019a). By connecting with carers' groups, students on placement are able to learn from, and support, those groups to bring about social change. This is compatible with the ABCD model (Shiggins et al., 2020, Harrison et al., 2019). Asset-based community development (ABCD) builds on the strengths of people and their communities to improve the quality of life of those communities (Harrison

MODELS OF CARER ENGAGEMENT

	Carer as a resource	Carer as co-worker	Carer as co-user of services	Unrecognised Carer role	Carers as equal expert partner
Carer contribution	Knowledge is a resource; may also provide practical help e.g. transport/bought equipment	Liaises with professionals and is actively involved in meetings about loved one's needs	Someone who is in need of services both in their own right and in relation to their loved ones	'Relative' not carer – perceived as not having an interest or role to play in the design of support services for loved one. Sees self as 'only' a relative, friend, partner, or neighbour	Skilled, knowledgeable experienced at dealing with health and social care systems and know the needs of loved ones.
Focus of contribution	Disabled person/child	Disabled person with some recognition of carer role	Carer – as someone in need of services	Disabled person – carer incidental or seen separately for own service needs	Both carer as a person in their own right and the needs of loved one. Also the plight of other carers
Community Connection	Sources of further help; e.g. technology, more equipment	Proactive member of professional team.	Accessing services for self and loved one	Potentially no access to community connections – if any, only disabled person accesses local support and carer is invisible	Facilitates and attends independent carers' networks; provides and receives peer support
Needs of carer	Recognition of resource contribution in the care and support of loved one	To be seen as a respected co-worker, contributing to the support plan	Requires service in own right (might have needs to improve their own 'wellbeing' for example)	To recognise their role as a carer themselves and to be recognised by others, particularly health and other professionals so that the carer can access support for self and loved one and connect with other carers for mutual benefit	To be treated in a holistic way as an 'equal expert partner' re loved one and also as someone in their own right who has needs and a life outside the caring role

Figure 11.1 Models of carer engagement. Adapted from Twigg and Atkin (1994, p 13) Carers Perceived: Policy and Practice in Informal Care. Open University Press.

et al., 2019; Russell, 2015; Payne, 2006). Local independent carers' groups are rich with knowledge of systems and '*experiential wisdom*' (Fox, 2019). Social movements, such as disability movements and carer movements, are user-led and identify what needs to change (Askheim, Beresford and Heule, 2017; Payne, 2014; Warren, 2007). By being aware of, and perhaps supporting, the establishment of independent carers' groups, a student on placement could draw together the needs of individual carers and the wider difficulties they may face with health and social care systems. Weiss-Gal, Levin and Krumer-Nevo (2014) have identified ways students can address social justice concerns within their practice. They suggest that the approach needs to include both the personal and political and the individual and society. This is a golden opportunity for students to make a difference. They can recognise the frustrations carers often feel at systems which are not working for them; work in partnership with them to connect with other carers and find a strong collective voice, and be aware of their status as outsider and observer as well as use language which carers understand and can connect with. Simultaneously, students can recognise caring has a toll on carers' well-being (Al-Janabia et al., 2019; Carers UK, 2019a) without devaluing the positive contributions carers make.

Independent community networks for carers usually exist locally (Eronen, 2020; NDTi, 2017) but are often not known about, valued or promoted. The voluntary sector is an umbrella for a range of formal and informal community support networks (Polivka and Polivka-West, 2020; NDTi, 2019a; Billis, 2010). Students can find out about informal support for carers and promote the information to isolated carers and other colleagues. When asked, carers often say that the most important support comes from other carers (NDTi, 2017; Cowie and Wallace, 2000). The student may encounter different perceptions held by the carer and loved one. Conflicting tensions within the caring relationship can impact on theories that address inequalities. It raises questions as to who the unequal person is within this scenario and how they can be supported. Brimblecombe et al. (2017) found that working carers perceived that their loved ones had higher unmet needs than was acknowledged by the loved ones themselves. Pickard et al.'s (2015) study shows that services at the right level are pivotal for working carers to remain in employment. If only the loved one's views are valued by the professional, the carer may be unable to continue paid work. Few-Demo and Allen (2020) draw attention to the importance of intersectionality which explores how gender, race, social class, sexuality and other forms of stratification impact on families. Carers play a central role within families and so intersectionality is key. Older female workers are twice as likely to be caring as men (Skopeliti, 2019; Office for National Statistics (ONS), 2019; ONS, 2013). There are societal expectations on women that they will be unpaid carers (ONS, 2019; Skopeliti, 2019). Older men are more likely to be caring for spouses whereas women could be caring for anyone, including non-relatives (ONS, 2019).

Feminist theory has traditionally been used to explore power dynamics within the domestic/private world (Few-Demo and Allen, 2020). Studies have found there is an expectation that daughters will care (Brimblecombe et al., 2017). Students on placement will want to consider how to support female and male carers differently. There could be merit in supporting male carers, for example, to set up a group because studies show that men are less likely to seek social support as a coping strategy (Ketcher et al., 2020). Brimblecombe et al. (2017) point out that Black and Asian Minority Ethnic (BAME) carers can experience barriers to accessing health and social care in the UK. Applying an intersectionality approach, students on placement should find out about BAME communities and networks and how carers within those communities can be identified and supported within culturally appropriate contexts.

Hurley and Taiwo (2019) argue that training provided to students is taught as micro-skills that are value-free. They say it is important that grasping relevant skills should include an in-depth understanding about how inequalities are internalised. If family carers, including those who face barriers as women, BAME and/or disabled people are to be supported, then independent carer groups need to be inclusive and reflecting diversity (Pizio, 2020).

Sicora (2019) explores what is meant when a student makes 'mistakes' while on placement; it examines how reflective practice can help the student to explore their 'mistakes' but observes that rarely does the student consider the role systems and institutions play in influencing those 'mistakes'. By reflecting on the theories referred to in this chapter, students should be able to make wider links between their own practice and the systems which make the lives of carers difficult. Their role can be to support carers through the minefield of understanding how systems work.

A study by Tanner et al. (2017) indicates that what students can do is influenced and shaped by the placement culture. This could limit the wider thinking encouraged here. A number of reflective models will support students to learn, influence and support a shift in thinking (if needed) in relation to the role of carers. For example, Schon's (1987) reflection IN action addresses the need to reflect in the present and Rolfe, Freshwater and Jasper's (2001) reflective framework (three questions: What? So what? What now?) enables practitioners to act on their reflections. These reflective frameworks will enable students to consider how they are able to connect carers to community support using the ABCD model, what barriers might exist and how they can be overcome.

The guidance below will help to identify carers and their contributions within the context of the placement and connect those carers and colleagues to each other and/or to further support. This will lead to better outcomes for the person with care and support needs and for the carer involved. It also enables the student and placement to recognise and learn from carer contributions.

Student advice

1. If your placement works directly with families, find out what local support, including peer support, is available for carers.
2. Find out whether support exists for particular marginalised carers, eg, BAME, young carers, LGBT carers, and how inclusive the existing independent support available is.

3. If your placement is indirectly in touch with the family, friends, partner, neighbour of the person with care and support needs, find out how you/your organisation can connect the carer to local peer or other support.

4. Have conversations with the person with care and support needs to find out whether they have informal support and enable them and your colleagues to recognise its importance (if they do not).

5. Increase your placement's understanding about the importance of valuing and including the multiple roles carers play in the lives of people with care and support needs.

Section two – service user feedback

Service user and carer involvement in higher education programmes for social care has long been regarded as an essential element in course design, content and admission processes (Hatton, 2017; Baldwin and Sadd, 2006; Robinson and Webber, 2013). However, there has been significantly less written about the why and how students obtain service user and carer feedback during practice placements. Where this is the subject of academic writing there is a focus on the content of feedback and less of a concern with the validity of how it may have been obtained and with what can be learnt from this feedback (Elliott et al., 2006). There is government guidance on the principles for gathering feedback from service users of social work services. This guidance specifically addresses the need for service user feedback to be tailored to the service user group in question and emphasises the need for collaboration with service users in the gathering of feedback. Although this guidance is social work specific, it is submitted that the principles will apply to the whole social care spectrum (Allen et al., 2016).

We live in a feedback culture. If one purchases a product or accesses a service, it is very likely that there will be a request for feedback. In the context of a culture that is saturated with feedback and requests for feedback, it is important that we are prepared to ask ourselves what might be the purpose of obtaining feedback. It is evident that feedback surveys can sometimes be used as advertising tools whereby the results are manipulated so that they can be used to promote the quality of a product or service (Bone, Lemon and Voorhees, 2017). It is also evident that employers sometimes use feedback surveys to manage and control their employees. Results that indicate less than a 'target satisfaction rate' may mean that an employee loses a bonus, has a poor appraisal or in some circumstances may even mean that the employee loses their job. It is therefore suggested that any person or organisation seeking feedback needs to do so with two key questions in mind: *will the methods used produce meaningful results? How might the results be employed as a genuine reflective learning tool?* This acts as a good starting point when constructing any approach to service user feedback in social care. The government guidance referred to above is predicated on the need to produce meaningful results (Allen et al., 2016). It follows logically that meaningful service user feedback acts as a sound basis for reflective learning by students.

Students in the wider field of social care who undertake practice placements are frequently required to demonstrate that they have obtained service user and carer feedback within their practice learning portfolios. As a practice educator, supervisor of practice educators and then more recently as a university tutor, the author's experience has been that students tend to focus on ensuring that they receive 'good' feedback. There is much less of a focus on constructing a method of obtaining feedback which produces valid and meaningful results. Even less frequently does one come across students who, without prompting, have taken pains to ensure that they reflect on what can be learnt from the feedback received. In a culture in which the key aim is to demonstrate 'how good I am' it is no surprise that students may require coaching to seek rather to demonstrate 'how I have learnt and what I have learnt'. If a student can be encouraged to approach a practice placement with this reframe of the placement's purpose, this will make it more likely that the placement in general and service user/carer feedback will become truly valuable. To assist practice educators to guide their students to think through an approach to the gathering of service user/carer feedback, a mind map has been constructed. It is suggested that individual practice educators will choose to adapt this mind map and develop an approach to reflection and analysis that becomes more customised to the placement setting and more customised to the sophistication of individual students. The need to customise service user feedback according to the nature of the service user group is highlighted in government guidance (Allen et al., 2016).

Below is an approach to assist students reflect upon their choices and conclusions regarding the gathering of service user feedback. This utilises the principles of double loop learning (Argyris and Schon, 1996). The approach could also be adapted for reflection in group supervision within the philosophy of action learning. Action learning involves the use of pertinent reflective questions to enable individuals, groups and organisations to solve problems (Revans, 1982).

Diagram A is a mind map that can be a useful tool for both student and practice educator to ensure that service user and carer feedback is being obtained in a meaningful way and has been used to create genuinely reflective learning. The mind map has been annotated to encourage reflective questioning of the student's approach to obtaining feedback.

Diagram B is a mind map illustrating the use of *spontaneous service user and carer feedback* as one example of the collection of service user and carer feedback. For these purposes, spontaneous feedback is defined as *'unsolicited comments or behaviour from a service user or carer that can be interpreted and reflected upon as feedback on the service received'*. Spontaneous feedback has been chosen because it has the potential to provide very clear indications of the uncontaminated thoughts and feelings of service users/carers. Beresford, Adshead and Croft (2007) have written about the vital importance of hearing the service user voice to ensure that services are appropriate and fit for purpose. The dark box annotations in this example highlight the learning that can take place for a student if there is a reflective and analytical approach to the gathering of feedback.

Involving others · **161**

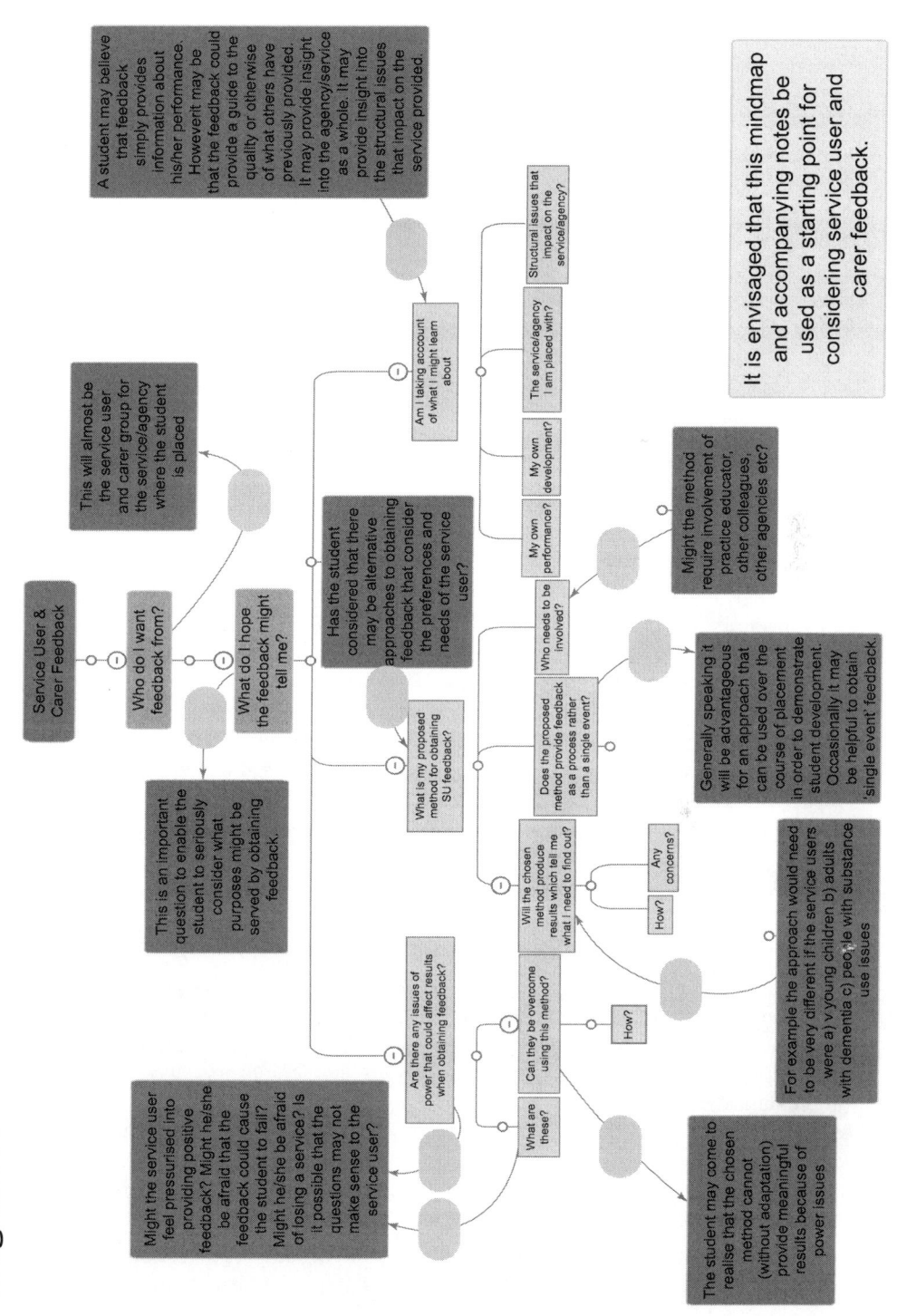

Diagram A

Notes to Diagram A

- **Who do I want feedback from?** This should be the most straightforward question to answer for the student as it will almost always be that feedback is required from the service users and their carers in the setting in which the student is on practice placement.
- **What do I hope the feedback might tell me?** Here we are starting to encourage the student to consider what is the purpose of feedback and that this is not necessarily a straightforward question. It may well be that as the placement develops and evolves the student will start to realise that the initial thinking and motivation concerning the gathering of feedback has become more sophisticated and much more of a learning tool. It is important that a student recognises that the point of feedback is not to demonstrate '*what a great student I have been*'. If this is the motivation, then the student is likely to fall prey to some of the temptations of gathering feedback in a marketised world. Bone, Lemon and Voorhees (2017) have provided evidence that the framing of questions in feedback surveys can impact on consumer behaviour. Therefore, supervisors should encourage students to consider whether the way in which they frame questions to obtain service user feedback might inadvertently impact on the answers given to those feedback questions.
- **Are there any issues of power that could affect results when obtaining feedback?** It is quite possible that the student had not considered that there may be some genuine concerns about power dynamics in relation to the gathering of feedback. It is likely to be useful to ask a student to consider all of the potential issues of power that could arise and impact on the validity of any results obtained. Might service users consider that negative feedback could impact on the future service they receive? Might the service user believe that the power and authority of anyone providing a service cannot be challenged? Might the service user fail to understand what is being asked because, for example, a questionnaire is full of jargon and inaccessible language? Anti-discriminatory and anti-oppressive practice is at the heart of effective social care, and it is vital that a student applies this thinking to the gathering of service user feedback (Thompson, 2016).
- **What is my proposed method for obtaining feedback?** If a student understands the potential power issues, they are much more likely to become both thoughtful and creative in devising a meaningful approach to obtaining feedback. Tailoring the method of obtaining feedback to the needs of the particular service user group in order to hear the authentic voice is essential (Allen et al., 2016).
- **Am I taking account of what I might learn about a range of issues?** Initially a student may have believed that feedback will simply provide evidence of their performance and skills. However, as reflection is more fully applied there may be a realisation that feedback may be a guide to how the service user/carer feels about his life and circumstances. It may act as a guide to more general feelings about the service/agency as a whole rather than the individual student. It might even act as a commentary on wider issues about the way in which society views the particular service user group. For this to occur, students need to form genuine professional listening relationships with service users (Beresford, Adshead and Croft, 2007; Beresford, 2012).
- **Does the proposed method provide feedback as a process rather than a single event?** It is not uncommon for both student and practice educator to start to consider the gathering of feedback as a one-time event near to the end of placement. It is almost always likely to be useful to encourage that service user/carer feedback is obtained as an ongoing process throughout placement. Treating feedback as a process rather than an event can provide a genuine guide to the developing performance and reflective skills of the student (Bolger and Walker, in Lishman et al., 2018).

Involving others · 163

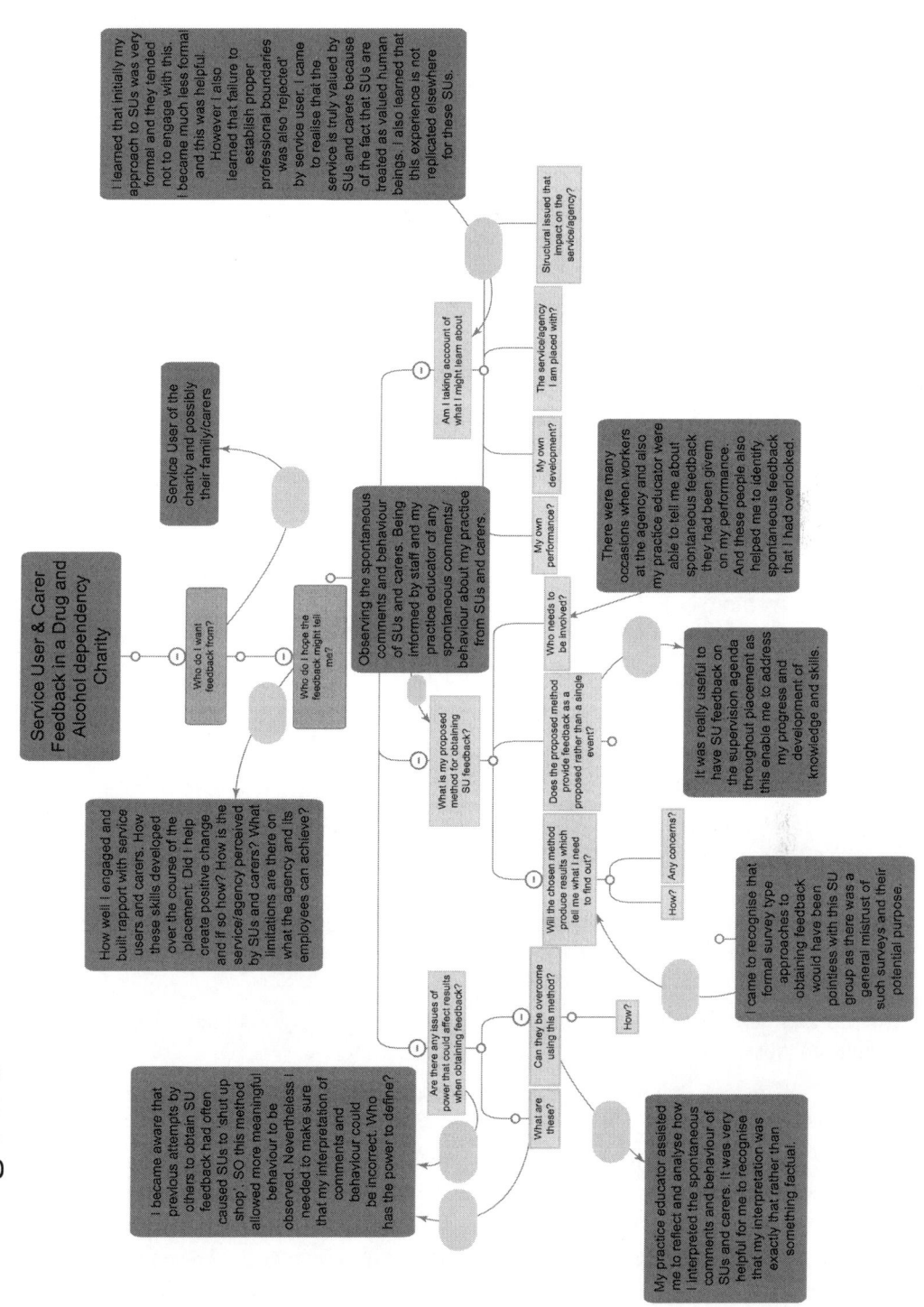

Diagram B

Service User & Carer Feedback in a Drug and Alcohol dependency Charity

Who do I want feedback from?
- Service User of the charity and possibly their family/carers

I learned that initially my approach to SUs was very formal and they tended not to engage with this. I became much less formal and this was helpful. However I also learned that failure to establish proper professional boundaries was also 'rejected' by service user. I came to realise that the service is truly valued by SUs and carers because of the fact that SUs are treated as valued human beings. I also learned that this experience is not replicated elsewhere for these SUs.

Who do I hope the feedback might tell me?
- Am I taking account of what I might learn about:
  - Structural issues that impact on the service/agency?
  - The service/agency I am placed with?
  - My own development?
  - My own performance?

How well I engaged and built rapport with service users and carers. How these skills developed over the course of the placement. Did I help create positive change and if so how? How is the service/agency perceived by SUs and carers? What limitations are there on what the agency and its employees can achieve?

There were many occasions when workers at the agency and also my practice educator were able to tell me about spontaneous feedback they had been given on my performance. And these people also helped me to identify spontaneous feedback that I had overlooked.

What is my proposed method for obtaining SU feedback?
- Observing the spontaneous comments and behaviour of SUs and carers. Being informed by staff and my practice educator of any spontaneous comments/behaviour about my practice from SUs and carers.

Does the proposed method provide feedback as a proposed rather than a single event?
- Who needs to be involved?

It was really useful to have SU feedback on the supervision agenda throughout placement as this enable me to address my progress and development of knowledge and skills.

Will the chosen method produce results which tell me what I need to find out?
- How? Any concerns?

I came to recognise that formal survey type approaches to obtaining feedback would have been pointless with this SU group as there was a general mistrust of such surveys and their potential purpose.

Can they be overcome using this method?
- How?

Are there any issues of power that could affect results when obtaining feedback?
- What are these?

I became aware that previous attempts by others to obtain SU feedback had often caused SUs to 'shut up shop'. SO this method allowed more meaningful behaviour to be observed. Nevertheless I needed to make sure that my interpretation of comments and behaviour could be incorrect. Who has the power to define?

My practice educator assisted me to reflect and analyse how I interpreted the spontaneous comments and behaviour of SUs and carers. It was very helpful for me to recognise that my interpretation was exactly that rather than something factual.

By reflecting on what feedback is, how it is obtained, its validity and what can be learnt from it, there are benefits, not simply for the student but for the placement setting and those who use services and those who care for them. When students engage in this critical and analytical approach to obtaining feedback, it is likely to be beneficial to the placement setting (often although not exclusively) via the practice educator/supervisor. It is also likely to benefit those who use services or care for those that do because it is likely to make these people feel more validated and valued. It is also likely to benefit these people because the future practice of the student will have a more accurate view of the perceptions of those using services and those who care for them. It will also make it more likely that the student will be more attuned to fully listening to the views of those who they seek to support.

Conclusion

This chapter has explored the value to social care students on practice placement of accessing the untapped expertise of family carers. It has also explored the benefits of a reflective and analytical approach to gaining meaningful feedback from those who use social care services and those that care for them. Students who are able to embrace the thinking and philosophy of these ideas will become more thoughtful and competent practitioners. Their engagement with those that they seek to support will become more meaningful and more equal. This will benefit not only their future practice but will also serve to encourage others who work in placement settings to consider how they themselves engage with those people who use their services.

References

Al-Janabia, H, McLoughlin, C, Oyebodeb, J, Efstathiouc, N and Calver, M (2019) Six Mechanisms Behind Carer Wellbeing Effects: A Qualitative Study of Healthcare Delivery. *Social Science and Medicine*. 23. https://doi.org/10.1016/j.socscimed.2019.112382.

Allen, R, Carr, S, Linde, K and Sewell, H (2016) *Making the Difference Together Guidance on Gathering and Using Feedback About the Experience of Social Work from People Who Use Services and Their Carers*. London: Department of Health.

Argyris, C and Schön, D (1996) *Organizational Learning II: Theory, Method and Practice*. Reading: Addison Wesley.

Askheim, O, Beresford, P and Heule, C (2017) Mend the Gap – Strategies for User Involvement in Social Work Education. *Social Work Education*, 36(2):128–40.

Baldwin, M and Sadd, J (2006) Allies with Attitude! Service Users, Academics and Social Service Agency Staff Learning How to Share Power in Running Social Work Education Courses. *Social Work Education*, 25(4):348–59.

Beresford, P (2012) What Service Users Want from Social Workers. *Community Care*. Available at: www.communitycare.co.uk/2012/04/27/what-service-users-want-from-social-workers/ (accessed 05 February 2020).

Beresford, P, Adshead, L. and Croft, S. (2007) *Palliative Care, Social Work and Service Users: Making Life Possible*. London. Jessica Kingsley.

Billis, D (ed) (2010) *Hybrid Organizations and the Third Sector: Challenges for Practice, Theory and Policy*. London: Palgrave Macmillan.

Bone, S, Lemon, K and Voorhees, C (2017) 'Mere Measurement Plus': How Solicitation of Open-Ended Positive Feedback Influences Customer Purchase Behaviour. *Journal of Marketing Research*, 54(1).

Bowlby, J (1969) *Attachment and Loss*. New York: Basic Books.

Bowlby, J (1980) *Attachment and Loss, Volume III. Loss: Sadness and Depression*. New York: Basic Books.

Brimblecombe, N, Pickard, L, King, D and Knapp, M (2017) Perceptions of Unmet Needs for Community Social Care Services in England: A Comparison of Working Carers and the People they Care for. *Health and Social Care in the Community*, 25(2):435–46.

Burton, M (2008) Grounding Constructions of Carers: Exploring the Experiences of Carers through a Grounded Approach. *British Journal of Social Work*, 38:493–506.

Carers UK (2019a) *Getting Carers Connected*. Available at: www.carersuk.org/for-professionals/policy/policy-library/getting-carers-connected-2.

Carers UK (2019b) *Facts About Caring*. Available at: www.carersuk.org/for-professionals/policy/policy-library/facts-about-carers-2019.

Cowie, H and Wallace, P (2000) *Peer Support In Action: From Bystanding to Standing By*. London: Sage.

Deans, E (2020) Group Work: A Haven for People Living with Mental Illness. *Social Work with Groups*, 43(1–2):141–44.

Elliott, T, Frazer, T, Garrard, D, Hickinbotham, J, Horton, V, Mann, J, Soper, S, Turner, J, Turner, M and Whiteford, A (2006) Practice Learning and Assessment on BSc (hons) Social Work: 'Service User Conversations'. *Social Work Education*, 24(4):451–66.

Eronen, E (2020) Experiences of Sharing, Learning and Caring: Peer Support in a Finnish Group of Mothers. *Health and Social Care in the Community*, 8(2).

Few-Demo, A and Allen, K (2020) Gender, Feminist, and Intersectional Perspectives on Families: A Decade in Review. *Journal of Marriage and Family*, 82:326–45.

Fox, J (2019). Being a Service User and a Social Work Academic: Balancing Expert Identities. *Social Work Education*, 35:960–69.

Hammond, M and McLean, E (2009) What Parents and Carers Think Medical Students Should be Learning about Communication with Children and Families. *Patient Education and Counselling*, 76:368–75.

Harrison, R, Blickem, C, Lamb, J, Kirk, S and Vassilev, I (2019) Asset-Based Community Development: Narratives, Practice, and Conditions of Possibility—A Qualitative Study With Community Practitioners, *SAGE Open*. Available at: https://journals.sagepub.com/doi/pdf/10.1177/2158244018823081 (accessed 02 May 2020).

Hatton, K (2017). A Critical Examination of the Knowledge Contribution Service User and Carer Involvement Brings to Social Work Education. *Social Work Education*, 36(2):154–71.

Haugland, B., Hysing, M and Sivertsen, B (2020) The Burden of Care: A National Survey on the Prevalence, Demographic Characteristics and Health Problems Among Young Adult Carers Attending Higher Education in Norway. *Frontiers in Psychology*, 10.

Henderson, J and Forbat, L (2002) Relationship-based Social Policy: Personal and Policy Constructions of 'care'. *Critical Social Policy*, 22(4):669–87.

Hurley, D and Taiwo, A (2019) Critical Social Work and Competency Practice: A Proposal to Bridge Theory and Practice in the Classroom. *Social Work Education*, 38(2):198–211.

Jones, R (2015) The End Game: The Marketisation and Privatisation of Children's Social Work and Child Protection. *Critical Social Policy*, 35(4):447–269.

Ketcher, D, Trettevik, R, Vadaparampil, S T, Heyman, R E, Ellington, L and Reblin, M (2020) Caring for a Spouse with Advanced Cancer: Similarities and Differences for Male and Female Caregivers. *Journal of Behavioral Medicine*, 43(5):817–28. https://doi.org/10.1007/s10865-019-00128-y.

Lishman, J, Yuill, C, Brannan, J and Gibson, A (2018) *Social Work: An Introduction*. London. Sage.

Maclean, S and Harrison, R (2015) *Social Work Theory: A straightforward Guide for Practice Educators and Placement Supervisors*. Staffordshire: Kirwin Maclean Associates.

Manthorpe, J, Moriarty, J, Brimblecombe, N, Knapp, M, Fernandez, J and Snell, T (2020) Carers and the Care Act: Promise and Potential, in Braye, S and Preston-Shoot, M (eds) *The Care Act 2014*. London: Sage.

McKimm, J and Phillips, K (2009) *Leadership and Management in Integrated Services*. Exeter: Learning Matters Limited.

Musson, P (2017) *Making Sense of Theory and Its Application to Social Work Practice*. St Albans: Critical Publishing

National Development for Inclusion (NDTi) (2017) Spotlight on a Carer's Journey, Available at: /www.ndti.org.uk/uploads/files/Carers_Journey.pdf.

National Development for Inclusion (NDTi) (2019a) *Supporting Carers: Sharing Best Practice in Integrated Approaches to Support*. Available at: www.ndti.org.uk/uploads/files/Carers_Shared_Learning_Final.pdf.

National Development for Inclusion (NDTi) (2019b) *Do You Care?: Preparing Carers to Get the Best from the Care Act 2014*. Available at: www.ndti.org.uk/uploads/files/Carers_guide_Final.pdf.

Office for National Statistics (2013) Full Story: The *Gender Gap* in *Unpaid Care Provision*: Is There an Impact on *Health* and *Economic Position*? Available at: www.ons.gov.uk/peoplepopulationandcommunity/healthandsocialcare/healthandwellbeing/articles/fullstorythegendergapinunpaidcareprovisionisthereanimpactonhealthandeconomicposition/2013-05-16 (accessed 2 May 2020).

Office for National Statistics (2019) *Living Longer: Caring in Later Working Life*. Available at: www.ons.gov.uk/peoplepopulationandcommunity/birthsdeathsandmarriages/ageing/articles/livinglongerhowourpopulationischangingandwhyitmatters/2019-03-15 (accessed 02 May 2020).

Payne, M (2014) *Modern Social Work Theory*. 4th ed. Hampshire: Palgrave Macmillan.

Payne, P R (2006) *Youth Violence Prevention Through Asset-based Community Development*. El Paso: LFB Scholarly Publishing LLC.

Pickard, L, King, D, Brimblecombe, N and Knapp, M (2015) The Effectiveness of Paid Services in Supporting Unpaid Carers' Employment in England: Analysis Using Large-Scale Survey Data and Implications for Policy. *Journal of Social Policy*, 44(3):567–90.

Pizio, J (2020). The Importance of Diversity and Inclusion in Health Care Compliance. *Journal of Health Care Compliance*, 22(2):21–26.

Polivka, L and Polivka-West, L (2020) The Changing Role of Non-Profit Organizations in the U.S. Long Term Care System. *Journal of Aging & Social Policy*, 32(2):101–07.

Revans, R (1982) *The Origin and Growth of Action Learning*. Brickley: Chartwell-Bratt.

Robinson, K and Webber, M (2013) Models and Effectiveness of Service User and Carer Involvement in Social Work Education: A Literature Review. *British Journal of Social Work*, 43:925–44.

Rolfe, G, Freshwater, D and Jasper, M (2001) *Critical Reflection for Nursing and the Helping Professions: A User's Guide*. Basingstoke: Palgrave Macmillan.

Russell, C (2015) *Asset Based Community Development : Looking Back to Look Forward – In Conversation with John McKnight About the Intellectual and Practical Heritage of ABCD and Its Place in the World Today*. [United States]: Cormac Russell. Available at: http://search.ebscohost.com.ezproxy.derby.ac.uk/login.aspx?direct=true&db=nlebk&AN=1004777&site=eds-live (accessed 03 May 2020)

Saleebey, D (1996) The Strengths perspective in social work practice: extensions and cautions. *Social Work*, 41:296–305.

Schon, D (1987) *Educating the Reflective Practitioner*. San Francisco: Jossey Bass.

Shiggins, C, Soskolne, V, Olenik, D, Pearl, G, Haaland-Johansen, L, Isaksen, J Jagoe, C, McMenamin, R and Horton, S (2020) Towards an Asset-Based Approach to Promoting and Sustaining Well-Being for People with Aphasia and their Families: An International Exploratory Study. *Aphasiology*, 34(1):70–101.

Sicora, A (2019) Reflective Practice and Learning from Mistakes in Social Work Student Placement. *Social Work Education*, 38(1):63–74.

Skopeliti, C (2019) Older Female Workers 'Twice As likely as Men' to be Informal Carers. *The Guardian*. Available at: www.theguardian.com/society/2019/mar/15/older-female-workers-twice-as-likely-to-be-informal-carers-ons-report (accessed 02 May 2020).

Tanner, D, Littlechild, R, Duffy, J and Hayes, D (2017) Making It Real': Evaluating the Impact of Service User and Carer Involvement in Social Work Education. *British Journal of Social Work*, (47):467–86.

Teater, B (2014) *An Introduction to Applying Social Work Theories and Methods*. 2nd ed. Berkshire: Open University Press.

Thompson, N (2016) *Anti-discriminatory Practice*. London. Palgrave Macmillan.

Warren, J (2007) *Service User and Carer Participation in Social Work*. London: Sage.

Weiss-Gal, I, Levin, L and Krumer-Nevo, M (2014) Applying Critical Social Work in Direct Practice with Families. *Child and Family Social Work*, 19:55–64.

Yeandle, S and Buckner, L (2015) *Valuing Carers 2015 – The Rising Value of Carers' Support*. Available at: www.carersuk.org/for-professionals/policy/policy-library/valuing-carers-2015.

12 Managing projects
Simon Williams

Introduction

Placement can be exciting for students as they can provide a range of opportunities for learning. Depending on the student's course and the level of placement, there may be opportunity to manage a project. Projects can be any size, and students may be more involved in the planning, delivery and evaluation stages. Managing a project on placement allows students to build and demonstrate a wide range of skills and their readiness for work. Some students may be required to project manage as part of course requirements, others might have the opportunity to engage in managing projects through connections made on placement, and some students will seek out opportunities to engage in project management for their own development. Additionally, having students manage projects can be part of an organisation's own development, as organisations might 'trial and error' a project to measure effectiveness and need, but also to provide evidence for funding.

This chapter will critically debate theory around project managing – including negotiation, planning, research and evaluation. These stages are underpinned by a collaborative stance through the involvement of staff, volunteers and individuals who access the agency to support project management. This chapter connects to other chapter discussions and develops skills to support project management and working with others.

The chapter discusses:

- Motivation for projects
- Defining aims and objectives
- Negotiation skills
- Needs analysis
- Planning

- Delivery
- Evaluation
- Reporting outcomes

Why might students be involved in managing projects?

While some organisations initiate projects, students on placement might be working with community members who set up their own projects (Webster, 2004); for example, a community group who want to set up a community allotment project, and seek support from an organisation to achieve this. The mixture of these motivations for projects raises the question, 'why is the student managing the project?' – is it for the student, the agency or for the individuals who access the agency? Therefore, students will need to demonstrate:

> Confidence and clarity when dealing with conflicts that can occur between professional principles and individuals, organisational or societal expectations and assumptions. (Sapin, 2009, p 170)

Managing projects can lead to potential conflicts, and these can be present even before the project planning takes place; for example, clashes of professional values, differences in perceived outcomes, and bias towards people, places and organisations. These might shift the focus and motivation of those involved, including the student, which can then affect engagement. This chapter seeks to lay out a theoretical framework to support effective management of projects. Having a clear aim and objectives that are carefully negotiated is a great place to start. Without this, a project is starting off on shaky ground, placing it at an increased risk of drifting or failing to do what it set out to do.

Aims and objectives

In short, an 'aim' is what you hope to achieve from the project; 'objectives' are the steps you will take to achieve the aim. Sapin (2013, p 174) refers to an aim as the *hope* of the project and objectives as activities undertaken; however, students need to reflect that 'hopes' are often different and rooted in bias and professional and personal agendas. Generally, an 'aim' is often quite broad and open, but 'objectives' should be more focused.

For example, a project might have the aim of reducing social isolation in the community.

The objectives to meet this aim might be:

- to open a weekday evening youth club for 11–16-year olds;
- to organise a monthly weekend social trip for all ages;
- to make use of social media to connect local people by communicating local opportunities to meet people.

Set 'objectives' can be revisited at each stage of the project, as they provide a framework to work towards, thus enabling resources to be focused effectively. The aim and objectives frame projects, and thus it is essential that enough time is allocated to exploring these fully, to make sure that they are clear and achievable; otherwise project managers can expect to encounter difficulty and confusion (Thomas and Hodges, 2010). There are several models designed to support effective planning. A useful one to look at is the FINER model, devised by Hulley et al. (2013). This is for research projects, but it can be applied for wider project types too. The model considers if the project is:

Feasible?

Interesting?

Novel?

Ethical?

Relevant?

When planning a project, it is useful to debate these questions to gain insight into the potential effectiveness of the project. However, a flaw of this model is that it lacks the voices of participants, which should be considered to increase participation in the project and to make sure the project is done 'with' and not 'to' individuals (Simmons, Birchall and Prout, 2011) – this is discussed later. Additionally, the answers to the questions in the model are subjective; what is interesting, novel or ethical to one person may not be for others, highlighting again the need for collaborative working. A project manager will need to consider who might be involved in collaborative working, and Table 12.1 shows some of the different stakeholders to project design.

Table 12.1 Stakeholders in project design

The wider community
Community members – potential participants of the project
You – the project manager
Staff/Volunteers – not just those that will be involved in the delivery of the project
Management – your supervisor, for example
Funding bodies – those paying/supporting the project
Senior management/Trustees
Other professional bodies – other agencies and/or students that are involved in/supported by the project

Negotiation

Stakeholders can be involved in projects in a formal or informal way. Formal stakeholders include contracted partners and funders; informal are those outside of contractual obligations yet still benefit from the project. For example, a project at a school working specifically with special educational needs (SEN) students might have specific funding and formal involvement from key members of the school. However, other teachers, parents, other support groups might be informally involved through offering advice and guidance, resources, contacts or general support like attending a showcase of work completed. This, however, means there could be a variety of individuals involved with a range of different agendas and values, potentially leading to conflict; therefore, careful negotiation is needed. Negotiation happens at each stage of project management and is a constant aspect throughout. As such, a student can find themselves 'ping-ponging' between people to find the solution that makes all parties happy – a 'perfect' project plan. Of course, no 'perfect' project exists, and as such, negotiation is the key to getting the project to (and off) its starting blocks.

> *Despite agencies having the culture and desire to support young people's rights, some members of staff saw this as an additional duty rather than a fundamental aspect of working with young people in an ethical context. I found that workload, resources and individual staff member enthusiasm heavily affected the progress of participation opportunities and rights-based practice.*
>
> Linzi, Youth Work and Community Development

Negotiation is defined as '*a way to resolve conflicts and disagreements*' (Zohar, 2015, p 540). Negotiation is often misunderstood as making everyone happy; however, Adirondack (2005) suggests negotiation is more about recognising individual needs and interests and mutually agreeing on a solution. Negotiation is not about coercing a group to agree but is encouraging reasoned debate to reach an acceptable plan of moving forward. Additionally, negotiation does not just happen at the start of the project – good practitioners will constantly revisit negotiation, using skills such as patience and awareness, at several points throughout a project's life (McGuire, 2004). However, negotiation for students can feel like a battlefield, and fears such as being viewed as 'just a student' can cause students to not challenge inappropriate ideas or oppressive practice. Furthermore, students can become concerned about meeting learning outcomes of their academic work that can lead to students pushing their own agenda above others. Therefore, students will need to be honest in the aspects of their negotiation with all parties to make sure they balance their own voice in project management (Provis, 2004) with maintaining ethical standards (Ogden, 2018), demonstrating skills of flexibility and adaptability (Jeffs and Smiths, 2010) to respond to changes.

Needs analysis

Part of successful negotiation is effective planning (Rich, 2011). For projects to be effective, sufficient time is needed to plan the several stages of the project. Assessing need is an essential place to start but does not just happen at the start of the project and will often need revisiting. The World Health Organization (2020, p 314) defines a needs analysis as:

> *Needs assessment is the collection and analysis of information that relates to the needs of affected populations and that will help determine gaps between an agreed standard and the current situation.*

A needs analysis finds out what are the key issues affecting groups; for example, a needs analysis of a group of young carers might find that the key issues for that group are isolation – this then provides an evidence base for organisations to have clear aims and objectives and raise funds to run projects. An analysis of needs can be informal, but for projects, the inclusion of more formal practices (collection and presentation of data) can provide a more solid foundation for accessing resources to support the project and providing an evidence basis of why practitioners make certain decisions. Different voices can get lost in busy agendas and often agencies do not have the time or resources to conduct a needs analysis, where a student can (Walkington, 2015; Wilkinson et al., 2015). However, for some students their placement may have already undertaken research and students are directed to a specific project by supervisors or management.

Needs analysis is primarily a piece of research for the agency, and as such, ethical guidance should be carefully followed (Itulua-Abumere, 2012; D'Agata, 2008). The needs analysis might use focus groups with service users, management and/or workers to explore what they feel are useful projects for the student to undertake, or an examination of effectiveness of policy and working practices. This practice of needs analysis, while useful for negotiation and gaining funding, can often provide solutions to the identified needs (Ke, 2013). However, students should be aware that they are not expected to solve all the problems or respond to all the needs raised as information and recommendations can be left with the agency once the student moves on.

Impact of policy

An important factor that affects aims, needs analysis and negotiation is policy. Organisations are impacted by a range of laws, policies and guidance (such as codes of practice) that might be national, or indeed global, which inform local working policies. These policies can affect several aspects of your project, eg, safeguarding, lone working and health and safety. All of these can impact the direction, delivery and process of a project. For example, a student who wants to set up a mentoring programme at the local hospital to support young people with lifelong conditions will be impacted by the policies of the government and the hospital to make sure the project is safe. The project will need to consider location, for example, not going outside hospital grounds, and lone working. For a student on placement this adds an extra dimension that they may not be aware of, so they need to engage fully in the support mechanisms of placement to make sure they follow policy guidance.

In the context of agencies, access to resources and impact of policy might mean that a project cannot be run under a certain organisation (Brunetto and Farr-Wharton, 2003), which can lead to the organisation sharing resources and skills to maintain projects; this reinforces the need for effective communication. Policies should help frame a safe and supportive working space but can also feel constricting.

Different organisations will have differing ideas of what good project management looks like but this example from the Corby Borough Council Project Management Policy and Procedure document (2006, p 1) is fairly typical; it states that good project management includes:

> *moving towards tighter financial management, procurement, asset and risk management and setting and meeting targets for achieving priorities.*

While this is useful to highlight some careful practices, for some projects it can move away from a community-orientated project or needs analysis to producing bureaucratic outcomes and priorities, especially in terms of financial control. Some projects will naturally fit this approach, while others may not. An example of this would be health professionals seeking to increase the uptake of vaccinations in their local area – their project is two-fold. The first would be to provide direct information (leaflets etc) to encourage people to take the vaccine; this can be easily measured in response to policy guidance and easily meets priorities. The second aspect of the project is forming community health clubs allowing space for networking, conversation (especially around vaccines) and developing confidence in medical professionals. These 'softer' aspects are an equal part of the project; however, they are much more difficult to measure and transfer into terms of policy and meeting priorities. Students need to be aware of the shifting 'priorities' of government, local authorities, organisation and service users, recognising barriers and responding with adequate preparation, team building, knowledge sharing and negotiation to deal with potential conflict (Wang and Wu, 2020).

Theory of planning and delivery

Once evidence of a need for a project has been compiled and ideas been negotiated, students can then move to the next planning stages of the project. Stuart, Maynard and Rouncefield (2015) suggested that planning should consider:

- context influences (why is the project happening and with whom?);
- methods (the way the project will be delivered);
- evaluation (the way the project will be measured as successful);

- ethics (the 'right and wrongs' of the project);
- power (who has the power to affect outcomes, participation and other key aspects of the project).

Taking this theory and applying it to practice helps highlight some key stages of planning. For example, students may ask, 'what is the context of our work, and will that affect engagement and delivery? What methods will be used to deliver the project, and how will it be evaluated?' However, students need to balance time for each stage of this model and recognise that stages will need to be revisited. For example, a project planned in a hospital to raise awareness of young people's services will examine the context of the hospital, but also consider the context of young people (outside the hospital) – such as whether they are with family or carers and if this will, therefore, impact on the methods. Negotiation with service users etc could cause a change to methods to make sure projects remain ethical. Additionally, recognising the power and influence of organisations, staff and participants can facilitate changes to projects (Langdon and Agyeyomah, 2013). A difficulty is that students can become lost in planning to the point that nothing will ever be delivered. Therefore, students will need to find a point at which they decide to start the project, but still need to be flexible to respond to change and feedback (Nancarrow, 2015).

Often the need to respond quickly to issues can cause a conflict with planning, as time is not allowed to develop deep and critical thinking (Whelan, 2010). That is where planning models are useful as they can provide a mental framework for action taken by students. The more students 'practice' a model the more memorable it becomes. However, due to the vast array of planning theories and models that are present, students will need to find theories that support their specific practice, but make sure time is taken elsewhere (such as supervision) to reflect and challenge their thinking in planning (Allbutt et al., 2017; Wilkins et al., 2018). It is important that students remember there is no 'perfect' way of delivery, but instead they need to be confident and be able to evidence why they took certain actions, underpinning their work with theory (Veeramah, 2016; Mitchell, 2011; Barth et al., 2011).

Recognising and using resources

Too often students undertaking placement can feel pressured to 'show off' – after all it will be affecting their marks! (Gavin, 2014). However, the reality is that all practitioners are constantly learning and developing their practice through feedback from other staff, volunteers, service users and interprofessional working (Cabiati and Raineri, 2016, Misener, 2017). Chapter 9 has already debated in greater detail the resources of self and Chapter 7 has debated the values of supervision; Chapter 6 has applied theory to practice in challenging environments. Therefore, here, when considering projects, students need to take time to observe and recognise the value of these resources – self, environment, supervision – and how this adds to the project development. Supervisors should be a key development force in supporting reflection (Tomlin, Weatherson and Pavkov, 2013). However, students and practitioners must also be aware of maintaining ethical boundaries and working in a way that does not lead to abuse of those valuable resources or becoming dependent on them. Students need to make sure that they always reflect on their professional values and potential conflicts with the agency's agenda or their own personal values (Ramos et al., 2014).

Anti-oppressive framework

Working towards professional values means that students need to maintain an anti-oppressive framework; Chapter 4 has discussed this in more detail. As discussed, when planning projects, students need to maintain their negotiation skills and continue to revisit the stages of their planning while also recognising the value of the resources around them, to continually evaluate their project to make sure it is accessible and adapted to all those who are involved. This is key to anti-oppressive practice, and collaboration with the voice of individuals and groups is not a tick box, one-off exercise. Part of maintaining an anti-oppressive framework is the ongoing involvement of others, including staff, volunteers and members of the community; otherwise projects have a danger of becoming top-down in their approach and can often fail as they do not meet the needs of the service users. However, to listen effectively takes time (Sutterfield et al., 2006; McLeod, 2007). Chapter 11 discusses involving and learning from others in detail.

I was working with two young people who had not worked well together before and had been excluded from schools. During a forest school session, we were working with knives and whittling away at some sticks to make into Thor's Hammer. One of the boys put his knife on the ground, in between the two of them. Another colleague then said, 'look at that, both of you boys are sat near each other, both using knives – and no one has stabbed anyone! Surely that can go as a positive outcome for you both!'

I felt that it showed that without an audience and without the pressures of conforming to society, they were just two boys sitting creating tools. Not two boys with reputations for violence and aggression, having been excluded from schools or having to be the man of the house. Just two boys. It shows how powerful and important these projects can be, and therefore the need to take the management of these projects seriously.

Ed, Youth Work and Community Development

Sometimes, anti-oppressive practice is a recognition of barriers to involvement such as disabilities, but it is also about challenging institutional oppression. Therefore, working anti-oppressively, students will sometimes need to challenge practice within organisations when managing projects (Collins, 2010), but they can also feel intimidated thinking that challenging practice will be viewed negatively and potentially affect their grade; however, placement agencies often seek students to challenge their practice as students encourage agencies to rethink working practices, supported by recent theory. An example of this is shown in my own experience on placement in a youth work setting. The young people choose what music was being played in the background, but in one session a young person played a song which encouraged sexual violence against women. I was really surprised that the lead worker allowed this and did not challenge this situation. I feared to raise this, as I thought it would affect my grade, but also knew I could not leave it unchallenged. I accessed the support of my academic tutor who talked me through how to challenge the situation and I was able to raise the issue constructively in a supervision. Overall, all practitioners need to remember that to not challenge oppressive practice is to support oppressive practice (Hafford-Letchfield and Cocker, 2014).

Current staff and volunteers

This chapter has already focused on the wide array of people needed to be negotiated with for project management, but here it will focus on existing staff and volunteers within an agency. Students on placement will work with people who are employed or who volunteer with the service or agency. These individuals can be an essential resource, from their base of knowledge, relationships with service users as well as their experience. This can be intimidating to students, but additionally existing staff and volunteers might also feel intimidated by students, who bring with them recent knowledge and a critical approach to practice. This could cause a sense of rivalry between staff and students. Therefore, students need to rely on their communication skills and make sure they let others know about their role and remit within the agency. Unfortunately, while students often expect that managers will let everyone know a student has started and the requirements of the placement, this does not always get transferred to other staff and rarely to volunteers. However, co-learning with existing staff and volunteers is always much better when the supervisor has explained to staff the student's role and engaged in negotiation with staff about hosting the student. This provides greater potential for co-learning, sometimes encouraging staff to take on higher qualifications and training, as well as more mutual informal learning, ideally replicating the university experience of students (Bovill, 2019; Le, Janssen and Wubbels, 2017). To make a successful co-learning experience, Bovill, Jarvis and Smith (2020, p 31) suggest the following are needed:

Shared goals

Shared decisions

Negotiation

Valuing student perspectives

Shared respect

Shared responsibility

Reciprocity

Bovill, Jarvis and Smith's (2020) work is based on students studying in university, but it can be applied also to placement. Developing these key elements, however, can take time and preparation and may need revisiting at different times throughout the placement.

Some of the worst experiences for students have been when they have been 'palmed off' to other members of staff, who do not know them or their reason for being there. However, this sits outside of the students' control and if this situation does appear, students will need to manage the situation by working through Bovill, Jarvis and Smith's (2020) ideas on their own to reach a stage of co-learning. For example, a student will need to set out to existing staff and volunteers their goals, but show how their goals also support the workers and agency, demonstrate negotiation by encouraging existing staff and volunteers to be part of projects, and be willing to go back and forth, adapt and change in response to existing staff and volunteers' experience and advice.

Evaluation and monitoring

Planning for the end of projects is often overlooked, yet it is as vital as all other stages. Abma (2006) suggests that effective evaluation is 'Responsive Evaluation' which focuses beyond outcomes for funders, but considers all parties involved in the project being sensitive to power relations. Putting this theory into practice requires students to be responsive to the audience of their evaluations; as such, students will need to consider using different methods to collect feedback, but also collect information that goes beyond meeting the outcomes (potentially planning for the next project). This will enable students to demonstrate skills, such as creativity for effective evaluation. Sadly, due to ineffective planning, evaluations end up using formats that are not suitable for respondents and do not collect effective data on developing next stages. Effective evaluation can be both formal (eg questionnaires) and informal (eg conversations) in its collection of feedback. To gather the wide range of data, a range of evaluation methods should be used. Additionally, service users need to be aware and involved in evaluation processes to be able to support the process. This will happen if service users have been involved in each step from the beginning, as allowing service users to be equally invested in the outcomes of the project (Fox, Grimm and Calderia, 2017; Omeni et al., 2014).

Effective evaluation is paired with effective monitoring – the systematic feedback loop as the project is ongoing. Effective monitoring enables evaluation methods to become a normal and active part of the project, rather than a final chore of the project. Reading the data of these evaluations should also use the range of people involved in projects to gain a fuller understanding.

I reiterated to staff the importance of young people having the opportunity to input into service delivery and improvements. As a result of the autonomy afforded to me within my

> *placement, I was able to instil opportunities, processes and policies that will outlive my placement.*
>
> Linzi, Youth Work and Community Development

Localisms and cultural speak can cause misunderstanding in the information, but a range of people, professionals and methods allow for a greater understanding of the effectiveness of projects; additionally, this collaborative evaluation allows individuals to develop their own skill set (Bovill et al., 2009).

Reporting outcomes

Project managers need to present evidence of the effectiveness of their project both formally and informally. For example:

- Formal – funding report using a required format
- Informal – Individuals sharing their success and participation in the project to their social networks, such as posting photos or a story on the services website

Adirondack (2005) suggests that we might need to communicate our results to groups of people such as trustees, managers, young people and the wider community. With a range of different audiences, a range of different communication methods are needed.

> *Good communication ... is provided in accessible formats and language, and that papers are circulated in good time for people to properly consider their response. (Gilchrist, 2003, p 28)*

Although this might seem obvious, project managers often get very busy with delivery and do not plan to communicate effectively for the end of projects; as such, this is done unsatisfactorily often requiring additional work. Applying what Gilchrist (2003) indicates, it is important for project managers to consider how they communicate the end of the project in their initial planning, which includes a recognition of whom the information is being shared with. Information can be presented in a variety of ways including written, verbal and other creative methods; however, information may need altering to keep confidentiality depending on the audience. Additionally, where the information can be found needs careful consideration, for example, if the information is freely available to all online or requires a secure location. Often effective IT skills are needed at this stage, highlighting the need for effective planning.

Conclusion

Project management encompasses a range of skills and attributes for students to develop. It allows opportunities for individuals and communities to become more involved in the situations affecting their lives. Clear analysis of needs, aims and objects is required if a project is to achieve what it has set out to do. If not managed well, projects can become oppressive and ignore the people they are intended to support. Thus, effectively managing projects is not reliant on a single individual but includes a cohesive working with individuals, communities and professionals to collectively respond, evaluate and define next steps, acknowledging the impact of service users, communities and policy which informs the scope and approach of a project. Theory of planning can be effective in helping develop a project, recognising resources and maintaining anti-oppressive practice, but all stages of the project need careful consideration, including the end of the project. Ongoing monitoring and negotiation are, therefore, an essential component of any successful project.

References

Abma, T (2006) The Practice and Politics of Responsive Evaluation. *American Journal of Evaluation*, 27(1):31–43.

Adirondack, S (2005) *Just about Managing*. 4th ed. London: Voluntary Service Council.

Allbutt, H, Colthard, I, El-Farargy, N, Sturgeon, C, Vallis, J and Lough, M (2017) Understanding Supervision in Health and Social Care through the Experiences of Practitioners in Scotland. *Journal of Integrated Care*, 25(2):120–30.

Barth, R, Greeson, J, Zlotnik, S and Chintapalli, L (2011) Evidence-Based Practice for Youth in Supervised Out-of-Home Care: A Framework for Development, Definition and Evaluation. *Journal of Evidence-Based Social Work*, 8(5):501–28.

Bovill, C (2019) Co-creation in Learning and Teaching: The Case for a Whole-Class Approach in Higher Education. *Journal of Higher Education*, 79:1023–37.

Bovill, C, Aitken, G, Hutchison, J, Morrison, F, Roseweir, K, Scott, A and Sotannde, S (2009) Experiences of Learning through Collaborative Evaluation from a Masters Programme in Professional Education. *International Journal for Academic Development*, 15(2):143–54.

Bovill, C, Jarvis, J and Smith, K (2020) *Co-creating Learning and Teaching: Towards Relational Pedagogy in Higher Education*. St Albans: Critical Publishing.

Brunetto, Y and Farr Wharton, R (2003) The Impact of Government Practice on the Ability of Project Managers to Manage. *International Journal of Project Management*, 21(2):125–33.

Cabiati, E and Raineri, M (2016) Learning from Service Users' involvement. *The international Journal of Social Work Education*, 35(8):982–96.

Collins, S (2010). Anti-Oppressive Practice and Social Work Students' Portfolios in Scotland. *Social Work Education*, 29(7):760–77.

Corby Borough Council (2006) Project Management Policy and Procedure. Available at: https://www.corby.gov.uk/sites/default/files/Overview%20_%20Scrutiny%20Panel.28-Mar-07.Project%20Management%20Policy%20and%20Procedure%20-%20Appendix%201.pdf (accessed 09 December 2021).

D'Agata, M (2008) Ethics: Contemporary Challenges in Health and Social Care. *International journal of Integrated Care*, 8(1).

Fox, C, Grimm, R, and Calderia, R (2017) An Introduction to Evaluation. *Nurse Education Today*, 26(7):564–71.

Gavin, J (2014) Placement Experience and Learning Motivations in Higher Education. *Journal of Applied Research in Higher Education*, 8(3):302–15.

Gilchrist, R (2003) Linking Partnerships and Networks, in Banks, S, Butcher, H, Orton, A and Robertson, J. *Managing Community Practice*. 2nd ed. Bristol: Policy Press.

Hafford-Letchfield, T and Cocker, C (2014) *Rethinking Anti-Discriminatory and Anti-Oppressive Theories for Social Work Practice*. London: Palgrave.

Hulley S, Cummings S, Browner W, Grady, D and Newman, T (2013) *Designing Clinical Research*. 4th ed. Philadelphia: Lippincott Williams and Wilkins.

Itulua-Abumere, F (2012) Ethical Issues in Health and Social Care Profession. *Journal of Humanities and Social Science*, 5(6):14–18.

Jeffs, T and Smith, M (2010) *Youth Work Practice*. London: Palgrave Macmillan.

Ke, C (2013) Research on Optimized Problem-Solving Solutions. *Journal of Applied Research and Technology*, 11(4):523–32.

Langdon, J and Agyeyoma, C (2013) Critical Hyper-Reflexivity and Challenging Power: Pushing Past the Dichotomy of Employability a Good Global Citizenship in Development Studies Experiential Learning Contexts, in Tiessen, R and Huish, R. *Globetrotting or Global Citizenship: Perils and Potential of International Experiential Learning*. London: Toronto Press.

Le, H, Janssen, J, and Wubbels, T (2017) Collaborative Learning Practices: Teacher and Student Perceived Obstacles to Effective Student Collaboration. *Cambridge Journal of Education*, 48(1):103–22.

McGuire, R (2004) Negotiation: An Important Life Skill. *The Pharmaceutical Journal*, 273:23–25.

McLeod, A (2007) Whose Agenda? Issues of Power and Relationship When Listening to Looked-After Young People. *Child & Family Social Work*, 12(3):278–86.

Misener, K (2017) Learning from the Experiences of Older Adult Volunteers in Sport. *Journal of Leisure Research*, 42(2):267–89.

Mitchell, P (2011) Evidence-Based Practice in Real-World Services for Young People with Complex Needs: New Opportunities Suggested by Recent Implementation Science. *Children and Youth Services Review*, 33(2):207–16.

Nancarrow, S (2015) Six Principles to Enhance Health Workforce Flexibility. *Human Resources for Health*, 13(9).

Ogden, J (2018) When do Negotiation Tactics Become Unethical? *Southern Journal of Business and Ethics*, 10:98–114.

Omeni, E, Barnes, M, MacDonald, D, Crawford, M and Rose, D (2014) Service User Involvement: Impact and Participation: A Survey of Service User and Staff Perspectives. *BMC Health Services Research*, 14(491):1–13.

Provis, C (2004) Honesty in Negotiation. *Business Ethics A European Review*, 9(1):3–12.

Ramos, F, Brehmer, L, Varga, M, Trombetta, A, Silveira, L and Drago, L (2014). Ethical Conflicts and the Process of Reflection in Undergraduate Nursing Students in Brazil. *Nursing Ethics*, 22(4):428–39.

Rich, C (2011) Successful Negotiation is 80 Percent Preparation. *Strategic Direction*, 27(3):3–5.

Sapin, K (2009) *Essential Skills for Youth Work Practice*. London: Sage.

Simmons, R, Birchall, J and Prout, A, (2011) User Involvement in Public Services: 'Choice about Voice'. *Public Policy and Administration*, 27(1):3–29.

Stuart, K, Maynard, L and Rouncefield, C (2015) *Evaluating Practice for Projects with Young People: A Guide to Creative Research*. London: Sage.

Sutterfield, J, Friday-Stroud, S and Shivers-Blackwell, L (2006) A Case Study of Project and Stakeholder Management Failures: Lessons Learned. *Project Management Journal*, 37(5):26–35.

Thomas, D and Hodges, I (2010) *Designing and Managing Your Research Project: Core Skills for Social and Health Research*. London: Sage.

Tomlin, A, Weatherson, D and Pavkov, T (2013) Critical Components of Reflective Supervision: Responses from Expert Supervisors in the Field. *Infant Mental Health Journal*, 41(2):166–77.

Veeramah, V (2016) The Use of Evidenced-Based Information by Nurses and Midwives to Inform Practice. *Journal of Clinical Nursing*, 25(3–4):340–50.

Walkington, H (2015) *Students as Researchers: Supporting Undergraduate Research in the Disciplines in Higher Education*. Available at: www.heacademy.ac.uk/system/files/resources/Students%20as%20researchers_1.pdf (accessed 07 April 2020).

Wang, N and Wu, G (2020) A Systematic Approach to Effective Conflict Management for Program. *Journal Indexing and Metrics*, 10(1):1–15.

Webster, G (2004) Sustaining Community Involvement in Programme and Project Development, in Banks, S, Butcher, H, Henderson, P and Roberston, J. *Managing Community Practice*. Bristol: Policy Press.

Whelan, M (2010) Detached Youth Work, in Batsleer, J and Davies, B. *What Is Youth Work*. London: Sage.

Wilkins, D, Khan, M, Stabler, L, Newlands, F and McDonnell, J (2018) Evaluating the Quality of Social Work Supervision in UK Children's Services. *Clinical Social Work Journal*, 46:350–60.

Wilkinson, A, Gollan, P, Kalfa, S and Xu, C (2015) Management: Voices Unheard? *The International Journal of Human Resource Management*, 26(14):1913–15.

World Health Organization (2020) *The Health Cluster Guide*. 2nd ed. Available at: https://www.who.int/health-cluster/resources/publications/hc-guide/en/ (accessed 23 April 2021).

Zohar, I (2015) The Art of Negotiation. *Procedia – Social and Behavioural Science*, 209:540–48.

13 Measuring impact
Tim Rosier

Introduction

In recent decades, the health and social care sector has transformed into a mixed market with services provided by public sector bodies, charities, private companies and social enterprises. The marketisation of the sector has increased the focus on 'targeted' programmes being tendered out, with payment-by-results mechanisms and 'delivery partnerships' reducing the risk and costs to the state. Students in health and social care are much more likely to be on placement in organisations outside of the public sector than just a few years ago and required to develop multiple relationships with stakeholders across the public–private sector continuum. Whether undertaking a placement in a frontline role or management position, students will need to contribute in some way to gathering data to help measure and demonstrate impact – a key feature of the marketised sector. Therefore, students need to be able to develop an understanding of the mixed market landscape and the sophisticated toolbox available for measuring impact and apply their theoretical knowledge to these practical realities.

This chapter discusses:

- The history and nature of the mixed market, and how neoliberalism combined with managerialism has created the marketised sector in which public services now operate

- The ethical challenges likely to be faced by students when balancing professional values with the realities of working in this landscape

- Creative and participatory methods of evaluation underpinned by the principles of evidence-based practice

- A range of quantitative and qualitative data gathering tools for use on the front line

The historical context of the mixed market approach to delivering public services

It is helpful for students on placement to have an appreciation of the historical landscape to fully understand the current and future policy influences, wider management responses, likely ethical and practical challenges and the expected impact on those with whom they are working (Table 13.1). For over a century, the health and social care sector has navigated its way through several development phases. Each of these has shaped the subsequent political and funding landscape and contributed to today's market-driven system.

The hallmarks and nature of the mixed market economy

Over the last 40 years, public services have gradually been opened up to free-market forces which has led to the contraction of the public sector and the increase of private and voluntary sector organisations delivering services through complex supply chains of tiered providers (Hood, 1991; Dorey, 2015; Lawler and Hearn, 1995; De st Croix, Mcgimpsey and Owens, 2019). The shift towards mixed market delivery gave rise to a radical new paradigm in public service delivery known as New Public Management (NPM) (Clarke, Gerwitz and McLaughlin, 2000; Diefenbach, 2009). NPM draws on the ideas, processes and techniques of the private sector and imposes them *carte blanche* on the public sector with the sole aim of making public services more business-like in driving greater efficiency, facilitating decentralisation, searching for continued excellence and focusing on public service orientation (Ferlie et al., 1996; Ward, 2011; George, 2017).

Advocates of NPM theory suggest there are ten key principles to this approach (see Table 13.2), including demonstrating your impact and being allocated resources based on results. The outworking of NPM theory is underpinned by two key ideological pillars: *marketisation* (or neoliberalism) and *managerialism* (De Vries, and Nemec, 2013; Shepherd, 2018). Marketisation is primarily concerned with economics while managerialism focuses on managerial techniques and holds that all problems have managerial solutions (Klikauer, 2015). Neoliberal ideas are implemented through the 'organisational glue' of managerialism resulting in NPM practice (Clarke, 2004; Hood, 1991). This two-pillar model provides a helpful framework for students on placement to gain an understanding of the theoretical underpinnings of the political landscape in which they will be practising. These are explored in more detail below.

Table 13.1 Historical context timeline

1760–1840	Industrial Revolution	Urbanisation, the erosion of close family support structures and the impact of poor working conditions, long hours and child labour led to greater health and social care issues. Unprecedented economic boom but lack of commensurate health and social care provision
1837–1914	Victorian and Edwardian philanthropy	The response to the Industrial Revolution led by wealthy business owners looking for opportunities to offload some of their wealth to philanthropic and religious organisations concerned with social issues
1914–45	World Wars I and II	Much of the nation's resources were ploughed into fighting the war efforts, leaving the country almost broke
1942–79	Big government – welfare state	Rise of the welfare state in response to the economic and social fallout from World War II, based on the principles of equal opportunity, equitable distribution of wealth and public responsibility for citizens unable to provide a minimum standard of living for themselves – Beveridge Report (1942)
1979–97	Big capitalism – small government	Watershed moment in response to discontent and struggles of the 1960s and 1970s. Contraction of government control and increase in privatisation of public assets and services. Promotion of New Public Management paradigm
1997–2010	Civic renewal – the 'Third Way'	A shift to the Centre Ground led to marrying together the ideas of a competitive society and successful economy with a just and decent society
2010–16	Austerity and the Big Society	Contraction in government shouldering the burden for funding public services during austerity following the global banking crisis. Promotion of society taking more responsibility for local public services through community empowerment, localism, social action and voluntarism
2016–19	Shared society and social financing	Increase in the development of social financing to 'harness the full potential' of charities and social enterprises in the delivery of public services
2019–	Post-Brexit, the end to austerity and the impact of Covid-19	The spending taps in a Post-Brexit Britain turned on fully, marking the end of the age of austerity. Within weeks, the global Covid-19 pandemic causes a sudden and devastating impact on national finances as the government returned to huge state control and financing of public services and businesses (big government). Start of a new period of uncertainty and possible austerity

Table 13.2 Ten principles of New Public Management theory (Osborne and Gaebler, 1992)

1. Governments should 'steer', not directly deliver, public services
2. Community-owned services – empower citizens towards self-governance
3. Competition is inherently good
4. Governments should be driven by their mission, not constrained by their rules
5. Judged on results (impact)
6. Choice is of highest value – citizens are *consumers* of public goods and *customers* of public service
7. Resources should be earned through demonstrating value (payment by results)
8. Public agencies concerned with prevention rather than cure – 'upstreaming'
9. Maximise participation in decision-making processes
10. Leveraging of market forces and strategies to fund services is to be encouraged

Keep an eye out for where theory links into your professional practice. You'll be surprised at how often your instinct on how to approach projects and challenges is a tried and tested foundation of health and social care practice. This gives you an opportunity to analyse your practice more critically, and use more in-depth sources to deal with the more tricky areas experienced on the front line.

Jo, Youth Work and Community Development

Measuring impact with integrity – some ethical considerations

There is now greater emphasis on the moral authority of practitioners and managers in the health and social care sector to make key decisions that balance upholding professional (and personal) values on the one hand and maintaining service delivery on the other (Jeffs and Smith in Banks, 2010).

I would recommend that you consider your red lines before they are crossed. Take a step back and look at your practice objectively and ask yourself what things clash with your professional values. How can you maintain a sense of balance between your professional values and the pressures from the context you are working in?

Natalya, Social Work

This balancing act can be described as 'principled pragmatism', recognising that the ideals of both extremes are often incongruent and require a creative and nuanced approach to finding a pragmatic way forward (Snyder and Vinjamuri, 2012). As a student on placement,

Table 13.3 Characteristics of New Public Management – two-pillar model

Pillar 1 – Neoliberalism (Marketisation)	Pillar 2 – Managerialism
Guiding principle: the free-market is the best mechanism to manage financial resources	**Guiding principle: management itself provides solutions to organisational problems**
The introduction of market-type mechanisms and competition	The adoption of a more business-like approach and private sector practices
The commodification of services	The establishment of a management culture
A focus on value for money and doing more with less (ie efficiency)	A rational approach to management (eg strategic planning and objective setting)
Central regulation and/or control	A strengthening of the line management function (eg performance management)
The adoption of an entrepreneurial culture	Adoption of human resource management techniques to secure employee commitment
A shift of priorities from universalism to individualism	A shift from inputs and processes to outputs and outcomes
An emphasis on service quality and consumer orientation and choice	More measurement and quantification of outputs (eg performance indicators)
Greater flexibility of pay and conditions	
The growth of contractual relationships (eg purchaser–provider)	
A blurring of public–private sector boundaries and increased scope for private sector provision	

Sources: Diefenbach (2009); Ferlie et al. (1996); Hood (1991); Pollitt (2003); Ranson and Stewart (1994), cited in Shepherd (2018).

it is good practice to critically reflect on the ethical and practical challenges that are likely to arise and consider how you might respond to them in a principled yet pragmatic way.

McCulloch and Tett's (2010) organisational climates for professional practice model helps students on placement consider the extremes and tensions that might arise between organisational bureaucracy and staying true to one's professional values and desire to practise with integrity (Figure 13.1).

Organisational climates for professional practice model (McCulloch and Tett, 2010)

Below are some examples of key ethical considerations which students are likely to face while on placement. These can be considered more carefully by using McCulloch and Tett's (2010) model as a tool for reflection.

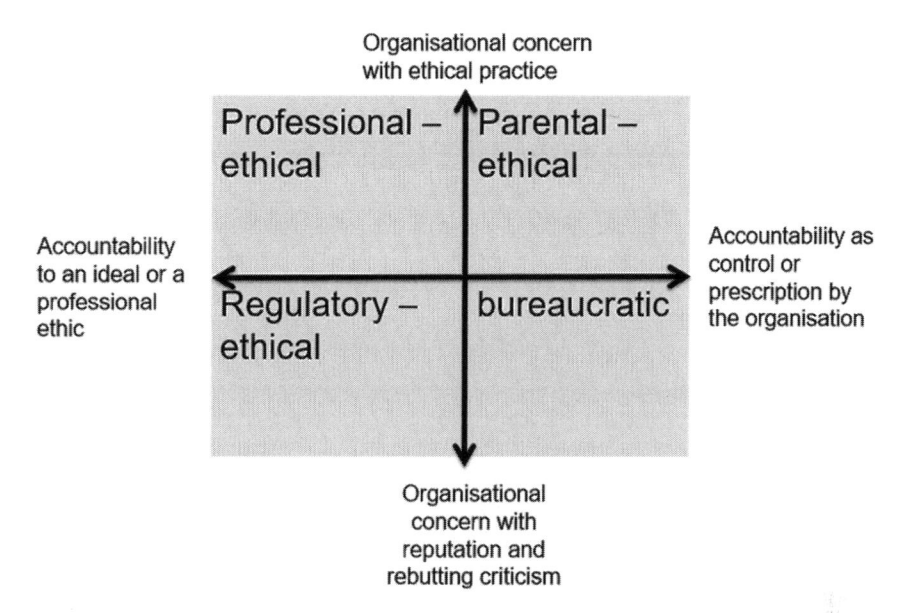

Figure 13.1 Organisational climates for professional practice model (McCulloch and Tett, 2010)

Top-down decision-making

One of the defining features of managerialism is the top-down nature of decision-making which often grates with the bottom-up informality and person-centred approaches traditionally adopted by our sector (Dart, 2004, cited in Doherty et al., 2014; Arbuckle, 2012). Predetermined outcomes and regulation systems required by management may mirror what is deemed to be required by funders and commissioners. However, these often clash with the frontline priorities of effective relationship building with service users and needs-led/patient-centred work commonplace in health and social care (Jones, 2012; George, 2017; Hampson and Howell, 2018). Students on placement can strengthen and champion ways of better hearing and listening to the voices and needs of service users as part of the organisation's strategic decision-making. This may require appropriately challenging processes within supervision structures or bringing fresh perspectives to practice through idea forums and departmental meetings. In ensuring this process is non-tokenistic and effective, the trust, confidence and strength of user-centred relationship can actually be enhanced (Hart, 1991).

Engaging appropriate funding streams

Marketisation has led to the need for small and medium-sized organisations to engage funding from multiple funding streams. As a student on placement, it is important to consider whether certain types of funding engaged by the agency are ethically cogent with the values of your profession (Jeffs and Smith, 2010) and relevant to the mission of the organisation (Ord, 2012). For example, accepting corporate sponsorship in exchange for promoting certain brands that contradict the organisation's ethos or drawing on money gained from investments that have negative health or environmental consequences raise difficult questions. The debate around whether National Lottery funding is acceptable for work with certain people is particularly troublesome for some faith-based organisations with their religious positions around gambling (Tondeur, 1996). The constant demand to seek available funding can lead to organisations experiencing 'mission drift' where they chase the money at the expense of organisational clarity (Ord, 2012). Students on placement can instigate or participate in fund-raising initiatives that better reflect the values and principles of their particular profession. For students with a management focus to their placements, discussions with their supervisor around scoping alternative, more ethical and relevant sources of funding can form the basis of a reflexive and impactful management learning project.

Collaboration vs competition

One of the greatest challenges created by marketisation and managerialism is the damage to the quality of human relationships and interactions, which is the bedrock of work within the health and social care sector. Operating in the free market often requires organisations to *compete* for funding rather than *collaborate* around health or social needs. This can lead to a breakdown of trust and collegiality between services who traditionally tended to work together (McCabe and Sambrook, 2019). This is especially problematic for those with multiple and complex needs who often require long-term engagement. Students on placement can sometimes feel like they are put in a difficult position relationally, particularly when there may be other students on placement with competing organisations. Drawing on theoretical knowledge around effective interprofessional working can help manage these tensions. Chapter 10 covers this in more detail.

The datafication of people

The involvement of service users in gathering and providing data to demonstrate impact required to support funding bids has led to dehumanising practices and the datafication of people (De St Croix, 2018; De St Croix, 2016), thereby undermining the holistic focus of health and social care work. This, according to some, has irrevocably damaged some organisations to the core (George, 2017). Some research methods are arguably exploitative and deskilling of their subjects (Packham, 2000) and rather than being seen as part of the essential toolbox to inform analysis to enable ethical practice (D'Cruz and Jones, 2004) can actually lead to a narrowing down of both the groups we work with and the methods used. Furthermore, state influence can often lead to practitioners fishing for 'policy-based evidence' based on the significant number of programmes driven by political ideology rather than the evidence base itself (Bradford and Cullen, 2012). For students on placement, there are considerable opportunities to bring fresh perspectives and creative ideas to measuring impact which can disrupt the preferred ways of working. For example, engaging more qualitative, storytelling methodology which involves practitioners and services users engaging in collective reflections around their lived experiences can capture rich data while not being constrained by the rigid belief that impact is always linear, formulaic or predictable (de st Croix, 2017; Knox and Cooper, 2014; Ord, 2016). Examples of more creative impact measurement tools are discussed in more detail below.

Attributing impact

Within the interprofessional sector of health and social care, it is very difficult to demonstrate agency contribution and ownership of outcomes and impact when multiple agencies have been involved. Ord (2016) argues that human development is a non-linear process rather than a direct correlation between input and outcome. While workers may provide specific interventions for specific needs (eg supporting breast-feeding), often programmes work with complex, multiple factors and interventions leading to success. The reality is that most outcomes are developed through and over time. Asthana and Halliday (2006) describe this latency effect in health-based interventions, but this is also true when discussing the impact of many other health and social care interventions in multi-professional contexts where the pressure for linear outcomes in the process of multiple relationships is deeply problematic (Taylor, 2017). For students on placement, this tension is impossible to overcome and therefore requires them to reflect on ways to live with it while seeking not to undersell their input and influence.

Evidence-based practice

While on placement, it is helpful for students to develop their knowledge of the different types of evidence that contribute to measuring impact and become familiar with the different monitoring and evaluation strategies and tools available to measure different outcomes. Evidence-based practice (EBP) can improve professional practice within health and social care through engaging with scientific research evidence that engages a more methodical approach to capturing and interpreting data (Lilienfeld and Basterfield, 2020; Newell and Burnard, 2010). As a student on placement, a commitment to EBP ensures equilibrium between maintenance of professional values in practice and improved outcomes for service users on the one hand, and increased credibility and accountability of services and enhanced cost effectiveness to commissioners on the other (Barnard, 2011).

Types of evidence and rationale for measuring

Any measurement strategy should address the following considerations (Royal National Institute for the Blind [RNIB], 2014):

Who? Which *people* will you be engaging to capture evidence? This includes hearing the voice of the service user (see Chapter 11).

What? Understanding the *prose* of what you are measuring. What do you need to measure, and what metrics will you be using to do it? This includes knowing the different evidence types and comparators available.

Why? What is the *purpose* of the different things you will measure? There are four key purposes of measuring outcomes and impact.

1. *A decision tool* – a focus on impact enables organisations to improve their strategic and operational decisions in line with organisational strategy and project objectives. Decisions about which services to maintain, change, expand or reduce should strongly consider evidence of which activities are creating changes in the lives of beneficiaries.

2. *A persuasion tool* – impact can demonstrate a track record of producing real change in the lives of people and the continual improvement of services over time. Providing clear evidence of impact can persuade new funders and supporters to invest.

3. *An accountability tool* – evidence of impact helps maintain strong relations with internal and external stakeholders by providing them with assurance that their money and support are being used well.

4. *A communication tool* – describing key sector-specific issues in terms of non-specific outcomes such as quality of life and social inclusion can enable understanding for all audiences.

When? What is the *pace* of your measurement? Understanding the difference between short- and long-term evidence, as well as the sequencing, timing and scheduling of it. Students will find management tools such as Ganntt charts and milestone structures helpful in managing these processes.

How? The following subsections outline some of the different tools available to help students measure and consider their impact.

It is helpful for students to recognise that capturing data involves more than just statistics. Opportunities for collective and creative engagement can not only build the relational element of our work with service users, but also add a depth to the overall assessment and presentation of our impact. These forms of evaluation can be broken down into two categories: quantitative and qualitative.

Quantitative evaluation

Quantitative research methods and measurement tools have dominated the health sector in particular for many years (Newell and Burnard, 2010). With a focus on the extent of a particular issue and the explanation of causes, quantitative data is statistical and extensive and used to deduce the level of impact in a linear and logical fashion (Vazquez-Navarrete, 2009).

Below are some examples of different quantitative tools available to students for use within the health and social care sector.

Tool name	Description
Warwick-Edinburgh Mental Wellbeing Scale (WEMWBS) University of Warwick (2006)	An academically developed and tested 14-item scale with five response categories covering various aspects of mental well-being. It is validated for use across the UK with those aged 16+.
Office for National Statistics well-being questions ONS (2018)	Since 2011, the Office for National Statistics (ONS) has included four questions about personal well-being in the Annual Population Survey. Because ONS asks these questions of large samples in the general population, there is good comparison data to compare your clients against.
Rosenberg Self-Esteem Scale (RSES) Rosenberg (1965)	RSES is a ten-item scale with four response options, measuring feelings of self-worth and self-acceptance, using positive and negative statements about the self.
General Self-Efficacy Scale Schwarzer and Jerusalem (1995)	The General Self-Efficacy Scale assesses respondents' sense of *self-efficacy* – their self-belief and perceived ability to cope with daily hassles and adapt to stressful life events. When used before and after an intervention, it can be used to assess change.
Duckworth et al.'s Short Grit Scale Duckworth et al. (2007)	The Grit Scale measures *perseverance* and *self-control* – the ability to sustain interest towards long-term goals, and the voluntary regulation of impulses.

Tool name	Description
The You Ladder Callaghan (undated)	The You Ladder is a basic, adaptable tool that asks clients to assign a 'rung' rating in two key outcome areas – originally housing and drug use – and give a reason for any change in ratings at repeat readings. The tool provides a useful visual way of engaging with clients about their progress.
Outcomes Star(s)	The Outcomes Star is a flexible approach to measuring distance travelled in a wide range of different outcome areas. Bespoke outcomes stars, such as the Family Star (Burns and MacKeith, 2013), can be developed to suit a particular programme or activity. Users judge their position along a series of ten-point scales in discussion with a key worker. Repeated readings are taken to track progress.
The Rickter Scale Hutchinson and Stead (1994)	The Rickter Scale is a method of measurement designed for work with young offenders, but customisable to a wide range of areas. The method consists of a physical grid with ten outcome areas and magnetic sliding scorers, which are controlled by the client. Various overlays can be ordered or customised to cover different outcomes.

Qualitative evaluation

In contrast to quantitative tools, qualitative measurement tools have a focus on people's perceptions of their situations and how change has happened over time. Qualitative evaluation can take place with individuals or groups and is about creating trustworthy yet nuanced methods to capture the lived experience of service users of a programme, project or intervention. Bringing fresh and new perspectives to the organisation, students on placement can reinvigorate potentially tired and ineffective approaches to evaluation. With the contribution of new, creative and more engaging ideas, service users' engagement may increase, thereby providing more comprehensive and reliable results (Stuart, Maynard and Rouncefield, 2015).

Below are some examples of different qualitative methods available to students to use while on practice.

Likert scales

Likert scales are useful for measuring degrees of intensity of feeling or perception, where participants score something on a range. This tool is best supported by open questions to understand why an individual chose a particular score (Brace, 2013).

Semi-structured Interviews

Semi-structured interviews follow a general plan with pre-tested questions and prompts. They can explore the answers through follow-up questions based on issues raised by respondents using prompts and probes and use the practitioner initiative to pick up, explore and record additional information (Alston and Bowles, 2013).

Focus groups

Focus groups facilitate discussion among a selected group of individuals about specific topics or issues, most commonly presented as a set of questions, although sometimes as a film, a collection of advertisements, cards to sort, a game to play or a vignette to discuss (Beck, Trombetta and Share, 1986; Wilkinson, 1998).

Case studies

A case study examines one 'case in a context' (Cohen, Manion and Morrison, 2018) and the extent to which a phenomenon within its context comes at the expense of generalisability

(Thomas, 2017). Case studies enable understanding of how participants see and make sense of their world (Yin, 2014), focusing on both actions taken and meanings given to them (McCulloch, 2007).

The advantage of the methods outlined above is that they can be adapted or developed to best fit a particular context or situation. Students on placement can make each of these methods more engaging and stimulating by adopting or adapting some of the creative tools below.

Tool name	Description	Research method used
Digital	Digital polls and apps	Surveys
Graffiti wall	Using Post-it notes or whiteboard pens, write your comments and feedback on a programme	Structured interviews/ focus groups
Flash cards	Select a flash card to describe how you feel about a service and explain why. They could be emojis, facial expressions, weather cards or more random abstract post cards	Structured interviews
Verbal games	Wish and a star, traffic lights, bin it keep it – allows participants to review the strengths and weaknesses of an intervention	Structured interviews
Values line	Read out statements with agree and disagree at opposite ends of the room. Ask the group to stand where they feel and discuss their perspective	Likert scale, structured interviews
Annotated art work	Use art material to try or annotate an experience of a service and talk through symbolism and meaning of art	Case study

Dissemination of data

Part of a programme, project or intervention ending well relates to the effective dissemination of evaluation results and communication of impact. By working with service users, students on placement can identify new or potential target audiences and use a range of formats beyond the traditional formal written report (Shaw, Brady and Davey, 2011). Students could develop a web page on the project or text for a blog, contribute to press releases, design posters for the benefit of the wider community, give presentations at community meetings, conferences or seminars, or find an experiential way to share findings at a fun day or community event. In doing so, students on placement can contribute to a greater impact for the individual and organisation by capitalising on the opportunity to develop and apply additional skills gained through their professional study as part of their wider learning journey.

Conclusion

This chapter has examined the history and nature of the mixed market and how the highly competitive and marketised political landscape shapes the delivery of health and social care services. It has also considered some of the ethical issues faced by practitioners working within this sector and how these can affect their ability and integrity to measure and communicate the impact of their work. Finally, this chapter has highlighted a range of qualitative and quantitative measurement tools that students on placement can utilise to support their impact measurement while maintaining the professional values that underpin their work.

For students on placement, an understanding of the ethical and practical considerations around measuring impact is vital to practice effectively and sustainably in the current climate. Ultimately, it is important for students on placement to involve as many people as possible in the evaluation process, to create ownership and commitment and insist on democratic and popular ways of working (see Chapter 12 for more detail). Agencies that develop good communications systems and feedback mechanisms that value and empower the people they work with, and make sure the information and recommendations are well supported with credible evidence, can truly demonstrate impact and celebrate the achievements and experiences for both service users and students on placement alike (Thompson, 2007).

References

Alston, M andand Bowles, W (2013) *Research for Social Workers*. 3rd ed. Abingdon: Routledge.

Arbuckle, G A (2012) *Humanising Healthcare Reforms*. London: Jessica Kingsley.

Asthana, S and Halliday, J (2006) *Researching Health Inequalities in What Works in Tackling Health Inequalities: Pathways, Policies and Practice through the Llifecourse*. Bristol: Policy Press.

Banks, S (2010) *Ethical Issues in Youth Work*. 2nd ed. London: Routledge.

Banks, S (2012) *Ethics and Values in Social Work*. 4th ed. Basingstoke: Palgrave Macmillan.

Barnard, A (2011) *Key Themes in Health and Social Care: A Companion to Learning*. London: Routledge.

Beck, L, Trombetta, W and Share, S (1986) Using Focus Group Sessions before Decisions Are Made. *North Carolina Medical Journal*, 47(2):73–74.

Brace, I (2013) *Questionnaire Design*. 3rd ed. London: Kogan Page.

Bradford, S and Cullen, F (2012) *Research and Research Methods for Youth Practitioners*. London: Routledge.

Burns, S and MacKeith, J (2013) *The Family Star Plus User Guide and The Family Star Plus: Organisation Guide*. Brighton: Triangle Consulting.

Callaghan, K (n.d.) *The You Ladder*. Available at: https://evaluationsupportscotland.org.uk/wp-content/uploads/2020/08/theyouladder.doc (accessed 9 December 2021).

Clarke, J (2004) *Changing Welfare Changing States: New Directions in Social Policy*. London: Sage.

Clarke, J, Gerwitz, S and McLaughlin, E (eds) (2000) *New Managerialism, New Welfare?* London: Sage.

Cohen, L, Manion, L and Morrison, K (2018) *Research Methods in Education*. 8th ed. London: Routledge.

D'Cruz, H and Jones, M (2004) *Social Work Research: Ethical and Political Contexts*. London: Sage.

De St Croix, T (2016) *Grassroots Youth Work: Policy, Passion and Resistance in Practice*. Bristol: Policy Press.

De St Croix, T (2018) Youth Work, Performativity and the New Youth Impact Agenda: Getting Paid for Numbers? *Journal of Education Policy*, 33(3): 414–38.

De St Croix, T, Mcgimpsey, I and Owens, J (2019). Feeding Young People to the Social Investment Machine: The Financialisation of Public Services. *Critical Social Policy*, 40(3):440–70.

De Vries, M and Nemec, J (2013) Public Sector Reform: An Overview of Recent Literature and Research on NPM and Alternative Paths. *International Journal of Public Sector Management*, 26(1):4–16.

Diefenbach, T (2009) New Public Management in Public Sector Organizations: The Dark Sides of Managerialistic 'Enlightenment'. *Public Administration*, 87(4):892–909.

Doherty, B, Foster, G, Meehan, J, Meehan, K, Rotheroe, N, Royce, M and Mason, C (2014) *Management for Social Enterprise*. Los Angeles: Sage.

Dorey, P (2015) The Legacy of Thatcherism - Public Sector Reform. *Observatoire de la société britannique*, 17:33–60.

Duckworth, A L, Peterson, C, Matthews, M D and Kelly, D R (2007) Grit: Perseverance and Passion for Long-Term Goals. *Journal of Personality and Social Psychology*, 92:1087–1101.

Ferlie, E, Ashburner, L, Fitzgerald, L and Pettigrew, A (1996) *The New Public Management in Action*. Oxford: Oxford University Press.

George, M (2017) The Effect of Introducing New Public Management Practices on Compassion within the NHS. *Nursing Times*, 113(7):30–34.

Hampson, J and Howell, T (2018) Managing Managerialism – How the 21st Century Manager can Truly Thrive. *Youth & Policy*. Available at: www.youthandpolicy.org/articles/managing-managerialism/ (accessed 28 May 2020).

Hart, S N (1991). From Property to Person Status: Historical Perspective on Children's Rights. *American Psychologist*, 46(1):53–59. https://doi.org/10.1037/0003-066X.46.1.53.

Hood, C (1991) A Public Management for all Seasons? *Public Administration*, 69:3–19.

Hutchinson and Stead (1994) *The Rickter Scale*. Available at: www.rickterscale.com/assets/docs/Rickter%20Paper%20Dr%20Deirdre%20Hughes%20Master%2017%20Nov%202010.pdf (accessed 9 December 2021).

Jeffs, T and Smith, M K (2010) Resourcing Youth Work, Dirty Hands and Tainted Money. Chap. 4 in Banks, S. *Ethical Issues in Youth Work*. 2nd ed. London: Routledge.

Jones, H (2012) Youth Work Practice in England, in Fusco, D (ed) *Advancing Youth Work*. New York: Routledge.

Klikauer, T (2015) What is Managerialism? *Critical Sociology*, 41(7–8):1103–19.

Knox, R and Cooper, M (2014) *The Therapeutic Relationship in Counselling & Psychotherapy*. London: Sage.

Lawler, J, and Hearn, J (1995) UK Public Health Organizations: The Rise of Managerialism and the Impact of Change on Social Services Operations. *International Journal of Public Sector Management*, 8(4):7–16.

Lilienfeld, S and Basterfield, C (2020). *History of Evidence-Based Practice. Oxford Research Encyclopedia of Psychology*. [online] Available at: https://oxfordre.com/psychology/view/10.1093/acrefore/9780190236557.001.0001/acrefore-9780190236557-e-633 (accessed 8 May 2020).

McCabe, T J and Sambrook, S A (2019) A Discourse Analysis of Managerialism and Trust Amongst Nursing Professionals. *Irish Journal of Management*, 38(1):38–53.

McCulloch, K and Tett, L (2010) Professional Ethics, Accountability and the Organisational Context of Youth Work, in Banks, S (ed) *Ethical Issues in Youth Work*. 2nd ed. Oxon: Routledge..

McCulloch, K H (2007) Living at Sea: Learning from Communal Life Aboard Sail Training Vessels. *Ethnography and Education*, 2(3):289–303.

Newell, R and Burnard, P (2010) *Research for Evidence-Based Practice in Healthcare*. 2nd ed. New Jersey: Wiley-Blackwell.

Office for National Statistics (2018) *Surveys that Use Our Four Wellbeing Questions*. Available at: www.ons.gov.uk/peoplepopulationandcommunity/wellbeing/methodologies/surveysusingthe4officefornationalstatisticspersonalwellbeingquestions (accessed 9 December 2021).

Ord, J (2012) *Critical Issues in Youth Work Management*. Oxon: Routledge.

Ord, J (2016) *Youth Work Process, Product and Practice*. Bristol: Policy Press.

Osborne, D and Gaebler, T (1992) *Reinventing Government: How the Entrepreneurial Spirit is Transforming Public Services*. Reading: Addison-Wesley.

Packham, C (2000) Community Auditing: Appropriate Research Methods for Effective Youth and Community Work Intervention, in Humphries, B (ed) *Research in Social Care and Social Welfare: Issues and Debates for Practice*. London: Jessica Kingsley.

Pollitt, C (2003) *The Essential Public Manager*. Maidenhead: Open University Press.

Ranson, S and Stewart, J (1994) *Management for the Public Domain: Enabling the Learning Society*. Basingstoke: Palgrave Macmillan.

Rosenberg, M (1965). *Society and the Adolescent Self-Image*. Princeton: Princeton University Press.

Royal National Institute for the Blind (2014) *Measuring Impact and Outcomes: Lessons from RNIB*. London: RNIB.

Schwarzer, R, and Jerusalem, M (1995) Generalized Self-Efficacy Scale, in Weinman, J, Wright, S, and Johnston, M. *Measures in Health Psychology: A User's Portfolio. Causal and Control Beliefs*. Windsor: NFER-Nelson.

Shaw, C, Brady, L and Davey, C (2011) *NCB Guidelines for Research with Children and Young People*. London: National Childrens Bureau.

Shepherd, S (2018) Managerialism: An Ideal Type. *Studies in Higher Education*, 43(9):1668–78.

Snyder, J and Vinjamuri, L (2012) Principled Pragmatism and the Logic of Consequences. *International Theory*, 4(3):434–48.

Stuart, K, Maynard, L and Roucefield, C (2015) *Evaluation Practice for Projects with Young People*. London: Sage.

Taylor, T (2017) *Treasuring, but not Measuring: Personal and Social Development*. Available at: www.youthandpolicy.org/articles/treasuring-not-measuring/ (accessed 2 June 2020).

Thomas, G (2017) *How to do your Research Project*. 3rd ed. London: Sage.

Thompson, N (2007) *Power and Empowerment*. Lyme Regis: Russell House Publishing.

Tondeur, K (1996) *What Price the Lottery?* Crowborough: Monarch Publications.

University of Warwick (2006) *The Warwick-Edinburgh Mental Wellbeing Scales*. Available at: https://warwick.ac.uk/fac/sci/med/research/platform/wemwbs/ (accessed 9 December 2021).

Vazquez-Navarrete, M L (2009). Qualitative and Quantitative Methods in Health Research. *International Journal of Integrated Care*, 9(5). http://doi.org/10.5334/ijic.377.

Ward, S C (2011) The Machinations of Managerialism: New Public Management and the Diminishing Power of Professionals. *Journal of Cultural Economy*, 4(2):205–15.

Wilkinson, S (1998), Focus Groups in Health Research Exploring the Meanings of Health and Illness. *Journal of Health Psychology*, 3(3):329–48.

Yin, R K (2014) *Case Study Research - Designs And Methods*. 5th ed. London: Sage.

Index

Abma, T, 177
academics, 2, 15–16
ACES, see adverse childhood experiences
Adamson, C, 37
Adirondack, S, 178
adverse childhood experiences (ACES), 84
agile working, 114
Allen, K, 157
Allport, G, 124
Angelou, Maya, 130
anti-oppressive practice, 3, 47–60
   conscious, 55–58
   diversity, 49–51
   empowerment, 54–55
   equality, 49–51
   example of, 57
   internalisation, 51–52
   oppression, tackling of, 52–54
   PCS model, 53, 55, 59
   in projects management, 174–175
   unlocking, 59–60
   value base for, 48–49
anxiety, 7, 10, 38, 132
Armstrong, H, 111
Armstrong, P, 111
asset-based community development (ABCD) model, 155–156
Asthana, S, 189
attachment, 125
attitudes, 8–9

BACP, see British Association of Counselling and Psychotherapy
Banham, V, 110
Bartlett, A, 86
Beard, C, 27–29
Beard's model of reflection, 27–29
Becker, H S, 50, 84
Becker's labelling theory (1963), 50
Beckford, Jasmine, 59
Beddoe, L, 37
Beesley, P, 73
'best hopes,' 8–9
Big Society, 70
Black and Asian Minority Ethnic (BAME) carers, 158
Blom-Cooper, L, 59

Bold, C, 102
Bolton, G, 131
Bone, S, 162
Bovill, C, 176, 177
Bowlby, J, 35, 125
Bradshaw, J, 129
Brimblecombe, N, 157–158
British Association of Counselling and Psychotherapy (BACP), 109
Bronfenbrenner, U, 108–109, 112, 117
Bronfenbrenner's (1974) model, 108–109, 112, 117
Brown, B, 130
Browning, A, 141
Burton, M, 155

CAIPE, see Centre for the Advancement of Interprofessional Education
Caldicott Principles, 143
Calkins, S, 97–99
Callaghan, K, 191
Cameron, David, 70
CAMHS, see child and adolescent mental health service
Care Act (2014), 69, 76
carers, 154–159
   BAME, 158
   contributions, 155
   engagement, models of, 156
   feedback, 159–164
   groups, 155, 157
   independent community networks for, 157
   in intersectionality, 157–158
   student advice, 158–159
   UK, 155, 157
   unpaid/family, 154–159
Carney, P A, 149
Case, S, 141
case studies, 192–193
Centre for the Advancement of Interprofessional Education (CAIPE), 140
Charities Act (2011), 74
Charity Commission for England and Wales, 74
charity sector, student experience and, 74–75
child and adolescent mental health service (CAMHS), 77, 82, 87
Children Act (1989/2004), 76, 86

Children and Social Work Act (2017), 76
children's services, 89
Chiripanyanga, S, 76
chronosystem, 116–117
Clarke, J, 69
clinical supervision, 100, 104
Cohen, S, 84, 89
Collishaw, S, 35
communication, 143–146, 178
Compassionate Mind Foundation, 9
competence, 16
  conscious, 23
  cycle, 23
  ladder, 16
  unconscious, 23
complexes, 127–129
confidentiality, 109
connections making, 41–42
conscientiousness, 40
conscious anti-oppressive practice, 55–58
consideration behaviour, 147
continuing professional development (CPD), 100
coping mechanisms, 36
coronavirus pandemic, 54
Covid-19 pandemic, 115–117
Cox, R, 97–99
CPD, see continuing professional development
Crenshaw, K, 111
Crime and Disorder Act (1998), 145
Croisdale-Appleby, D, 83
cultural iceberg, 56

Danesh, H, 142
Danesh, R, 142
data protection, 109, 143, 145
Data Protection Act (2018), 143, 145
Davidson, P M, 117
Davies, J, 141
Davys, A, 37
D'Cruz, H, 24
'deficit' model, 155
Dewey, John, 22
digital divide, 115
digital literacy/technology on placement, 3, 108–118
  agile working, 114
  chronosystem, 116–117
  definition, 113
  exosystem, 114–116
  individual student, 109–111
    ethical/legal responsibilities, 109–110
    information technology by, 109–110
    technology and accessibility, 111
    working with risk, 110–111
  macrosystem, 116–117
  microsystem, 112–114
digital native, 113
discrimination, 48, 53–56
dispositional optimism, 9
diversity, 49–51

Django Unchained (2012), 51
Donzelot, J, 89
Driscoll, J, 100
Duckworth, A L, 191
Dweck, C., 76
Dwerk, C, 8, 124

EBP, *see* evidence-based practice
education, 55
  interprofessional, 75, 140–141
  oppression and, 55
  supervision in, 96
Education Act (2002), 76
emotional intelligence (EQ), 10–12, 39–40
emotional resilience, 3, 34–43
  components of, 35–36
  definition, 35–37, 40
  development, students in, 38
  emotional intelligence and, 39–40
  importance for placement, 37–38
  learning need and, 38–39
  overview, 34–35
  in practice, 39–43
    connections making, 41–42
    report writing, 42
    supervision, 42–43
    talking, 41–42
    university and placement, 40–41
emotional well-being, 41
emotions, 10
empathy/sensitivity, 11–12, 40, 129–131
empowerment, 54–55, 85
EQ, *see* emotional intelligence
equality, 49–51
Equality Act 2010, 14
Eraut, M, 30
ethnicity, 15–16
evaluation/monitoring, projects management, 177–178
evidence-based practice (EBP), 189
exosystem, 114–116
experiences, 38
exploitation in society, 53–55

family carers on placement, 154–159
Farnsworth, V, 89
feedbacks, service user, 159–164
feminist theory, 157–158
Few-Demo, A, 157
FINER model, 170
Firmin, C, 56
fixed mindset, 8
focus groups, 192
Fook, J, 24
Foucault, M, 89
Frankl, V, 83
Freeth, D, 140
Freire, P, 53, 54, 57, 60
Freshwater, D, 158
Frost, N, 77
Frost, Robert, 128

Gaebler, T, 70
Gardner, H, 10
Garmezy, N, 35
General Self-Efficacy Scale, 191
Gewirtz, S, 69
Gibbs model of reflection, 25, 29
Giddens, A, 102
Gilbert, P, 132
Gilchrist, R, 178
Gillespie, J, 141
Gillingham, P., 24
Gladwell, M, 124
Glassman, U, 51
God complex, 129
Goffman, E, 52, 84, 87
Golding, B, 143
Goleman, Daniel, 10–11, 39–40, 43
Gould, N, 30
Graham, L J, 111
Granheim, B M, 143
Grant, L, 41
Gray, R, 76
Greer, J, 41
grief, stages of, 91
growth mindset, 8, 85, 124

Hales, H, 86
Hallberg, R, 35
Halliday, J, 189
Handy, H, 42
Hawkins, P, 100
Hawkins and Shohet model, 100–101
Hayes, J, 71
Health and Social Care Bill (2021), 149
Heaney, C, 15
HESA, *see* Higher Education Statistics Agency
Higher Education Statistics Agency (HESA), 77
Hollis, J, 128, 133
homelessness organisations, placements within, 90–91
Homelessness Reduction Act (2017), 91
Hood, R, 141
hospices, placements within, 91
'hot desking,' *see* agile working
Howell, W S, 22
Hulley, S, 170
human development, 189
Human Rights Act (1998), 143, 145
Hurley, D J, 35, 158

impact measurement, 182–194
  dissemination of data, 193
  evidence and rationale for, 189–190
  evidence-based practice (EBP), 189
  mixed market, 185–186
  professional practice model, organisational climates for
    attributing impact, 189
    collaboration *vs.* competition, 188
    datafication of people, 188–189
    funding streams, 187–188
    top-down decision-making, 187
  quantitative research methods for, 190–191
incompetence
  conscious, 22–23
  unconscious, 22
individual pathology, 89
inequality in society, 47, 49, 51, 54–55
influence/rapport, 40
information sharing, 143–146
information technology (IT), 109–110
Inskipp, F, 96
intelligence, 15–16
intelligence quotient (IQ), 15, 16
Internet access, 115
interpersonal skills, 36, 88
interprofessional education, 75, 140
interprofessional group, 146
interprofessional learning/working, 3, 67, 75–77, 139–150
  accountability for, 149
  barriers, overcoming to, 141–150
    agenda clashes, 141–142
    communication, 143–146
    funding and resourcing, 149
    information sharing, 143–146
    knowledge of other professionals, 143
    professional meetings, 147–148
    teamwork, 146–147
    technology, 148
  community/strategic level, 145
  definitions of, 140
  medical *vs.* social model, 142
  time commitment in, 149
intersectionality, 111, 157–158
intra-personal intelligence, 11
intrapersonal traits, 36
intuition, 40
IQ, *see* intelligence quotient
IT, *see* information technology

Jackson, Samuel L, 51
Jacobs, M, 123
Jappe, E, 31
Jarvis, J, 176, 177
Jasper, M, 158
Jerusalem, M, 191
Johari window model, 126
Jung, C G, 83, 127–128

Kabat-Zinn, J, 9
Kadushin, A, 88, 102–103
Kadushin model, 102–103
Kahneman, D, 72
Kinman, G, 41
Kleanthous, I, 89
Knott, C, 22
knowledge, 30
Knowles, M, 38
Kolb, D A, 26–27, 29, 102
Kolb's experiential learning cycle, 26–27, 29
Kropp, M., 8

Krumer-Nevo, M, 157
Kubler-Ross, E, 91

labelling theory (1963), 50
learning
  approach to, 38–39
  children vs. adults, 38
  deep, 38
  need, resilience and, 38–39
  surface, 38
Lemon, K, 162
Levin, L, 157
Lewin's theory of change, 75
Light, C, 97, 99
Likert scales, 192
literacy in social care, 41

macrosystem, 116–117
Malin, N A, 104
managerialism, 97, 183, 186
Mansah, M, 143
mapping technology application, 112
Marmot, M, 115
Martin, L, 35
Marton, F, 38
maternal deprivation theory, 35–36
Mayer, J D, 11
Maynard, L, 173
McCarthy, D J, 89
McCulloch, K, 186–189
McKinsey's 7s model, 147
McLaughlin, E, 69
meditation, 9
Meier, J D, 8
Melendez, S, 24
Mental Capacity Act (2005), 76
Mental Health Act (1983), 86
microsystem, 109, 112–114
mindfulness, 9, 12
mindset for placement, 7–10, 17–18
  attitudes, 8–9
  'best hopes,' 8–9
  definition, 8
  emotions, 10
  fixed, 8
  growth, 8
  mindfulness, 9
  realism, 10
  tolerance for difficult feelings, 10
  types, 8
mixed market
  to delivering public services, 183–185
  economy, hallmarks and nature of, 183, 185
  historical context of, 183–184
  impact measurement, 185–186
models of carer engagement, 156
models of reflection, 25–29
  Beard's, 27–29
  Gibbs's, 25–26, 29
  Kolb's, 26–27, 29

  Schon's, 25–26, 29
Morrison, T, 39–40
Moss, B, 129
motivation/drivers, 11–12, 40
Murphy, K, 10
mutual humanisation, 53, 57

Neck, C P, 142
needs analysis, for projects management, 172
Neff, K, 133
negativity, 132
negotiation skills, 171
neoliberalism (marketisation), 183, 186
network theory, 146
New Public Management (NPM), 183
  characteristics of, 186
  managerialism, 183, 186
  neoliberalism (marketisation), 183, 186
  principles of, 185
NMC, see Nursing & Midwifery Council
Northouse, P G, 147
NPM, see New Public Management
nurses' clinical supervision, 104
Nursing & Midwifery Council (NMC), 95

Office for National Statistics well-being questions, 191
oppression
  challenge, 51
  definitions of, 48
  education and, 55
  inequality and, 55
  internalisation of, 51–52
  structural, 59
  tackling of, 52–54
optimism, 8–9, 36
orality in social care, 41
Ord, J, 189
organisational cultural norms, 85–86
organisations
  digitisation of, 112
  health and social care
    charity sector, student experience and, 74–75
    interprofessional working, 75–77
    political drivers for, 68–70
    service delivery, 70–71
    student expectations, 72–73
  homelessness, placements within, 90–91
  in placements, 1, 68–78
  policy, knowledge of, 143
  public sector, 69
  strengths, weaknesses, opportunities and threats (SWOT)
    analysis of, 71
  voluntary, 72, 74
  youth services, 68–69
Osborne, D, 70
Outcomes Star(s), 191

Parker-Rees, R, 99
Pavlov, I P, 31
PCS model, 53–55, 60

Peckover, S, 143
Pelden, S, 110
personal effectiveness, 10–12
personality, 124
PEST analysis, 71
Peters, L M, 9
Peterson, J, 132
Petrie, P, 147
Petty, G, 30
Pickard, L, 157
placements in health and social care sector, 1–2, 82–83, 168
   challenges, 14, 82–92
      children/families, structural issues in settings with, 89–90
      children/young people's secure care settings, 86–89
      homelessness organisations, 90–91
      hospices, placements within, 91
      self-awareness, 83–84
      strength-based approach, 84–85
      whistleblowing, 3, 85–86
   digital literacy on, 3, 108–118
   emotional resilience for, 37–38
   external stakeholders, 98
   within homelessness organisations, 90–91
   within hospices, 91
   impact of technology on, 3
   internal stakeholders, 98
   as learning opportunity, 2
   managing difficulties, 97–98
   mindset, 7–10, 17–18
   organisation in, 1, 68–78
   overview, 7
   pitfall, 73
   preparation for, 2, 7–18
      applying theory to practice, importance of, 16–17
      emotional intelligence, 10–12
      ethnicity, 15–16
      intelligence, 15–16
      mindset, 7–10, 17–18
      personal effectiveness, 10–12
      practical, 13–14
      SWOT analysis, 12–13
      theory, 14–15
   process of, 99–100
   professional practice, 69
   PVI sector, 83
   reflection on, 2–3, 21–32
   student in, 1, 7, 13–14 (see also students, in health and social care)
   students family carers on, 154–159
   university in, 1–2, 40–41
   work experience, 97–98
policies, projects management, 172–173
political drivers, for organisations, 68–70
Pollard, K, 75
poverty, 16, 54, 84, 142
power, 3, 24, 43, 47, 50–54, 59, 84–85, 95, 99–100, 128–129, 142, 144, 146, 148, 150, 157, 162
practical preparation for placements, 13–14
preparation for placements, 2, 7–18
   applying theory to practice, importance of, 16–17
   emotional intelligence, 10–12
   ethnicity, 15–16
   intelligence, 15–16
   mindset, 7–10, 17–18
   personal effectiveness, 10–12
   practical, 13–14
   SWOT analysis, 12–13
   theory, 14–15
Price, A, 101
privacy, 109
problem-solving abilities, 36
problem-solving techniques, 43
Proctor, B, 96
professional knowledge, 30
professional meetings, 147–148
professional practice model, organisational climates for, 186–189
   attributing impact, 189
   collaboration vs. competition, 188
   datafication of people, 188–189
   funding streams, 187–188
   top-down decision-making, 187
projects management, 168–179
   aims/objectives, defining of, 169–170
   anti-oppressive framework, 175–176
   evaluation/monitoring, 177–178
   FINER model for, 170
   motivation for, 169
   needs analysis for, 172
   negotiation skills for, 171
   planning and delivery, theory of, 173–174
   policy, impact of, 172–173
   reporting outcomes, 178
   resources, recognising/using, 174–175
   staff and volunteers for, 176–177
public sector organisations, 69
PVI sector, 83

qualified right, 143
qualitative evaluation, 192–193
   case studies, 192–193
   focus groups, 192
   Likert scales, 192
   semi-structured interviews, 192
quantitative research methods, 190–191

Rai, L, 42
realism, 10
reflection, 3, 21–32, 38, 99–102
   on action, 59–60
   conscious competence, 23
   conscious incompetence, 22–23
   definitions, 22–24
   importance of, 22–23
   on learning, 30–31
   models of, 25–29
      Beard's, 27–29
      Gibbs's, 25, 29
      Kolb's, 26–27, 29

Schon's, 25–26, 29
  in practice, 30–31
  SAROL, 31–32
  self, 131–132
  types of, 22–24
  unconscious competence, 23
  unconscious incompetence, 22
reflection-in-action, 131
reflection-on-action, 131
reflective practice, 2–3, 12, 21–32, 59–60, 76, 101–102
reflective practitioner toolkit, see SAROL reflective/reflexive process
reflexive practice, 24–25
reflexivity, 131
report writing, 42
resilience, 35–37, 72, see also emotional resilience
  definition, 35–37
  learning need and, 38–39
  as optimism, 72
  to work, 3
The Rickter Scale, 191
Robb, M, 30, 102
Robinson, M, 77
Rogers, C R, 31, 60
Rolfe, G, 158
Rose, C, 126–127
Rosenberg, M, 191
Rosenberg Self-Esteem Scale (RSES), 191
Rothwell, C, 97, 99
Rouncefield, C, 173
Ruch, G, 36
Rutter, M, 35
Ryn, M, 15

Säljö, R, 38
Salovey, P, 11
Salvador, J T, 104
SAMR model, 112–113
Sapin, K, 169
SAROL reflective/reflexive process, 32
Schein, E, 75
Schon, D, 59–60, 99, 131, 158
Schon's model of reflection, 25–26, 29
Schwarzer, R, 191
SCIE, see Social Care Institute for Excellence
SCR, see serious case reviews
Scragg, T, 22
self, professional, 3, 24, 122–133
  attachment, 125
  compassion, 132–133
  complexes, 127–121306
  definition of, 123
  empathy, 129–130
  external factors of, 123–124
  internal factors of, 123
  Johari window model, 126
  personality, 124
  reflection, 131–132
  self-awareness, 125–127
self-awareness, 11, 21, 23–24, 40, 83–84, 99, 125–127

self-care, 91
self-compassion, 9, 132–133
self-concept, 52
self-confidence, 13
self-development, 38–40, 82
self-disclosure, 88
self-efficacy, 38
self-kindness vs. self-judgment, 133
self-motivation, 36
self-regulation, 11
Sellman, D, 75
semi-structured interviews, 192
serious case reviews (SCR), 75
service delivery, 70–72
  partnerships in, 70
  social enterprise in, 70–71
service user feedback, 159–164
seven-eyed process model, 100
SFBT, see solution-focused brief therapy
SHARE model, 42
Shaw, J M, 143
Shohet, R, 100
Short Grit Scale, 191
Sicora, A, 158
Six Cs value model, 133
Skinner, B F, 31
Slee, R, 111
Smith, K, 176
Smith, W J, 142
Social Care Institute for Excellence (SCIE), 110
social enterprises, 70–71
social justice, 157
Social Services and Wellbeing Act (2014), 76
social skills, 11–12
social transformation, critical consciousness for, 54–55
social welfare system, 89
society, 47
SOLER model, 88
solution-focused brief therapy (SFBT), 8
Spivey, C A, 41
statutory sector, 67
stereotype, 50
strength-based approach, 84–85
strengths, weaknesses, opportunities and threats (SWOT) analysis of, 71
stress, 7, 10, 13–14, 37, 38, 41, 91
stress management, 10
Stroud, J, 76
Stuart, K, 173
students, in health and social care
  anti-oppressive practice, 3, 47–60
  areas for development, 3
  dissemination of information, skills of, 3
  diversity, 49–51
  emotional resilience, awareness of, 34–43
  equality in, 49–51
  expectations, 72–73
  family carers on placement, 154–159
  on frameworks, 3
  interprofessional working, 3, 139–150

involvement of others and, 3
personality attributes in practice, 3
in placements, 1, 7–18 (*see also* placements in health and social care sector)
planning skills of, 3
preparation for placements, 2, 7–18
  applying theory to practice, importance of, 16–17
  emotional intelligence, 10–12
  ethnicity, 15–16
  intelligence, 15–16
  mindset, 7–10, 17–18
  personal effectiveness, 10–12
  practical, 13–14
  psychological, 9
  SWOT analysis, 12–13
  theory, 14–15
in projects management, 168–179
service user feedback and, 159–164
skills of negotiation, 3
strengths, 3
supervision and, 95–106 (*see also* supervision)
and supervisor, relationship between, 3
support, 3
student–supervisor relationship, 95–106
supervision, 42–43, 76–77, 87, 95–106
  clinical, 100, 104
  definition, 95
  difficulties management, 97–98
  in education, 97
  expectations of, 96–97
  formative function of, 96
  function of, 96, 99
  models of, 100–104
  normative function of, 96
  outcomes from, 104–105
  restorative function of, 96
  seven-eyed process model, 100
supervisors, 3, 99–100
  dynamics, 97
  management, 99–100
  roles and responsibilities, 96, 99
  and supervisee, relationship between, 96–97
Sure Start projects, 89
SWOT analysis, 12–13

Taiwo, A, 158
talking, 41
Tanner, D, 158
Taylor, D, 42
Taylor, I, 30
teamwork, 146–147
technology, 3, *see also* digital literacy/technology on placement
  digital, 108–118
  in interprofessional working, 148
Tett, L, 186–189
theories, 2, 14–15
  of attachment, 125
  Becker's labelling theory (1963), 50
  cycle of development, 16–17

feminist, 157–158
maternal deprivation theory, 35–36
network, 146
New Public Management, 185–186
of planning and delivery, 173–174
to practice, importance of, 2, 16–17
Schon's theory of reflection on action, 59–60
Thomas, T, 75
Thompson, N, 10, 12, 24–25, 53, 55, 60, 143–144
threat, 132
Three Ps model, 31, 89, 148
Three 'Ts,' 84
'through-the-mirror' approach, 131
time management, 10, 13
tolerance, 10
top-down decision-making, 187
Trevithick, P, 123
Tsang, N M, 41
Tuckman, B W, 27
Turney, D, 36
tutelary complex, 89

Ungar, M, 36
Universal Declaration of Human Rights (1948), 48
university placements, 1, 13–14, 40–41
unlocking anti-oppressive practice, 59–60

Vélez-Agosto, N M, 109
Vernard Harrington, K, 142
voluntary organisations, 72, 74
voluntary sector placements, 83
Voorhees, C, 162
Vygotsky, L S, 92

Wacker, J, 15
Ward, A, 36
Warner, L, 86
Warwick-Edinburgh Mental Wellbeing Scale (WEMWBS), 191
Watson, James, 15
Weiss-Gal, I, 157
Weller, F, 91
Wenger-Trayner, E, 89
Werbach, A, 71
Werner, E E, 35
Westergaard, J, 99
whistleblowing, 3, 85–86
Wilks, S C, 41
Worden, J W, 91
work experience placements, 97–98
Working Together to Safeguard Children (2018) guidance, 76, 141
working with agency, 3, 67–70
wounded healer, concept of, 83

Yalom, I, 130
YOI, *see* young offender institution
The You Ladder, 191
young offender institution (YOI), 87
young people's secure care settings, 86–89
youth services, 68–69